SHE CAN READ

SHE CAN READ

Feminist Reading
Strategies for
Biblical Narrative

EMILY CHENEY

TRINITY PRESS INTERNATIONAL
Valley Forge, Pennsylvania

Trinity Press International, P.O. Box 851, Valley Forge, PA 19482–0851
Trinity Press International is part of the Morehouse Publishing Group

Library of Congress Cataloging-in-Publication Data

Cheney, Emily, 1952–
    She can read : feminist reading strategies for biblical narratives
/ Emily Cheney.
      p. cm.
    Includes bibliographical references and index.
    ISBN 1–56338–167–2 (pbk. : alk. paper)
    1. Bible – Feminist criticism. 2. Bible – Reading. I. Title.
    BS521.4.C48   1996
    220.6′082 – dc20   96–24734
                                     CIP

Printed in the United States of America

96   97   98   99   10   9   8   7   6   5   4   3   2   1

To my mother,
Ruth (Emily) Ramsay Cheney

CONTENTS

PREFACE

Reading and listening to stories have been a significant part of my life as long as I can remember. During my girlhood, my mom would often end our evening meal by placing a lit candle in front of her and telling my sister, my three brothers, and me the story "The Crooked Mouth Family." Dramatically, my mother would act the parts of the mother, the father, a daughter, a son, another daughter, and another son, who tried but failed to blow out the candle flame so that they could go to bed. We would giggle at our mom's silly faces and anticipated the final role of the eldest son who had come home from college and whose mouth was not crooked as the mouths of the others were. When she played his part, she blew out the flame in front of her. Then she would say, "That, my children, is the value of a college education." For a few silent moments, we contemplated her words.

As an adult, I feel ambivalent about this story. On the one hand, it recalls childhood fun and my mother's playfulness. The story has inspired me to value education as much as my mom does and to attain some of the power that education offers. On the other hand, the story has required that I pretend to be male when I identify with the eldest son and make his aspiration my own. The story conveys the idea that educational power can be used to put people in the dark so that they can go to sleep. The story designates an "educated" man superior to all the "uneducated" women in the story: his mother and sisters. Pretending to be male, using the power of knowledge to control others, and affirming written knowledge as superior to unwritten knowledge are positions I want to reject and challenge. What must I do with a story like this one? Do I discard it because of its detrimental implications? Do I retain part of the story, remembering and treasuring its initial inspiration, and then examine and reinterpret it? Can I do more than expose its seemingly negative view of women? Can I retell it in a more positive way? How?

Such questions are crucial for telling, hearing, and reading special stories; they are crucial for reading those in the Bible. Biblical narratives pose many of the same challenges. They inspire me. At the same time, they usually require me and other female readers to pretend to be male, to subordinate women to men, and to affirm dualistic categories needlessly. Over the past few years, this dilemma has led me to pursue different ways of reading, ways that allow me and other female readers to affirm ourselves and other women as we read. I have searched for reading strategies that can also help us assess the oppressive positions of the narratives so that we can avoid appropriating them and affirm only their liberating stances and values.

Committed to appropriating the Bible in a liberating manner and yet quite aware of its pervasive patriarchal context, I have attempted in this book to develop three reading strategies for group or individual study of biblical narrative. More specifically, I offer these strategies for women like myself whose ecclesiastical traditions expect them to base their sermons on biblical texts and who want their sermons to reflect their feminist consciousness and compassion. In chapters 3, 4, and 5, reading strategies that focus on gender reversal, analogy, and women as exchange objects are developed and tested on several texts without female characters from the Gospel of Matthew. At the end of each chapter are some suggestions for using the strategies in the preparation of sermons. Chapter 6 complements the preceding three chapters with its application of the three strategies on Mt. 1:18–25, a text with a female character.

Since these strategies build upon the work of feminist biblical scholars and utilize the research of feminist literary critics, chapters 1 and 2 evaluate their major contributions and establish the need for the strategies I propose. The Introduction reviews briefly the audience-oriented literary critical approach that undergirds the strategies. The Conclusion reflects upon what role the authority of the text plays when readers utilize these strategies.

Many people have contributed to the completion of this book, which was first presented as my doctoral dissertation and has been revised. I thank Fernando Segovia, Daniel Patte, Peter Haas, and Phyllis Frus for their endorsement of my project. Most of all I am grateful to Mary Ann Tolbert, who taught me how to read biblical texts as rhetorical writings and to view my own writing as a rhetorical enterprise. For suggesting ways to strengthen my positions in this book, I am particularly appreciative. Harold Rast, Laura Barrett, John Eagleson, and the staff at Trinity Press International have been especially supportive. Colleagues and friends have also provided encouragement. I thank Ron Liburd, Gaylyn Ginn Eddy, Vicki Phillips, and Adeline Fehribach, who became my community where my views were challenged and reformulated. My husband Jeff Skinner and my son Matt can never be thanked enough for all the countless things they have done for me as I have finished this project.

As I make the final revisions, I know that education and scholarship can change a person and give that person power, power to think and write differently than before, strength to be a different person in the world, abilities which do not have to be used to put people to sleep. Power can help people discover their own strengths. To the one who set me in this direction, who told the story "The Crooked Mouth Family" and instilled in me the desire to learn, I dedicate this book.

LIST OF ABBREVIATIONS

AnBib	Analecta Biblica
ATRSup	*Anglican Theological Review Supplement*
BTB	*Biblical Theology Bulletin*
CBQ	*Catholic Biblical Quarterly*
CrossCur	*Cross Currents*
Int	*Interpretation*
JSNT	*Journal for the Study of the New Testament*
JSNTSup	Journal for the Study of the New Testament Supplement
JSOT	*Journal for the Study of the Old Testament*
JAAR	*Journal of the American Academy of Religion*
JBL	*Journal of Biblical Literature*
JFSR	*Journal of Feminist Studies in Religion*
JJS	*Journal of Jewish Studies*
JLT	*Journal of Literature and Theology*
JR	*Journal of Religion*
NewLitHis	*New Literary History*
NTS	*New Testament Studies*
NovTest	*Novum Testamentum*
NovTestSup	Novum Testamentum Supplement
RIL	*Religion and Intellectual Life*
RB	*Revue Biblique*
SBLDS	SBL Dissertation Series

SBLSP	SBL Seminar Papers
StTh	*Studia Theologica*
ThTo	*Theology Today*
USQR	*Union Seminary Quarterly Review*
WBC	*The Women's Bible Commentary*
ZThK	*Zeitschrift für Theologie und Kirche*

INTRODUCTION

For the past twenty-five years, feminist biblical scholars have struggled with how to read the Bible, which has been interpreted to justify the oppression of women; the marginalization of blacks, Jews, gays, and lesbians; and the colonization of third world countries. The problem of how to read the Bible, however, extends beyond the correction of interpretations. The problem involves how to respond to the patriarchal biases and misogynous views of women in the texts themselves. Although feminist biblical scholars differ in their estimation of the degree of patriarchy, most begin their reading of the Bible with the stance that the social context for the Scriptures is patriarchy: the view that political, social, and economic power is hierarchically structured and male-oriented.[1]

Despite their awareness of the destructive interpretations of the Bible, its patriarchal context, and its misogynous views of women, feminist biblical scholars have persisted in their research for various reasons. Some feminist biblical scholars have grappled with the problem of the patriarchal context of the Bible because the people with whom they work and live regard the Bible as an authoritative guide for their lives. They want to find ways to read and interpret the Bible that allow them to expose the oppression of women and other peoples as contrary to God's plans for humanity. Other scholars have persisted in their studies because they want to remain within the Christian tradition. They recognize both the misogynous views toward women in biblical texts and the messages of hope, renewal, and social change in them. They want to hold on to the latter and challenge the former. Still others have remained committed to the study of the Bible because they recognize the continuing influence of the Bible on secular society. They want to mitigate the oppression of women and other groups, which people have justified on the basis of the Bible. Some feminist biblical scholars share all of these concerns.

I count myself among those who are concerned with all of these issues. As a middle-class, white, Protestant, Presbyterian (PCUSA) clergywoman, who was born and has lived in the Bible Belt of the U.S. for most of my life, I am very much aware of the influence of the Bible on Southern culture and the authority that the Bible holds for many people in this area. I have persisted in finding different ways to read the Bible, partly because my ecclesiastical tradition has conditioned me to interpret its message and partly because I want to lessen its destructive impact. I care about people whose lives have been diminished by the way they have interpreted the Bible or the way other people have read the Bible for them in study groups, sermons, and classrooms. I would be remiss if I failed to say that personal needs have also motivated my research. As I have studied the Bible, I have become convinced of how pervasive the patriarchal context of the Bible is and how easily I can hurt myself if I read the Bible uncritically.

This awareness has led me to search for ways of reading where I can affirm myself and other women as I read. Since I remain within a tradition of Bible study, I am searching for reading strategies which will help me assess the misogyny of texts and their liberative value and avoid the former while affirming the latter. This present study develops such strategies for myself and for women in similar situations who are looking for ways to reread the Bible for liberation, strategies that women can also use to write sermons based on biblical texts. Of course, all readers use strategies to comprehend biblical texts, but they are usually so culturally familiar to readers that they are unaware that they have learned them and are using them. My interest is in highlighting some of these culturally conventional ways of reading and in developing strategies that go against these conventions so that women can read the Bible for liberation.

My search for such reading strategies has led me to read the works of feminist biblical scholars who have already explored ways that women can read the Bible and the writings of those feminist literary critics who share similar concerns about the difficulty of reading male-oriented texts. What I have concluded as I have reviewed this research is that reading is both a restricted and a creative process.[2] Although women have an active role in constructing the point of view of a biblical text or a story, textual elements, such as the plot, the narrator, and the characters, also determine this construction.[3] Cultural and literary conventions, found in the text as well as outside it, consciously or unconsciously selected, influence readers' responses to texts as well.[4] The ideal reader as male, a convention that has persisted, is one of the key conventions that has shaped women's responses to literary works, including biblical texts.[5] This convention is especially problematic for female readers because it is usually so embedded in the story line and the point of view of texts that they cannot totally alter its effects..

The convention of the ideal reader as male restricts women in constructing the point of view of texts in a way that allows them to acknowledge and affirm that they are female, not male, readers. They must pretend they are male as they follow the story line; such reading, as I will discuss in chapters 1 and 2, has had and can still have detrimental influences on women. Since reading biblical texts has also affected women favorably, rather than flatly rejecting biblical texts because of the negative effects, women can choose another alternative. Female readers can carefully examine and clarify the viewpoint of the texts by deliberately applying reading strategies that affirm their female identities and experiences as they read.[6] Reading strategies that focus on gender reversal, analogy, and women as exchange objects, I propose, can help women assess certain aspects of the point of view of biblical texts. To evaluate their usefulness, I have selected the Gospel of Matthew as a test case, a text that has generally been viewed as unsupportive of the presence and role of women.

The application of these strategies rests on two assumptions. First, female readers will consciously accept the role of the implied reader[7] until assessment of its viewpoint indicates that they must abandon it or they are led to read against the direction of the implied reader's constructed role. In this way, women who have experienced positive identification with the protagonists in biblical texts can use the strategies to decide in what ways they will reaffirm or renounce their identification with the protagonists. Secondly, these strategies assume that analysis of biblical narrative is not purely an academic task. These narratives do more than describe events; they urge their readers to adopt certain values and perspectives that, when accepted, really do affect them and, in turn, influence their communities. The goal of this analysis, therefore, is to enable women to read and see options; they can choose liberating values and perspectives.

Because of these two assumptions, I must explain more fully how modern female readers are expected to position themselves when they attempt to analyze biblical narratives with these strategies and avoid oppressive values. I will refer to the Gospel of Matthew in this explanation, thus providing some pertinent background material on this gospel, and focus on the theme of discipleship, a theme central in the discussion of the impact of this gospel on its audience. Discussion of discipleship in the Gospel of Matthew will provide the opportunity to mention briefly Susan Sniader Lanser's reading model that undergirds the reading strategies.

Discipleship and the Role of the Reader

Some of the most recent studies and essays on biblical narrative indicate that scholars differ on whether readers simply identify with the
characters or they readily accept the assistance of the narrator in appropriating the views of all the characters. Studies on the Gospel of
Matthew, for example, include references to or discussion about the
protagonists with whom readers ought to identify. Some scholars have
maintained that readers are encouraged to identify with the small group
of selected disciples. John Paul Heil claims that readers identify with
the disciples in Mt. 28:16–20 and in the process develop "an authentic
faith in the absolute authority of the risen Jesus."[8] As Jesus urges his
disciples to make disciples, modern readers are likewise invited to mold
people into disciples of the risen Jesus. J. Andrew Overman, who discusses the response of an ancient audience to the Gospel of Matthew,
acknowledges that Jesus is the central character, but argues that the
life and ministry of the disciples would have been the focal points of
the narrative for Matthew's community. The disciples, who can learn,
understand, and teach, are the ones whom the members of Matthew's
community were encouraged to imitate.[9]

Other research defines discipleship in the Gospel of Matthew as the
values upheld by Jesus and affirmed in various characters rather than
just those traits that the group of male disciples embody and attempt
to embrace. Janice Capel Anderson argues that readers, male and female, are urged to assume the role of the implied reader, evaluate all
the characters, and accept the views and values of those characters
whom Jesus and the narrator support.[10] Robert Harry Smith, Michael J.
Wilkins, David B. Howell, and Jack Dean Kingsbury, whose studies are
more recent than Anderson's, concur with this analysis of discipleship
in the Gospel of Matthew.[11] Daniel Patte, who utilizes a different literary methodology, also focuses on the values, which he calls convictions,
that the author wants the readers to affirm. For him, too, discipleship
is connected only partially with the twelve male disciples. The goal of
the whole gospel is to train scribes for the kingdom.[12]

Andrew T. Lincoln and Richard A. Edwards combine both issues,
the role of the implied reader and the impact of the dominant role
of the disciples on readers. Lincoln recognizes that Jesus is the central character and that the narrator encourages readers to adopt Jesus'
point of view.[13] The implied readers' identification, Lincoln argues, is
nonetheless with the disciples rather than with Jesus because the readers' situation is more analogous to that of the disciples. For Lincoln,

the Gospel of Matthew is told to prepare readers to become missionary teachers. Edwards agrees that Matthew's gospel demands that readers pay attention to the disciples. The narrator emphasizes the disciples' role in the narrative by making continual references to the disciples from the initial call to four of them in Mt. 4:18–22 until the end when Jesus commissions them.[14]

Although discipleship in Matthew need not be reduced to one distinctive task (such as teaching), I agree with Lincoln and Edwards that we must be attentive to the flow of the text and the impact of the narrative on readers. The author of Matthew is engaging his audience throughout his account so that at the end they want to appropriate the views and behavior of the eleven men (although they know more than the eleven disciples) and win converts. Ancient authors, such as the author of Matthew, wrote to teach, persuade, and entertain people, not for purely aesthetic or contemplative purposes or even for providing accurate historical records.[15] Because they intended their works to be read aloud, they composed them with rhetorical strategies that would enable the audience to hear the arguments of their position and be convinced of their validity.[16] For the most part, however, the audience I will be discussing will be a modern one. My focus is on modern readings of biblical narrative, specifically the Gospel of Matthew, not primarily on the very different ways an ancient audience would experience this gospel.

Concurring with Lincoln and Edwards that readers are expected to give special attention to the disciples, I also agree that readers must assume the role of the implied reader and pay attention to Jesus' and the narrator's evaluation of the disciples and other characters. Reading biblical narrative without taking into account the dynamics of the implied reader and the narrator can prevent female readers from seeing that they stand outside the story-world and are being influenced in a different way than the characters. Lanser's reading model makes it possible to see the complex relationships among the implied reader, the narrator, and various characters and to analyze what values the author is urging the audience to accept. For this reason, I turn to discuss Lanser's model of narrative discourse, which can foster an emphasis on the rhetorical character of Matthew and will form part of the basis for examining the point of view of the selected pericopes in chapters 3, 4, 5, and 6.

Lanser's Model of Narrative Discourse

Susan Sniader Lanser's model of narrative discourse offers a way to understand the audience's position in a text and the dynamics among the author, the audience, the narrator, and the characters.[17] Adapting speech act theory, in particular Roman Jakobson's model of communication, to narrative discourse, she examines the dynamics of narrative discourse and distinguishes narrative levels in a text on the basis of who is telling the story and to whom the story is told. These levels can be visualized as "Chinese boxes" so that each level encompasses the subsequent ones.

Although theoretically the levels are limitless, only five need to be discussed. At the extrafictional level, the real author tells his story to his real audience. On the next level, located both in and outside the story world, the implied author[18] speaks to the implied audience. In the story-world, the first level is that of the narrator speaking to the narratee. Both can be characters in the story; but in Matthew, they are not characters. On the second level are characters talking with other characters, who can function as private narrators and private narratees. Jesus would be called a private narrator in Matthew. The third narrative level occurs when characters converse with each other in a story told by a character on the second level. Some of the characters in Jesus' parables fall into the third level.

The value of Lanser's model for examining the point of view of biblical narrative, in particular Matthew's view of discipleship, is that it enables us to focus on Matthew's implied audience and discern how they are persuaded to believe that they must identify with the disciples and win new converts. This analysis has concrete implications for modern female readers, since according to Lanser's model, Matthew's real audience would be expected to position themselves in the level of the implied audience. Because the narrator and narratee are not characters in the Gospel of Matthew, there is very little distinction between the implied author[19] and narrator and between the implied reader and the narratee; henceforth, I will combine them and refer to this level as that of the narrator and the audience.

Located at the level where the narrator speaks to them, the audience knows more than the disciples, since the disciples cannot hear the narrator. Before the calling of the disciples (Mt. 4:18–22; 9:9; 10:1–4), the audience already knows who Jesus is and how they ought to respond. The narrator has told them in Mt. 1:1–4:17. The narrator as a third-person omniscient, intrusive narrator[20] knows everything:

Jesus' identity and background (Mt. 1:1–17), the fulfillment of the Scriptures in events (Mt. 1:23; 2:15, 17–18, 23; 3:3; 4:14–16), God's words to Jesus (Mt. 3:17), the private dialogue between Jesus and the devil (Mt. 4:1–11), the dreams of Joseph and the magi (Mt. 1:20–21; 2:12, 13, 19–20, 22), and the inner thoughts and motivations of characters (Mt. 1:19, 24; 2:3, 16; 3:14a). The audience continues to receive information from the narrator that the disciples cannot have.

Although Jesus as a character also does not hear the narrator's commentary, the narrator allows Jesus to share some of his abilities. Jesus can interpret events as the fulfillment of the Scriptures (e.g., Mt. 11:10; 13:14–15; 15:8–9), express people's thoughts (Mt. 9:4; 12:25–37), and predict events (Mt. 16:21; 17:22–23; 20:17–19; 21:2). This elevation of Jesus and his ability to do mighty deeds presents him to the audience as someone divine, powerful, authoritative, and worthy of following.

Insofar as the audience accepts the narrator's perspective, the audience will identify with Jesus' as well. That Jesus' perspective corresponds to the narrator's facilitates this identification.[21] As the audience reads about the responses of the minor characters, they know with which ones they ought to identify because the privileged knowledge provided by the narrator and the corresponding perspective of Jesus tell them to identify with those whom the narrator and Jesus accept. Evaluating Jesus' encounters with the religious leaders who are "flat characters"[22] is also easy. The audience quickly knows they must reject their viewpoint because it never changes and Jesus always reprimands them.

Evaluating Jesus' involvement with the disciples is more complex. Since they are "round characters," that is, they display both positive and negative traits, the audience will sometimes identify with them and sometimes distance themselves from them, depending on Jesus' response to them and the narrator's comments.[23] Jesus, therefore, plays a critical role in whether or not the audience will identify with the disciples. The narrator, however, never allows the audience to distance themselves so much from the disciples that they will be unwilling to identify with them in the final scene.[24] Of all the characters, including Jesus, the disciples are the ones with whom the audience is expected most often to identify, even though the audience's knowledge of Jesus' perspective surpasses that of the disciples.[25] Because Jesus continues to teach his disciples after their failures, the audience must view Jesus' reprimands to them differently from those directed toward the religious leaders. The reprimands are a part of their schooling as "learners"[26] and, consequently, the audience's schooling.

The utilization of Lanser's model to read the Gospel of Matthew accentuates the role of the narrator. Throughout this gospel the narrator urges the audience to value what he values, in particular, to value what Jesus values and what Jesus teaches the disciples to value. Since several recent studies on the Gospel of Matthew apply audience-oriented literary criticism to their analyses, I only need to list these values and perspectives.[27] In the Gospel of Matthew, the narrator presents Jesus, the Messiah, the Son of God, as the one who can best interpret the Scriptures and events. The audience must listen to Jesus' teachings, read the Scriptures in light of his teachings, and depend upon his risen presence to teach them. The audience must hand down these teachings to all the peoples of the world. As disciples, the audience must be willing to travel, face suffering and death, argue with opponents, leave behind possessions and their families, and obey God's will so that they can heal others and provide them Jesus' teachings. They must be servants and treat others as their equals. I must repeat that the audience, however, is always at a better vantage point than any of the characters to understand that discipleship involves these values and so to implement them.

Conclusion

When modern female readers read biblical narratives, they too are invited to accept the role of the (implied) audience and adopt these values and perspectives as relevant to their lives. How some of the values and teachings in the Gospel of Matthew affect modern female readers and how women can appropriate the behavior of or identify with the "learning" disciples are dynamics that I will examine when I apply each of the strategies to selected pericopes from this gospel in chapters 3, 4, 5, and 6.[28] I will devote most of each chapter to demonstrations of how these strategies can help women reread and assess the designated texts. I am assuming that if clergywomen have different strategies for reading biblical texts such as the ones I present here, then they can write sermons that avoid the perpetuation of oppressive values and attitudes and encourage the cultivation of liberating ones; but at the end of these chapters, I will include some suggestions about sermon preparation.

Before applying the strategies that focus on gender reversal, analogy, and women as exchange objects to the texts, in the next two chapters I must review and reflect upon what is already available to help women reread male-oriented texts. The work of feminist biblical scholars and feminist literary critics has influenced significantly the development of the three strategies I offer.

Chapter 1

THE NEED FOR
READING STRATEGIES

Reading and evaluating the research of feminist biblical scholars has been integral to my search for different ways to read the Bible. The efforts of feminist biblical scholars to appropriate the Bible can be divided into three major approaches. In the first approach women use a certain strand or theme of biblical tradition as the criterion for accepting or rejecting other biblical texts. In the second approach scholars reconstruct the earliest religious communities from critical readings of biblical texts so that female readers are knowledgeable about women's historical participation and leadership in those communities. Women can use these reconstructions to assess the oppressive function of specific biblical texts. The third approach focuses on biblical texts about women to correct previous negative interpretations, to provide alternative ways of reading these texts, or to underscore their misogynous views of women. Some of the issues addressed in the third approach resemble those that feminist literary critics raise, which I will discuss in the next chapter.

As a first step in developing critical reading strategies for women, strategies that women can apply during individual or group Bible study and clergywomen can use in the preparation of sermons, this chapter will review the three appropriations and the questions that the research raises. This study will reveal that, although feminist biblical scholars have provided rich resources for reading the Bible and writing sermons, additional reading strategies are needed.

Three Approaches in Feminist Biblical Scholarship

Prophetic-Liberating Traditions

Some feminist biblical scholars have decided to focus on the liberating messages of particular texts as the way to undercut or neutralize the patriarchal biases of other biblical texts. Rosemary Radford Ruether was the first to articulate this way of appropriating oppressive, misogynous texts in *Sexism and God-Talk: Toward a Feminist Theology*.[1] According to Ruether, women can use the prophetic-liberating traditions in the Bible, which contain normative principles for assessing the patriarchal biases of other Scripture texts, to determine whether other texts or parts of them ought to be accepted or rejected as authoritative.[2] The prophetic strand can be the criterion to evaluate texts because Ruether expands its call for the liberation of the oppressed to include women and deems its social critical process as similar to that which she finds in feminism.[3] Both feminism and the prophetic traditions criticize unjust social structures and envision a world where peace and justice prevail.

Her expansion of the oppressed to include women is, as she herself admits, a move she makes as a feminist.[4] She continually acknowledges that the prophetic-liberating traditions in the Bible never openly addressed women's oppression and offers two reasons why women can aptly use the critical process of these traditions. First, she claims that "a sociology of consciousness" accompanies movements which criticize social and religious structures.[5] The spokespersons for such movements are always limited by their specific social contexts so that they are inattentive to the ways that they perpetuate the oppression of members of their own group or justify injustice against another group. That the prophetic-liberating traditions overlook women's oppression reflects this negative aspect of such movements, but does not discount the positive value of their ongoing critique of religion and its deformations.

Although a sociology of consciousness can explain the absence of a prophetic voice against women's oppression, the concept inadequately explains its repeated absence throughout the Bible. Her second reason for using the critical process of the prophetic-liberating traditions is more convincing. She argues that modern women are not the first who have claimed access to prophetic critiques of their patriarchal oppression. Throughout history women have continually affirmed their self-worth in the face of patriarchal demands. The absence of women's prophetic voice against their own oppression in the Bible is due to male-defined traditions that repeatedly omitted and reinterpreted women's prophetic participation.[6] The question must be raised, however, whether accounts of women's participation in biblical prophetic movements, if they were available, would present us with a similar critical process or display a different one.

Ruether thinks that Christian feminists could benefit from including themselves among the oppressed depicted in the Scriptures and gain much from using the critical process of the prophetic-liberating traditions to evaluate nonprophetic texts. She does not illustrate how women might apply this critical process to other texts nor does she examine some of the complexities of separating it from the prophetic traditions. Some prophetic texts are so misogynous that some women may find it impossible to identify with the prophets' call for social reform and pointless to discern the critical process reflected in them. For instance, they may find it difficult to separate the critical principles in Isaiah's and Jeremiah's judgments of the Israelites' behavior from the use of female sexuality to symbolize sin, despite their awareness of the metaphorical use of such sexual imagery (Isa. 1:21, 47:1–15, 50:1–2; Jer. 2:20, 3:1–10). Renita Weems, although not specifically evaluating Ruether's appropriation of prophetic texts, demonstrates that the marriage metaphor in Hosea, which is used to describe God's faithfulness and to critique Israel's relationship with God, is dependent upon sexual violence against women.[7]

If women read the female imagery in texts metaphorically and suppress the misogynous aspects, what are the effects of this type of reading on them? The critical principle in other prophetic judgments, such as the command to shake the dust off your feet when people will not receive you in Mt. 10:14 and Lk. 9:5 (cf. Lk. 10:11), can offer battered women a way to critique the submissive behavior required in the household codes in Col. 3:18 and Eph. 5:21–23; but they must set aside the rest of the commands in the commissioning scenes.[8] Women who affirm Mt. 10:14 must ignore the subsequent demands to die and suffer for Jesus' sake. Certainly real readers always ignore some aspects of a text and focus on others in the reading process; nevertheless, women need to consider the negative as well as the positive effects on themselves and other women when they disregard certain aspects of the prophetic traditions.

In addition, the consequences or implications of the vision of liberation in some prophetic texts may be cast in such a patriarchal manner that some women may doubt the usefulness of the critical process of prophetic texts for evaluating the patriarchal biases of nonprophetic texts. For example, the vision of a new world in Rev. 14:1–5 is one

where the faithful 144,000 who worship the Lamb are men who have
not defiled themselves by sexual involvement with women. How must
women read this text in order to include themselves in its vision of a
new world? As Tina Pippin observes, they must pretend they are male
and believe sexual involvement is undesirable.[9] Even if women read the
sexual imagery metaphorically, that is, as loyalty to the true God, they
must still deny their female identities.

In Mt. 20:16 the vision of liberation is a reversal of the present social
structures: the last will be first. In this case women do not have to pretend to be male to be included, but some women may refuse inclusion
because they believe the end of oppression means more than a reversal
of power. Ruether argues that Jesus did not support a simple reversal of
power; instead, he called for a more radical vision of society where all
relationships are based on service (Mt. 20:26–27; 23:11).[10] The prophetic pronouncement of service is to be given greater weight than
the one about the reversal of power in Mt. 20:16 and those of other
prophets, since it is more radical.[11] How radical is Jesus' evaluation of
society for those female readers who have always been in a position of
service to other people? If this is as radical as the prophetic process
gets, how useful can the prophetic principles be for these women as
they assess the biases of nonprophetic texts?

Separating the content of the prophetic traditions of the Bible from
the social critical process in them is quite problematic.[12] To make this
move, women in some cases must simply ignore the sexual and familial
violence in which the prophetic critical process is contextualized. To
identify with the vision that the prophetic critical process can project,
women must remain in subservient roles or forget those specific visions
where the social critical principle required them to pretend to be male.
In these instances, the prophetic critical process must be stripped of its
patriarchal context to be useful. Katherine Doob Sakenfeld commends
Ruether's approach, yet comments that one of its drawbacks is that
people could lose sight of "the patriarchal character of the liberation
texts as they were written."[13] Overlooking the patriarchal context of
the prophetic critical process means female readers may avoid asking
in what ways the prophetic critical process itself encourages them to
perpetuate oppressive relationships.

Reconstructions of the Earliest Religious Communities

Elisabeth Schüssler Fiorenza, who exemplifies the second approach to
how women appropriate misogynous, authoritative texts, views the to-

tality of the Scriptures as patriarchal and dismisses any attempt to find a portion of Scripture that can serve as a feminist textual tradition as Ruether does.[14] Although all biblical texts and traditions have been generated out of male-oriented constructs of reality, she thinks that an examination of their social and historical contexts will reveal women's historical participation in the earliest Christian communities. In her major work *In Memory of Her: A Feminist Theological Reconstruction of Christian Origins*, she reconstructs the early Christian community as one of egalitarian discipleship.[15] Women are absent or marginal in biblical texts because their active role was erased or reinterpreted by authors whose patriarchal mindset ignored or subordinated female contributions but who nonetheless could not completely suppress their leadership and participation.[16]

According to Schüssler Fiorenza's approach, women must read and examine biblical texts in order to discover the dynamics of the earliest communities whose women found power and liberation in their involvement in the Christian movement. Grammatically masculine language used to describe the Christian communities must be assumed to include women until disproved.[17] Specific references to women must be understood as conveying only a small portion of women's participation and leadership in early Christianity.[18] Women, Schüssler Fiorenza concludes, must read biblical texts with "a hermeneutics of suspicion," refusing to believe that they say everything about women's involvement.[19]

Schüssler Fiorenza's examination of the biblical material suggests that the communities addressed by the New Testament books are perversions or inevitable patriarchal developments of the earliest communities.[20] She insists that her reconstruction does not depict a pristine beginning but the struggle of the Christian movement for egalitarianism in the midst of a predominantly patriarchal culture, a struggle continuing for some women in mainstream churches today.[21] Whether or not later Christian communities are perversions of the earliest communities or communities with similar conflicts will not be debated here. The pertinent question is how this approach can assist women in the process of reading the Scriptures.

Schüssler Fiorenza claims that reconstruction of the positive, visible, and active role of women in the earliest communities can help women assess the oppressive functions of biblical texts.[22] Female readers, however, might be led to overlook the more subtle expressions of oppression in biblical texts. For example, Schüssler Fiorenza reconstructs Mary's and Martha's roles in the early church to demonstrate

how the Lukan author used the account about Mary and Martha in
10:38–42 to silence women and limit their leadership and authority in the church.[23] She focuses on the competitive relationship of
Mary and Martha in Luke by contrasting their portrayal to the story
found in John. In this comparison, the negativity of the Lukan account is so great that the different way in which the author of John
oppresses women seems unnecessary to examine, although John too is
a patriarchal text with rhetorical strategies and purposes. A view of
the early communities as egalitarian thus in this case hampers scrutiny
of texts such as John 11–12, where women appear to be treated as
equals.

Female readers might also be led to accept too readily texts that
sound egalitarian, which on closer scrutiny of their grammatically
masculine language are probably addressing a male audience. In Mt.
23:8–10, for instance, Jesus commands the crowds and his disciples not
to be called rabbi or call anyone master or father. He tells them they
have one teacher and are all "brothers" (ἀδελφοί adelphoi) with one
father and one master. Since the text sounds egalitarian, female readers might assume adelphoi has a generic meaning and not question its
specific function. However, Matthew's generic use of adelphoi is incon-
sistent. For example, in Mt. 12:49 the author of Matthew uses adelphoi
generically because in Mt. 12:50 he specifies that whoever does the will
of his Father is his "brother" (ἀδελφός adelphos), his "sister" (ἀδελφή
adelphē), and his "mother" (μήτηρ mētēr). That Jesus sends the women
in Mt. 28:10 to tell his adelphoi to meet him in Galilee yet the eleven
male disciples are the ones who meet him suggests that the author of
Matthew does not use the term adelphoi generically in this chapter. The
term adelphoi in Mt. 23:8 is probably referring to egalitarian status only
among the men whom Jesus is addressing, since women would not be
called rabbi or master in the first place.

In spite of Schüssler Fiorenza's stance that the context of the
Scriptures is totally patriarchal, women who read the New Testament
and reconstruct its earliest egalitarian religious communities might fail
to take seriously its patriarchal context. Female readers might not
examine thoroughly enough the dynamics among the characters in
a text. Female readers might not carefully study the grammatically
masculine language. Such oversights could mean including themselves in patriarchal contexts where they will perpetuate oppressive
relationships.

Rereading Biblical Texts About Women

Both Ruether and Schüssler Fiorenza recognize that the patriarchal context of the Bible is a problem that women must address; yet, the manner in which they make use of biblical texts can sometimes hamper women from fully examining the problem. Ruether's work also does not provide women a way to understand why they have been able to read patriarchal biblical texts and experience some of them as liberating without subjecting them to the social critical principles of the prophetic-liberating traditions. Schüssler Fiorenza does not explain why women can read and find liberating meanings in some texts, such as those about the Last Supper (Mt. 26:20–29; Mk. 14:17–25; Lk. 22:14–39), where the exclusion and absence of women is highlighted when they are read to reconstruct the earliest Christian communities. Schüssler Fiorenza admits that some texts may express liberation for women and men; but the only explanation she offers for why women have found liberating meanings in these texts is that the texts do not reinforce oppressive values in the women's specific cultural situations.[24] In her more recent book *But She Said: Feminist Practices of Biblical Interpretation*, she addresses this issue briefly. Her book follows the work of many other feminist biblical scholars who have focused on how women can read and appropriate biblical texts about women. I will return to her comments in the course of this discussion.

The earliest studies that emerged during the resurgence of feminist biblical scholarship in the 1960s and 1970s focused on the retrieval of unnoticed texts about women and the correction of negative interpretations of texts about women. The early work of Phyllis Trible was a significant contribution to these endeavors. Trible acknowledged the patriarchal context of the Scriptures, but claimed that "the intentionality of the biblical faith ... is neither to create nor to perpetuate patriarchy but rather to function as salvation for both women and men."[25] In her essay "Depatriarchalizing in Biblical Interpretation," she identified biblical themes and exegeted Gen. 2–3 and the Song of Songs to demonstrate that the Bible itself contained depatriarchalizing principles, that is, principles that support human equality and negate patriarchy.[26] These principles were the basis of her claim about the intentionality of biblical faith. Trible's reinterpretation of Gen. 2–3 was a serious challenge to those exegetes who insisted that the text affirmed male dominance and female subordination. Reinterpretation, she explains in a later essay, is the way that she can read the Bible and find liberating meanings in it.[27]

Trible emphasized that depatriarchalizing principles were not applied to biblical texts; a careful analysis of biblical texts would reveal these principles in some texts.[28] Women could read patriarchal biblical texts and find liberating meanings in some misogynous texts because they could employ exegetical tools and tease these meanings out of the texts. In *God and the Rhetoric of Sexuality*, where she elaborated on her essay, Trible refers to her new interpretations as the exposing of "counter-voices" within a document whose patriarchal nature could never be expunged.[29] The uncovering of countervoices in the Bible is an exegetical task that some feminist biblical scholars have adopted. Also noteworthy is her claim that the varied interests of interpreters mean multiple interpretations of a text are possible but texts nonetheless put limits on these interpretations.[30] Other feminist biblical scholars have continued to evaluate the role that the reader plays in the interpretive process.

Janice Capel Anderson has noted countervoices in the Gospels of Matthew and Luke, which she calls tensions within the text where patriarchy is both undercut and reaffirmed.[31] She has examined how tensions in the portrayal of Mary in the birth narratives recur in the portrayal of female characters in the rest of Luke and Matthew.[32] Female characters in Matthew are usually depicted positively and often excel the male disciples; at the same time, they remain in subordinate positions and never become members of the character group of disciples. In Luke women are disciples yet seldom assume public roles as the male disciples do. She claims that Jesus' teachings and speeches display both patriarchal and nonpatriarchal values.[33]

Anderson, who utilizes an audience-oriented type of literary criticism, suggests a way that women can read Matthew and avoid adopting its patriarchal values and perspectives. Rather than identifying with only the female characters, which she notes has sometimes revalidated and maintained patriarchy, women can assume the role of the implied reader.[34] When they assume the role of the implied reader, they can accept the narrator's and Jesus' direction and assess the ideological viewpoints of all the characters, female and male, and sometimes evaluate their patriarchal assumptions.[35] As discussed in the Introduction, Anderson proposes that discipleship in Matthew be understood as the values and norms that the implied reader is guided to affirm rather than as identification with one character group, such as the twelve male disciples.[36] In order to become a disciple, the implied reader needs the traits of the women and other minor characters whom Jesus and the narrator commend as well as those of the male disciples.

Anderson claims that her analysis of the role of the implied reader helps to account for why some readers of Matthew have been referring to the female characters as disciples. Her understanding of the role of the implied reader appears to provide a way for women to continue to identify with the exemplary behavior of the female characters without affirming their subordinate status in the narrative. Three aspects of her reading strategy, however, are troublesome. First, although she claims that Matthew assumes a male audience, she does not perceive that modern female readers will have a problem when they assume the role of the implied reader. Even if the implied reader cannot be equated with the male disciples, the implied reader/audience would still be male. What her strategy overlooks is that women must pretend to be male and cannot affirm their female identities as they include themselves.

Secondly, Anderson claims modern women who have always included themselves among the audience of such texts as the Great Commission (Mt. 28:16–20) and the Missionary Discourse (Mt. 10) would be denying themselves if they read them more narrowly as directed to men.[37] Careful study of what the audience is encouraged to do in those texts, however, could persuade these women to desire a different kind of discipleship, one that is less patriarchal.

Thirdly, although the implied reader/audience cannot be equated with one character group in Matthew, it is incorrect to lump all the characters together. Every narrative has protagonists. In Matthew and Luke and to some extent in Mark, Jesus and the twelve male disciples are the characters with whom the implied reader is invited to identify more than any other characters. Assuming the role of the implied reader and judging all the ideological positions cannot in itself delete the subordinate status of the female characters in the narrative. Assuming the role of the implied reader means privileging the male protagonists. Privileging the male protagonists means that modern women imagine a continuity between their own experiences and those of the male protagonists rather than those of the female characters.

Other feminist biblical scholars have recognized that the gender of the protagonists is critical. For them, one of the major difficulties of the patriarchal context of the Bible is that women must usually identify with the experiences and views of male protagonists in order to follow the plot of the text.[38] According to Kerry Craig and Margret Kristjansson, readers must often identify with "the strong, active male characters rather than with the weaker, obstructive female characters."[39] Joanna Dewey observes that the women who traveled with Jesus are mentioned

too late in the Gospel of Mark to alter women's earlier reading experience significantly.[40] Women readers have already constructed their
picture of Mark's narrative world as one where only men follow Jesus.

Dewey offers a remedy. She concludes that the women who are
identified for the first time in Mk. 15:40–41 need to be mentioned
as explicitly present in earlier verses, such as Mk. 1:5, 1:27, 1:36, 2:2,
2:15, and 2:23, where the Greek refers to groups of people or disciples and not specifically to men or the twelve male disciples.[41] These
inclusive translations would enable modern female readers who are
reading the earlier chapters to imagine female disciples doing what
male disciples do. Dewey recommends this kind of translation in the
Gospel of Mark because she thinks that even though Mark is androcentric, its narrative world is "relatively unpatriarchal."[42] Its advocacy
for the servanthood of all people and its repudiation of hierarchical familial relationships have been supplemented with the marginalization
of women. A translation that restores women's presence before Mk.
15:40 would correct this marginalization. She recommends a different
treatment of Acts. Since the narrative world of Acts *is* patriarchal,
the specific reference to women in its translation would reconfirm
patriarchy and so ought not to be made.[43]

Although I appreciate Dewey's concern about the role that gender
plays in the reading of a text, her strategy disregards why some women
have already included themselves among the male disciples and would
find the different translation unnecessary. For those women who read
Mark and do feel excluded, her strategy would still not make the reading experience positive enough for them. She does not take seriously
enough the patriarchal context of Mark. Mark's narrative world may be
more patriarchal than she recognizes. The explicit inclusion of women
in earlier texts would fail to restore them to egalitarian roles. The subordination of female disciples would persist in Mark because, as Peggy
Hutaff observes, translation cannot restore women's presence to an account such as the Last Supper, a text which plays a prominent role in
many Christian ecclesiastical traditions.[44] In the Last Supper account
in Mk. 14:17–25, the Greek can only be translated as the twelve male
disciples.

Inclusive language would also alter the rhetorical strategy of the
Marcan text so that women readers would be more comfortable with
the text and less likely to examine the patriarchal perspectives in Mk.
1:1–15:39. The omission of the women's presence until the end can be
read as Mark's ploy to convey to his audience the kind of discipleship
they ought to have. Mary Ann Tolbert argues that the sudden specific

reference to the women and their almost immediate failure are meant to prod the audience, men and women, to respond to Jesus' request.[45] Although the twelve disciples and the women failed, the audience will deliver Jesus' message. In addition to pushing the audience to respond, the delayed reference to the women until Mk. 15:40 might reflect the author's knowledge of the gender roles in his society. The audience would have been less convinced that they ought to deliver Jesus' message if the author had not utilized conventional male and female gender roles associated with travel. Implicit in Dewey's translation project is her identification with the male disciples and their gender role and her desire to extend this gender role to the female characters.

Both Anderson and Dewey have dealt with the problem of the patriarchal context of the Scriptures by looking to the text itself for some remedy. Anderson argues that women can critique the positions of the various character groups and some of their patriarchal assumptions, yet she relies only upon the narrator and Jesus to do this. Dewey contends that women can correct the androcentric perspective of some texts through different translations. Although I agree with Anderson and Dewey that biblical texts themselves at times reject patriarchal values, I think women readers must allow themselves to play a more active role in the reading and appropriation of biblical texts. Anderson's and Dewey's more recent critiques reflect this shift. Anderson argues that women can assess the patriarchal perspectives of biblical texts, read their viewpoints differently, and alter them for feminist use.[46] Dewey claims women must proceed past the Gospel of Mark to create the discipleship of equals that Mark teaches but fails to portray in his characters.[47]

Schüssler Fiorenza also recommends a more assertive type of reading. In *But She Said: Feminist Practices of Biblical Interpretation*, she advises women readers to identify with the dissident, suppressed voices in a text and recreate these voices through the use of their imagination and historical critical methods so that they challenge the male-oriented perspectives.[48] Schüssler Fiorenza, of course, is not the first to recommend that women identify with the female characters rather than accept the narrator's invitation to identify with the male characters. Phyllis Trible in her later book *Texts of Terror* had invited her readers to identify with Jephthah's daughter and the Levite's wife.[49] The value of Schüssler Fiorenza's method over Trible's is that she claims it is necessary not only to focus on the female characters in texts, but also to study the entire narrative to discern how its rhetorical strategies support and legitimate patriarchal structures.[50] Without this contextual study of the female character(s), women can unknowingly affirm oppressive viewpoints.

When Schüssler Fiorenza illustrates her reading strategies with a study of Lk. 13:10–17, she recommends that women refuse to identify with Jesus as the narrator urges them. They must avoid this type of reading, she asserts, because it will perpetuate the patriarchal perspectives of the texts.[51] She is especially critical of how identification with Jesus's suffering and death in the gospel accounts can lead women to accept domestic violence.[52] Her study of specific biblical texts leaves the impression that female readers must only identify with female characters; yet, she does not offer her reasons for this position. If women have read the Bible as "common literature," containing "humanist" values and perspectives, as she claims, they might identify with male dissident voices because they identify with the "humanist" values and perspectives of those characters.[53]

Schüssler Fiorenza rejects the stance of some feminist literary critics that women's unawareness of their own needs and aspirations have misled them to identify with great literature such as the Bible.[54] Her rejection of their position would seem to leave the possibility that women could also identify with male protagonists such as Jesus and the disciples. Schüssler Fiorenza, however, consistently affirms that identification with the subject positions offered in the text (that is, the characters with whom the narrator encourages the reader to identify), will only lead women to affirm its patriarchal views. She, therefore, does not provide a way for women to retain their desire to identify with the "humanist" perspectives of male protagonists. I think reading strategies are needed to enable women who feel drawn to the "humanist" values of male characters to explore how and whether they can affirm these values. It may not be necessary to reject the male character(s) in every case.

Schüssler Fiorenza's emphasis is on female characters, not male characters. At any rate, she does not presume that women can overcome the patriarchal nature of the Scriptures by simply identifying with female characters. She recommends four reading strategies: (1) analysis of the function of the female characters in texts, (2) reconstruction of women's roles in the earliest Christian communities, (3) evaluation and rejection of texts that perpetuate oppressive relationships, and (4) imaginative recreations of the voices of the female characters.[55] Imaginative reinterpretations, she has observed, must also be subjected to a hermeneutics of suspicion, for they too can contain gender role expectations that impede women's liberation.[56]

Identification with female characters in biblical texts requires careful scrutiny of the texts. A number of feminist biblical scholars have studied the function of female characters in biblical texts to help their readers examine the patriarchal context and decide with which ones they want to identify. Katheryn Pfisterer Darr, for instance, examines rabbinical and feminist interpretations of Ruth, Sarah, Hagar, Vashti, and Esther and concludes her book with an invitation to her readers to evaluate in what ways they want to imitate these women.[57] Alice Laffey's survey of the women in the Old Testament emphasizes their influence, power, and courage in patriarchal culture so that readers can appreciate and identify with many of them.[58] Some of the essays in the The Women's Bible Commentary and the second volume of Searching the Scriptures: A Feminist Commentary present women's positive roles in biblical narrative so that readers value the women and want to identify with them.[59]

Such books and essays are helpful because a major problem with reading biblical accounts about women is that so many of them evoke such ambivalent responses that identification with the women is problematic. Some of these studies stress the positive literary function of female characters in biblical texts. The women serve as catalysts for change in men's lives or illustrate the author's themes. Amy-Jill Levine argues that Tamar, Rahab, and Ruth, found in the genealogy in Mt. 1, each taught a man about higher righteousness, a recurring theme in the rest of the gospel.[60] Mary Ann Tolbert claims that most of the women in the Gospel of Mark belong to the group who respond to Jesus' message and bear good fruit.[61] Both Levine's and Tolbert's analyses emerged from larger studies that included, but did not focus solely on, the role of female characters.[62] In neither study, however, does Tolbert or Levine discuss the complexities of modern women's identification with these female characters and the effects of such identification, since these are not their interests at this time. Such discussion would complement their studies and make them even more helpful to women.

More studies that scrutinize what values the female characters represent in a narrative and that take into account the complexities of the reading process for women can help women know whether or not they want to identify with the female characters. Susan Tower Hollis, for instance, observes that Potiphar's wife, who appears to be only a destructive woman, actually initiates Joseph's transformation and his subsequent rise to power.[63] Hollis does not question what values Potiphar's wife represents that modern women might want to claim, for her purpose is to compare the account with similar tales. It would have been interesting to learn what power this female figure represents, especially since in two tales she is divine.

Other research projects have attempted to understand the women's actions by placing them in their social context. These studies indicate that female characters function to model the kind of behavior that was desired in women and sometimes men. Alice Laffey, for example, suggests that Vashti's banishment in Esther 1 was meant to caution upper-class, Israelite women against disobeying their husbands.[64] The new queen Esther models the more desired deportment of women.[65] In light of Esther's compliance with patriarchy and Vashti's noncompliance, Laffey concludes that some feminists have decided that Vashti is the one worthy of emulation. Sidnie Ann White, on the other hand, broadens the context and argues that Esther is a positive model for how Jews, male and female, could live successfully in the Diaspora.[66] White's affirmation of Esther as a model for Jews in the past implies that there may be contexts in which modern women will want to emulate her. Both their critiques are reminders to women that female characters do not necessarily reflect historical women. Awareness that female characters function to convey desirable behavior can help women in their reading, especially if they extend this knowledge to examine those male characters to whom they feel drawn to emulate.

J. Cheryl Exum makes similar judgments about the function of biblical accounts. The Samson story, she observes, served to reinforce societal values: good women are mothers and bad women behave like foreign women.[67] She concludes that Sarah and Rebekah, whose assertive actions secure their sons' inheritance, are presented positively to readers as models of the self-sacrificing mother.[68] Exum, who insists on the multiplicity of interpretations, makes no comments about whether or not female readers ought to identify with the women in these accounts; instead, her analyses remind female readers who do want to appropriate biblical texts that, if they choose to identify with the female characters, they must still keep in mind the patriarchal context. The narrator ultimately negates women's assertiveness by containing it within accepted gender roles.

Exum's alternative readings of biblical texts in *Fragmented Women* resemble the kind of analyses that Mieke Bal has provided. Bal, coming from the field of literary criticism, has played a major role in applying poststructuralist theory to biblical texts. Using narratology and Freudian psychoanalytic theory, she debunks standard interpretations of biblical texts and offers alternative readings. Her work has focused on the women in Judges and biblical love stories (e.g., David and

Bathsheba).[69] She starts with a detail in a biblical text that resists recuperation and allows that detail to play a central role in her interpretation.[70] Bal indicates that her analyses are meant to do more than challenge biases in exegetical tools and traditional interpretations; she wants to demonstrate that there are many possible readings of a text.[71] Debunking the assumption that a text has one meaning means "women can creep in and rewrite themselves back into the history of ideology."[72] She succeeds in her goals; however, her analyses offer little assistance to women who see the possibility of various interpretations and want to appropriate biblical texts in their lives.

Obviously, in order to read patriarchal biblical texts and appropriate them, something positive must be seen in them. Some feminist biblical scholars see biblical texts so intertwined with male perspectives and values that the only recourse is to expose the patriarchal bias operative within them. Esther Fuchs has analyzed biblical narratives to demonstrate how the less obvious literary devices and strategies in them promote patriarchal ideology.[73] In her analysis of six annunciation scenes in the Hebrew Scriptures, she explains how the women are subordinated and marginalized even as they are exalted for their motherhood. She argues that the narrator in Judg. 11 tells the story to win the reader's sympathy for Jephthah. Fuchs concludes that recognition of the literary techniques used to focus on Jephthah's losses more than his daughter's means readers must resist giving Jephthah the attention that the narrator urges them to give.

Pamela Milne has questioned whether women can recuperate any part of the Bible.[74] Structural analyses of Gen. 2–3 have shown her that the Bible is "structured as male mythology."[75] Feminists, according to Milne, have only two options: to accept the Bible as a sacred text and disclose its patriarchal character or to unveil its patriarchy and dismiss it as authoritative. Poststructuralist analyses which intend to understand power relations and change them, Milne observes, can help feminists identify patriarchal structures in the Bible but cannot help women change them in the text. Women, Milne explains, cannot alter and transform the Bible in the same ways they can political and social structures in their communities. They cannot add feminist writings to the Bible as they might to other literary collections. The biblical canon is closed.

Susan Durber also relinquishes the possibility of rehabilitating biblical texts. As she examines the parables in Lk. 15, she shows how texts produced in patriarchal societies have immasculated their readers.[76] She argues, however, that the main problem with biblical texts such as Lk. 15 is not that they portray women in a patriarchal manner or that they present the reader with a male point of view; the primary problem is that every reader, male or female, must allow themselves to be constructed as a male reader in order to make sense of biblical texts. She is following the assessment of the French feminist literary critics Julia Kristeva and Luce Irigaray, who hold that there can be no female readers, since women's subjectivity has been constructed in a masculine symbolic order. Consequently, she rejects poststructuralist claims, such as those of Chris Weedon, that women can become shaped by the discourse of feminism, refuse to allow the texts to construct them, and read patriarchal texts innovatively. According to Durber, women have only three alternatives: to read as men, to refuse to read the text, or to write new texts.

The works of such scholars as Exum, Bal, Fuchs, Milne, and Durber provide a reminder that the patriarchal character of the Bible cannot be explained away. Their analyses can give women a sharp awareness of the subtlety of patriarchal ideology in biblical texts and prod them to read biblical texts with sophistication. Their works, however, are not particularly helpful at the point when women have recognized the pervasive patriarchal context of the Bible and then still want to appropriate its messages of hope and compassion in their lives and convey these messages in sermons. Durber's insistence on the impossibility of innovative readings of biblical texts is not particularly beneficial for women who want to read biblical texts and also affirm themselves as women.

Summary

Some feminist biblical scholars have found ways to affirm what they perceive as liberating meanings in biblical texts. They have focused on the prophetic-liberating traditions, reconstructed women's historical roles in religious communities, reinterpreted biblical texts, assumed the role of the implied reader, used inclusive translations, identified with the suppressed voices in the text, analyzed the literary role of female characters in the text, and placed the texts in their social context. Other feminist biblical scholars have concentrated on exposing the patriarchal perspectives of biblical texts and/or challenging established interpretations with multiple readings. Evaluation of a portion of the work of feminist biblical scholars has revealed the need for additional reading strategies.

Since the affirmation of liberating meanings in biblical texts has at times led female readers to pretend to be male or to suppress oppressive elements, reading strategies that enable them to affirm their female identities and examine these suppressed elements must be developed. Because assuming the role of the implied author or identifying with certain characters has in some cases led feminist biblical scholars to minimize the patriarchal perspective of the text, reading strategies that expose the pervasive patriarchal context of biblical texts are still necessary. Also, since female readers, feminists and nonfeminists, are continuing to resonate with the experiences of the protagonists in biblical texts, they need reading strategies that help them analyze to what degree the texts reinforce accepted gender roles. The emphasis of some feminist biblical scholars on multiple interpretations of a biblical text indicates the need for reading strategies that take into account how women can decide which texts to accept or challenge and even reject. Strategies that address these issues would enable clergywomen to read biblical texts differently so that they can write sermons that honestly recognize the patriarchal context of the Scriptures and affirm the women in their churches.

The research of feminist biblical scholars in many cases has been affected by that of feminist literary critics. Feminist literary critics have wrestled with similar issues. They too have examined some of the problems that occur when the reader of patriarchal literature is a woman. Since their work offers a way to move toward developing additional reading strategies for reading biblical texts, I will discuss some of their observations and concerns about female readers in the next chapter.

Chapter 2

SCHOLARSHIP OF
FEMINIST LITERARY CRITICS

The work of feminist literary critics has been quite varied over the past twenty years. I will begin with a discussion of Elaine Showalter's and Judith Fetterley's approaches to reading androcentric American literature and then evaluate more recent developments in feminist literary criticism in relation to Showalter's position. Although Showalter's work is dated, a critique of some of her assumptions about literature will be helpful for female readers of the Bible who want to identify with the characters in biblical texts and affirm themselves as they read. After this critique, I will suggest and illustrate three reading strategies that take into account Showalter's and other feminist literary critics' observations about female readers.

Showalter's and Fetterley's Views of American Literature

The early research of feminist literary critics such as Elaine Showalter and Judith Fetterley suggests that education would account for why women would read any androcentric text, including the Bible, and find liberating messages in them. Showalter claims that the typical curriculum for a freshman course on American literature and composition would teach a woman how to think as a man because she would be expected to identify with the male experiences and perspectives in the literature and assume these are normative and universal.[1] Seldom would she find her own experiences reflected and supported in the selected texts, mostly male-authored.[2] Few women, she argues, would be able to maintain or gain positive female identities while reading literature written by men in a course usually taught by a male professor. The long-range effects of her education would be alienation from her own experiences and perceptions.

Judith Fetterley agrees with Showalter that women who read the canon of classical American literature are led to identify with male experiences that are presented as universal; yet she goes further than Showalter in her assessment of women's reading experience.[3] She explains that the male experiences are often told in a way that female readers must identify against themselves.[4] The story line requires female readers to identify with the male protagonist whose character is often defined by his power over women, usually abusive power. Women readers are asked to suppress any empathy with the female characters and to perpetuate stereotypical portrayals of women. Fetterley argues that "the cultural reality is not emasculation of men by women but the immasculation of women by men."[5] Fetterley confirms Showalter's observations. The long-range effects of the process of immasculation on women are "self-hatred and self-doubt"; "intellectually male, sexually female, one is in effect no one, nowhere, immasculated."[6]

Since female readers cannot revise literature so that it mirrors their reality, Fetterley claims women must choose to be resisting rather than assenting readers so that they expose the point of view of male-authored literary works as male-oriented, not universal or normative.[7] Her analyses of "Rip Van Winkle" and The Great Gatsby bear some resemblances to those of feminist biblical scholars, such as Esther Fuchs' study of the story of Jephthah's daughter. Fetterley argues that a consciousness of the male perspectives in literature can empower women readers because the literature will affect them differently. A different relationship to the literature can lead them to interact with their culture differently and make changes.

Fetterley's appeal to female readers to become resisting readers sounds similar to Schüssler Fiorenza's suggestion to female readers of biblical texts to begin with a hermeneutics of suspicion. Fetterley, however, does not encourage women to find anything about themselves and their history in male-authored American literature. Female characters in male-authored literature do not reflect the lives of real women; they are stereotypes. Feminist literary critics have continued to emphasize that the actual behavior of women was probably more rich and complex than their behavior in literature. I will return to this issue later.

Showalter's response to male-authored American literature was to lay it aside and concentrate on female-authored literature. She proceeded to collect women's writings and called her study of female-authored texts "gynocriticism."[8] According to Showalter, for women to gain positive self-images, they need to know that female experiences can be portrayed differently. She designed her literature courses to enable female college students to arouse and affirm their female identities and experiences, to unlearn harmful behavior and habits, and to find their experiences mirrored and validated.[9] Fetterley seems to agree with this stance toward literature written by women. She admits in the introduction to her collection of writings by nineteenth-century American women writers that she wants to foster openness rather than resistance between her readers and these texts.[10]

If Showalter's and Fetterley's observations of the reading of male-authored texts are applied to male-authored biblical texts, then women who read biblical texts, such as Rev. 14:1–5 and Mt. 23:1–12, and find liberating messages in them, find them because they are reading them the same way they have been taught to read other male-authored texts. They submerge their female identities, pretend they are male, and identify with the male perspectives of the texts. They are unaware of how they have been taught to imagine themselves as male. According to Fetterley, women need to resist the biblical text and expose its male-oriented perspectives, unless it is a female-authored text. According to Showalter's position, the Gospel of Mark, the special material of the Gospel of Luke, the Letter to the Hebrews, and the Acts of Paul, texts sometimes attributed to female authorship,[11] are the biblical texts to which women ought to turn to see themselves more accurately mirrored.

Critique of Showalter's Position

Some feminist literary critics have been quite critical of Showalter's assumptions about female-authored literature. Gayle Greene and Coppélia Kahn disagree with her assumption that gynocriticism is less ideological than the study of male-authored texts. They argue that feminism which has insisted that all positions are ideological must steer clear of any claims that its own stances are value-free.[12] Toril Moi criticizes Showalter for her refusal to submit female-authored literature to the kind of analysis other critics would require of male-authored texts.[13] Some feminist biblical scholars would join Moi in her criticism, although from a different angle. Schüssler Fiorenza, for instance, values how female authorship of biblical texts might disrupt the rigid, established views of apostolic authorship but cautions against assuming women who have also been socialized in a patriarchal culture would write differently than men.[14] Female readers would still need to read such texts with a hermeneutics of suspicion.

I think that women's need to read the literature of women writers and have their female identities and aspirations affirmed must not be underestimated. Especially when this realistic literature provides women a female protagonist with whom they can identify, women can gain a sense of their own power and self-worth. They no longer have to identify against themselves. Instead of being intellectually male but sexually female, they can be intellectually and sexually female as they read. They can be embodied minds. Luce Irigaray, for instance, writes of the mental and physical effect that a statue had on her when she realized that it was not a statue of Mary with the child Jesus but a statue of Mary as a child with her mother Anne.[15] Female-authored literature, including writings which would be classified as realism, can provide female readers an experience similar to Irigaray's. Pam Morris maintains that female-authored literature does not always merely perpetuate patriarchal ideologies; it can function, and has functioned, to counter negative, denigrating portrayals of women and to affirm female readers' female identities.[16]

At the same time I agree with Moi and other feminist literary critics who think that women must read female-authored literature critically.[17] Privileging female-authored works over male-authored works assumes that women write differently than men and that this literature reflects life for women. Discussion of these two assumptions is pertinent because sometimes feminist biblical scholars have attempted to pinpoint a group of biblical texts as more appropriate for women to read and encouraged women to identify only with certain female characters.

Privileging female-authored literature over male-authored literature assumes that women have used language differently than men. They have used language in a way that is more liberating or nonpatriarchal. Some feminist literary critics, such as Julia Kristeva and Luce Irigaray, emphasize that language, as it is currently structured, always suppresses "the feminine." In light of this view of language, female authors also subordinate women because language itself has been built on this asymmetry. These feminist theorists base their position on the psychoanalytic theory of Jacques Lacan. A summary of his theory can help us understand their critiques of language.

According to Lacan, the acquisition of language occurs at the time of the child's separation from the mother.[18] The child moves from a period when no distinction is sensed between itself and the mother (called the Imaginary) to a period (called the Symbolic Order) when the child views him(her)self as a separate entity. The father plays a key role in this differentiation. As the father breaks the dyadic unity between mother and child, the phallus (which stands for the threat of castration) represents the loss of the mother. From this point on, the child, that is, a boy child, must repress the desire for unity with the mother and identify with his father. When the child says "I am" and recognizes others as separate, the child has acknowledged that he has assumed his place in the Symbolic Order. In other words, precisely to be a speaking subject, a boy must suppress his desire for his mother. Idealized representations of woman are offered to mitigate the loss of the mother. Girls also enter the Symbolic Order, yet somewhat differently. When separation occurs, a girl does not identify with her father; instead, she envisions herself as her father and other men envision her. Speaking women, therefore, only speak as men and speak in terms of how men view and desire them. They speak but never become speaking subjects.

It is on the basis of Lacan's psychoanalytic theory that Kristeva will make such statements as, "A woman cannot be; it is something which does not even belong in the order of being."[19] For Kristeva, the place where the repressed mother or "the feminine" can be found is in the breaks or ruptures in a text. Irigaray contends that in the present structures of languages "the feminine" cannot be articulated. Women can opt to speak "as a sexualized male or as asexualized."[20]

Kristeva's and Irigaray's views about language seriously challenge the stance that the female-authored American literature in Showalter's collection would be automatically affirming for women to read. Although not blatantly misogynous, the works would reveal their subordination of women if they were subjected to critical study. The female writers would have been unable to write otherwise. Kristeva's and Irigiray's views undermine any notions that women can read parts of the Bible uncritically. Their views affirm what biblical scholars such as Schüssler Fiorenza have claimed for some time: all biblical texts are patriarchal, regardless of whether or not they are blatantly misogynous. All biblical texts must be read critically.

What Kristeva's and Irigaray's critiques also convey is the impossibility of reading biblical texts as women, that is, as embodied minds. Not only is there no way a woman can speak as a woman, there is also no way a woman can read as a woman. As Susan Durber observed in her exegesis of the parables in Lk. 15, women can only read them as men.[21] Of course, not all feminist literary critics have agreed with Kristeva and Irigaray. Some have assessed language differently and suggested that women can read as women. Others have concentrated on locating the ruptures and breaks in texts and reading subversively. I will address the latter approach to reading texts first, since it allows me a way to address the second complaint against Showalter.

Several feminist literary critics have contested Showalter's supposition that women's experience is immediately obtainable in female-authored texts.[22] In response to Showalter and critics such as Sandra Gilbert and Susan Gubar who hold a similar position, Nelly Furman argues that poststructuralist analyses of language have challenged the position that writing simply conveys specific experiences or thoughts and represents speech.[23] Literature can be understood as providing an account of reality, yet it can also be viewed as a linguistic construct.

Furman illustrates the two ways to view literature with a discussion of two ways to understand the minister's or officiate's pronouncement of marriage in a wedding ceremony. She argues that although the selection of the words in the pronouncement of marriage ("I now pronounce you man and wife" or "I now pronounce you husband and wife") may not necessarily describe the experience of marriage, the words do reveal how the couple perceives or envisions their new relationship.[24] The choice of words matters because the selected words can either help reinforce sexist biases or help promote equality in that couple's marriage. When a text is understood as a literary construct, Furman continues to explain, it is seen as a dynamic discourse between the narrator and the reader and can affect the reader to act in certain ways (as the choice of words in the marital pronouncement can encourage a couple to interact in certain ways). A literary text, therefore, is not a fixed entity but the result of dialogue and interaction between the reader and writer. Since reading is an activity, every reading is different.

Furman concludes that feminists ought not to ask whether the author of a literary work is a woman or whether the text mirrors their experiences. They ought to ask how they can read a text from a feminist stance. For her, reading means ignoring "the author's presumed intentions or the assumed meaning of the text," exposing biases, and overturning their power.[25] Her position sounds similar to the views of Exum, Fuchs, and Bal, and to some extent resembles Schüssler Fiorenza's, since Schüssler Fiorenza proposes that readers identify with the dissident voices.

Furman's discussion has two implications for female readers of the Bible. First, in her comparison of what occurs in the reading process to what happens in a wedding ceremony, Furman emphasizes that words or texts do not necessarily describe the actual behavior of men and women. Texts reinforce what men and women ought to do. Simone de Beauvoir and feminist literary critics after her have studied the social construction of gender and gender roles and the ways that literature functions to confirm accepted gender roles.[26] The work of anthropologists has contributed to this research. Jane Collier, Michele Rosaldo, and Henrietta Moore, for instance, found that ideas about gender roles reflected political strategies that the men and women used to promote their interests; these ideas did not describe the people's actual social and economic positions.[27] In light of these literary and anthropological studies of gender roles, female readers who want to identify with the characters in biblical texts must continue to question what gender roles are being presented to them to emulate or reject.

Secondly, Furman stresses that each reading is new and unique. Her statement reflects a basic tenet of poststructuralist theory. Words do not have fixed meanings; their meaning must always be redefined as the context shifts. Not only discursive contexts, according to Chris Weedon, but also social and institutional contexts shape the meaning of words and texts.[28] Language in various specific forms (magazines, books, movies, etc.) and contexts (work, home, school, etc.) offers us subject positions, that is, ways of being an individual through which we can live our lives. Different readings are possible because of the various subject positions which the reader brings to interact with the subject positions offered by the narrator. Since individuals are not unified, coherent selves, but are continually offered an often conflicting array of subject positions with which to interpret texts, their interpretations must be understood as temporary. How this plurality of interpretations can help female readers appropriate biblical texts will be addressed after I discuss briefly women's subjectivity.

Literary critics explain the construction of subjectivity in different ways. In some feminist poststructuralist theory, as already mentioned, subjectivity is determined by the child's separation from the mother. Chris Weedon rejects this position and therefore views language differently.[29] Weedon maintains that women's subjectivity is a product of the society and culture in which women live, but it can continue to be reshaped as women encounter alternative ways of being individuals. She refers to education, political activism, and "consciousness-raising" experiences as discursive occasions where women gained insight about the social forces upon them and learned ways to bring about change.[30] Weedon insists that a woman can choose among the various subject positions competing for her attention; she is "capable of resistance and innovations produced out of the clash between contradictory subject positions and practices."[31]

Weedon's type of feminist poststructuralism has both advantages and disadvantages for female readers of the Bible. Female readers can affirm the new ways of reading texts that experiences among women's groups have brought them, ways that I think must be prized as long as they are not misled to think that they can erase the patriarchal context of the Bible with these strategies. Also, as some feminist biblical scholars have already demonstrated, poststructuralism provides a way to undermine set interpretations and examine women's resistance to patriarchy within biblical texts.

Poststructuralism nevertheless in its very strength to offer fresh interpretations presents the problem of how to appropriate these interpretations and promote changes in people's lives. Linda Alcoff, for instance, refers to three interpretations that Derrida gave on Nietzsche's writings, one of which exposed feminist propositions and countered charges of misogyny in Nietzsche's works. Using Derrida's interpretations as an example, Alcoff questions the usefulness of the position of undecidability (the unfixed meaning of texts) for feminists who need to have "their accusations of misogyny validated rather than rendered 'undecidable.'"[32] The position of undecidability, Alcoff observes, can have the effect of suggesting that feminists have grounded their assessments of sexism on distorted, limited analyses and have misread themes and contexts as misogynous that are actually beneficial for women.

Within poststructuralist theory, feminists have no recourse to counter such positive readings and declare that Nietzsche's writings or biblical texts are harmful for women. Meaning is undecidable. Feminists can only continue to give alternative readings. They cannot claim in the name of women that certain readings are harmful because the word "women" does not have a fixed meaning. Gender, as previously mentioned, is a social construct. Claims that women's personality is inherently different from men's and that all women have the same innate qualities such as peacefulness have been proved untenable. Poststructuralism poses a major dilemma in political activism.[33] As Alcoff has argued, certain needs such as satisfactory child care and legal abortions cannot be demanded without using the category of women.[34]

Poststructuralism also poses a problem to female readers of the Bible who are interested both in reinterpreting biblical texts and in appropriating them. Female readers who recognize that biblical texts have been used to hurt people are not provided any tools to read and evaluate which biblical texts to accept, challenge, or reject. The deficiencies of poststructuralism reveal the need for reading strategies that do not allow gender to become invisible or reading to be separated from praxis. Reading strategies that encourage women to see reading as a political activity are paramount. Not only must female readers become aware of what they are being persuaded to do or not to do, but they must also consciously question and evaluate the effects of the text on themselves and the people they know. In this way, the appropriation of the text does not become an entirely separate step after reading. At the same time, these reading strategies must help female readers affirm their female gender without, of course, assuming that all women read the same way. Reading is understood as both a physical and a mental activity and as a gendered activity.

Strategies

Female readers need reading strategies to help them decide which biblical texts to accept, challenge, or dismiss. Several feminist biblical scholars and feminist literary critics have voiced that dialogue with other women can provide female readers ways to reread patriarchal texts. Mary Ann Tolbert urges women to help each other identify the androcentric viewpoint of biblical texts and teach each other to read in new ways.[35] According to Chris Weedon, "consciousness-raising groups" are one form of feminist discourse that can enable women to resist harmful subject positions and make changes.[36] Susan Schibanoff, another feminist literary critic, recommends that women claim dialogue with other women as a valuable source to learn how to read "as women."[37] Jean Kennard observes that in feminist communities new interpretive strategies become established and make different interpretations possible.[38] Dialogue with other women about the Bible has led me to read the research of feminist literary critics and use their resources to formulate reading strategies. Their works along with conversations with my colleagues have suggested how I might begin this development.

According to Jean Kennard, when women know and use different interpretive strategies and reading conventions, they can read a story in a new way. She argues that interpretations do not change because readers discover and highlight what has always been in the text; they change because readers choose to apply reading conventions previously unavailable. For example, reading conventions associated with patriarchy, madness, space, and quest were reversed and then established in feminist communities. These new, reversed conventions had enabled Elaine Hedges, Annette Kolodny, Sandra Gilbert, and Susan Gubar to read Charlotte Perkin Gilman's "The Yellow Wallpaper" (1892), formerly categorized as a grotesque horror story, as a positive story of a woman's quest for identity.[39] Kennard claims that other female readers and writers have reversed the established, oppressive literary conventions so that they can evaluate or portray female characters in a way that reflects more honestly their view of female experience.

One of the main reasons that the different strategies and reading conventions produced a positive interpretation of Gilman's "The Yellow Wallpaper" is the gender of its implied audience. The story does not assume that its audience is male. It must be kept in mind that most male-authored literature is directed primarily toward a male audience: readers are invited to identify with the male protagonist(s). Even literature written by men, for women is often written for men since it affirms the kind of women suitable for men.[40] This particular reading convention, the ideal reader as male, limits female readers in how much they can creatively reread such literature to reflect their own experiences, including those biblical texts which assume men are their primary audience. The more recent interpretative strategy among feminists, for instance, reading against the grain and identifying with female characters, still requires examining in what ways the female characters convey patriarchal perspectives. The strategy of putting the female character in the center of the analysis reveals her significant role in conveying the perspective of the text but does not remove her subordinate status in the story.

The three strategies which I am proposing in this study assume that female readers will accept the role of the implied reader until evaluation of the perspective of the text reveals that they must relinquish it and then either read against the grain of the implied reader's constructed role or dismiss the text. My reason for proceeding in this fashion is to help female readers decide whether they want to continue to identify with the protagonists in biblical texts, dismiss the texts, or challenge the texts to encompass other concerns.

The first strategy that I propose to develop employs gender reversal to evaluate the actions of the characters in biblical texts. Jean Kennard observes that some female writers changed the point of view found in literature by reversing the gender of the characters in their own literary works so that the implications of an old convention were disclosed.[41] Erica Jong, for instance, in *Fear of Flying* portrayed men rather than women as sex objects and highlighted the abuse of that old convention toward women. Jong, of course, was dependent upon her audience's knowledge of the accepted conventions of gender role stereotypes to grasp the implications of the reversal.

One of the conventions embedded in modern reading is the acceptance of the experiences of the protagonist in a narrative as normative. Gender reversal can help women assess the abuses of this convention. When female readers reverse the gender of the characters in biblical texts, they can test whether the experience presented to female and male readers as normative is really normative. If the experience of the protagonist is based on accepted gender role behavior, then it is very possible that the text is addressed to an audience with the same gender as the protagonist.[42] To assess to what degree the characters in a biblical text are reinforcing accepted gender roles, other ancient writings must be studied to determine what some of the acceptable gender role behaviors might have been.

Let me give two examples to illustrate this analysis.[43] In Esth. 8: 3–6 the narrator encourages both male and female readers to identify with Esther as she pleads to the king to save her people. Her experience is presented as normative for both male and female readers. After reversing the gender of Esther, other texts would be studied to see whether kings or any men ever pleaded to their wives to persuade them do something or whether this behavior was more typical of women. If Esther's behavior reflects the accepted gender role behavior for women, then probably the text functioned to reinforce similar behavior in women in that ancient cultural milieu. Men might have been expected to appropriate the behavior of Mordecai and King Ahasuerus. On the other hand, in Ex. 3 the narrator encourages male and female readers to identify with Moses as God calls him and accept his experience as universal. After reversing Moses' gender, other texts would be studied to see how women and men were engaged in service to God. If Moses' experience reflects the accepted gender role behavior for men, then probably only an ancient male audience would have been expected to appropriate his behavior.

After this kind of analysis, female readers would need to decide whether or not they want to continue to identify with the protagonist. If female readers, for instance, come to the book of Esther with the position that begging maintains women's subordination to men and is unacceptable gender role behavior in their particular communities, then they might want to renounce their empathy with Esther. On the other hand, if pleading is a useful maneuver to bring change in their contexts, they might want to emulate her. Female readers who have a strong sense of call and service to God must assess the book of Exodus to see to what extent Moses' call overshadowed and excluded women's commitments. If Moses' call is dependent upon the subordination of women's vocations, female readers may not want to denigrate themselves by identifying with him.

The application of a reading strategy that focuses on gender reversal differs significantly from Dewey's recommendation of inclusive translation. This strategy can be applied to most biblical narrative texts and alters the rhetorical strategy only momentarily in order to clarify more sharply its perspective. The female reader is not primarily seeking to enter into the narrative world of the text and be included; she examines its demands upon her.

The second strategy, which I will develop, focuses on analogy; and it does allow female readers to enter into the narrative world of the text. In this strategy, role reversal or gender reversal is the first step in those texts where the narrator urges the reader to identify with male protagonists. (In those biblical texts where the narrator invites the reader to identify with a female protagonist, this step is not necessary.) The purpose of the strategy is to allow female readers to recuperate some biblical texts, those that portray desires and experiences common to women and men.[44] Female readers can affirm those texts that they find analogous to their lives and aspirations.

This strategy is based in part on the observations of the feminist literary critic Patrocinio Schweickart. She sensed that the reading process was more complex than Fetterley had claimed, since sexist literature, such as D. H. Lawrence's *Women in Love*, continued to appeal to her even though she agreed with the feminist critiques of its sexism.[45] In one scene in *Women in Love*, she observed that she unconsciously reversed the roles of Birkin and Ursula and ignored the absurd elements because she was drawn to the portrayal of autonomous selfhood and the desire for love and relationships in the character Birkin, a view of self consistent with her feminist aspirations. She implies that a *conscious* reversal of the characters, such as Birkin and Ursula, and a *conscious* suppression of the absurd aspects will enable her to match her aspirations to those of the male protagonist and escape the abusive designs of the text to make her identify against herself.

Schweickart's approach reaffirms in many respects the analogous way that women have always been taught to read biblical texts. Her way of reading differs in that readers must pay attention to those texts that continue to appeal to them and become conscious of what they will choose to ignore in these texts. I think that the reading process requires still another step. Deliberately and consciously omitting what she calls "the patriarchal trappings" of a story may be insufficient for grasping the thrust of the story. Birkin's autonomy and desire for love, with which Schweickart identifies, is dependent upon a patriarchal relationship with Ursula, which she ignores. I suggest that after the appealing portion or thrust of the story is separated from the suppressed elements and examined, the suppressed elements be analyzed for how they positively and negatively shape the rest of the story and women readers' imaginations. Feminist biblical scholars have become increasingly aware that insufficient attention to detail can unwittingly keep women in their place.[46]

For example, when female readers reverse the gender of the eleven male disciples and Jesus in Mt. 28:16–20 and claim questing as a female activity, they must suppress the fact that no men are present. For some women who have never imagined fulfillment without dependence upon a man, recognition of their absence could challenge them to imagine new and exciting possibilities. Women whose primary relationships are with other women could feel themselves affirmed. For other women, a quest without men may represent a lonely journey, a trip to avoid, the same old road of poverty.

The third strategy, which I plan to develop, focuses on the use of female characters as exchange objects. Female characters, according to some feminist literary critics, can function as a way to bond the reader and the author. For instance, Schweickart argues that American literature for male readers is "a meeting ground of the personal and the universal."[47] Male readers are urged to identify with the male protagonists and their experiences and endorse these experiences as universal by affirming their difference from the female characters. Drawing from Claude Levi-Strauss' anthropological theory, Schweickart comments that the female characters function as exchange objects and have the effect of changing the text into a woman so that this text/women creates a bond between the author and male readers.[48]

Female characters can also function as exchange objects between male characters. Eve K. Sedgwick has analyzed the involvement of female characters in the relationships between male characters in several novels written from the mid-eighteenth to the nineteenth centuries.[49] In these novels, she explores the varying representations of the bonds between men and the ways in which social and political relationships are sexualized. She demonstrates in her study of William Wycherley's *The Country Wife* how Pinchwife, Sparkish, and Horner each in their own way use women to relate to and gain power over other men. Underlying Sedgwick's analysis is Gayle Rubin's interpretation and critique of Levi-Strauss.[50] According to Rubin, relationships between men and women involve the use of the women mainly for the purpose of creating and strengthening bonds between other men.

Schweickart's and Sedgwick's observations that female characters function as exchange objects in American literature can help women examine the function of female characters in biblical texts. Since often small portions of biblical texts are selected and interpreted, a study of how female characters function as exchange objects in biblical texts requires in many instances reading those pericopes that precede the selected text. Consequently, what needs to be explored is the inverse of Rubin's perspective: in every relationship of a man with a man, a woman has been used to make it possible. For example, when women study a biblical text with only male characters, such as Jesus' Last Supper with his male disciples, they examine how a female character in a previous pericope functions to establish the close relationship between the male characters. One advantage this strategy gives female readers is the ability to see that the manner in which female characters are presented cannot be separated from the central thrust of the story even when female characters are absent. Women can see how sexuality and gender are used politically.

In summary, when women study the ways that female characters in biblical texts function as exchange objects, they analyze the dynamics among the male and female characters either in the selected pericope or in the preceding pericope(s), if the selected text contains no female characters. They also examine the response that the audience is invited to make toward the characters and the effect of that response on their reading of subsequent texts. For example, the dynamics among the characters in Mt. 28:1–10 (the two women, Jesus, and the angel) and their influence on the audience's response to the eleven disciples and Jesus in Mt. 28:16–20 would be studied. Using this analysis and evaluating the needs of their communities, female readers can decide how they will appropriate the text, that is, whether they will identify with the eleven disciples, challenge its perspective by combining what the two women represent with the perspective of the disciples, or dismiss the text.

Conclusion

For some women it is still important to read the Bible as authoritative, and for some clergywomen it is desirable that they also write sermons from their study of it. The three strategies I will develop are offered as ways to help these women examine a text and decide with which texts they want to identify, which ones they wish to challenge, and which ones they want to dismiss. For those clergywomen who want to preach with integrity, that is, preach in a way that acknowledges the pervasive patriarchal context of the Scriptures, these strategies allow them ways to be straightforward and yet affirm themselves and other women as they read the Bible and write sermons based on Scripture texts.

I have emphasized that these strategies are offered so that women will affirm themselves and other women as they read. Women must not hurt themselves by identifying against themselves. However, in using the terms "the female reader," "the woman reader," and "female experiences," I do not mean that all women read the same way.[51] All female readers have been and continue to be shaped by their gender identities, the experiences of their biological sex, and the social constructions of femininity. Other factors, such as race and class, are also integral parts of their womanhood.[52] I am focusing on the gender of the reader, not because class and race are less important, but because I think women need to become more aware of what occurs in the reading process that encourages them to identify with the male-oriented perspectives of biblical texts. I think that if women become more aware of the gender dynamics in biblical texts, they have more choices available to them as they decide how they will use the text to affirm and promote life in their specific contexts.

In order to develop and illustrate these three reading strategies, I will apply them to selected texts in the Gospel of Matthew, a gospel that has generally been viewed as unfavorable toward women. To be sure that these strategies fit most biblical narratives, I will first look particularly at texts without female characters.

Chapter 3

GENDER REVERSAL

At the end of the Gospel of Matthew, the audience, who knows more than the eleven disciples, is expected to identify with them as Jesus tells them to go out and make disciples of all the Gentiles. When modern female readers identify with the disciples, they are reading the way they have been taught to read biblical texts. They are assuming that the experiences of the disciples are normative for them as well as male readers. What female readers too seldom realize is that the text in its own cultural milieu was reinforcing male gender role behavior and addressing a male audience.

To recognize more sharply that biblical texts were directed to men, modern female readers can apply a reading strategy that focuses on gender reversal. The strategy can help female readers assess to what degree biblical writers utilized the conventional gender role behavior of their time to portray the experiences of the protagonists and persuade the audience to share their perspectives. Female readers can decide in what ways their identification with the protagonists, both male and female protagonists, would entail the acceptance of a role that includes self-denigration. This analysis, I propose, is one way clergywomen can read biblical texts differently so that they can draft sermons that affirm themselves and other women.

In this chapter, the usefulness of gender reversal for reading biblical narrative texts, which contain male protagonists, will be demonstrated. A discussion of how gender reversal must be adapted for biblical texts will be presented first. Then the strategy will be applied to Mt. 10:5–15, 28:16–20, 23:1–12, and 26:20–29. Some suggestions for how the data from this strategy can be helpful for sermon preparation will conclude the chapter.

Development of the Strategy

When modern women, including those who recognize the patriarchal context of the Bible, read biblical texts, they often identify with the protagonists and approach them as real people. Reversing the gender of the characters with the assumption that they are real people provides readers little insight into the dynamics of the text. The usefulness of gender reversal depends upon the readers' perception that literature, including biblical texts, reinforces acceptable gender role behavior and does not merely recount interesting stories. Therefore, when readers reverse the gender of the characters, their task is to assess to what degree the biblical text functions to reproduce conventional gender role behavior. An understanding of the formation of gender roles will help women know why they need to make such an assessment of biblical texts.

Most feminists disclaim that gender roles and the behavior that is associated with them are inherent in women's and men's social or biological natures. They maintain that particular roles and values about these roles have become associated with women and men through cultural ideologies, that is, systems of beliefs, assumptions, and practices that shape people's relationships to their material conditions. Ideologies influence people to view gender roles as universal and natural rather than as socially constructed. In Western society, for example, ideologies have usually presented the role of childrearing as a natural role for women rather than men since women bear the children. Actually, the role of mother is socially constructed.[1]

The cultural construction of gender has dominated the research of a number of female anthropologists. In her exploration for the reasons for women's subordination, Sherry Ortner, for example, concluded that women were subordinate to men in most cultures because women and their social roles (often restricted to the domestic sphere) were seen as closer to nature, which was devalued. Men and their social roles (usually placed in the public sphere) were linked with culture, which was esteemed.[2] Although her theory has been challenged,[3] her analysis initiated a way to examine how certain ideas and valuations become associated with men and different ones become connected with women as the result of cultural ideologies, rather than innate or physical qualities in men and women.

Some anthropologists have examined the relationships between men and women by investigating both the economic[4] and political processes in that society and the cultural ideas about women's and men's behavior. Jane Collier and Michelle Rosaldo concluded that gender roles did not directly reflect social or economic relationships but stemmed from political relationships.[5] Henrietta Moore found from her study on the Marakwet people of Kenya that cultural ideas about women's and men's behavior did not mirror the actual social and economic positions of the men and women.[6] The Marakwet used gender stereotypes in various social contexts as political strategies to further their interests. For instance, although the men knew that not all women were childlike, they continued to use that stereotype because it could explain and preclude women's participation in particular activities. Moore argues that the "power of gender stereotypes is not just in the mind, for they have a perfect material reality, which helps to reinforce the social and economic conditions within which they are developed and employed."[7]

Also central in much of feminist literary criticism is the theme that gender and gender roles are socially constructed.[8] Since one of the ways that cultural ideologies about gender roles are transmitted and reinforced is through literature, feminist literary critics have analyzed the ways that literature reinforces conventional gender role behavior. They have concurred with anthropologists that gender role stereotypes function to reinforce certain behavior and, although not necessarily reflections of real women's actions, have restricted the boundaries of real women's actions and behaviors.[9] They are aware that even potentially subversive literature has validated the prevailing cultural ideologies and pushed women to peripheral positions.[10]

Cultural ideologies, which include gender role stereotypes, influence people to act in ways that are not always in their best interests. Since cultural ideologies attempt to make gender roles look natural and normative, then strategies are needed to make them appear less natural and less normative. One way, which I am proposing, that female readers can begin to become more aware of the abuse of conventional gender role behaviors in biblical texts is by reversing the gender of the characters.[11] This strategy arises from Jean Kennard's observation that some female authors have attempted to challenge the abuse of gender role stereotypes in literary works by reversing the gender of the characters in their own writings.[12] For example, in *Fear of Flying*, Erica Jong portrayed men as sex objects to expose the abuse of that stereotype of women.

What Kennard and other literary critics fail to mention when they refer to gender reversal is that when authors have reversed the gender of characters to expose and criticize misogynous views toward women, the authors expected the audience to know the accepted conventions

of gender role stereotypes. Erica Jong, for instance, relies upon her readers to use their knowledge that women are usually viewed as sex objects
to comprehend the purpose of her depiction of men as sex objects.
When Joanna Russ illustrates how most plots of Western literature
sound odd or funny when the gender of the protagonist becomes female, she likewise assumes that readers can sense the oddness because
of their familiarity with gender stereotypes.[13]

When female readers reverse the gender of the characters in biblical
texts, they will probably be too unfamiliar with the gender stereotypes
of the cultural milieu of the text to determine whether the reversal of
the characters would create a gender role disruption that would sound
unusual to ancient audiences. A knowledge of ancient literary and cultural conventions about gender roles is therefore necessary in order to
sense that a protagonist of the reversed gender would be unusual for the
action of a story or scene. Since stories, as already discussed, function
to reinforce gender behavior, other ancient writings can be examined
to determine what some of the acceptable gender role behaviors might
have been.

Therefore, after reversing the gender of the male disciples in the four
Matthean texts, I will compare the dominant action of these scenes to
the portrayals of women and men in a selection of ancient writings to
assess the conventional role behavior attached to that dominant action.
The depictions of women and men in the Hebrew Scriptures, ancient
romance novels, and ancient biographies will be examined, since the
Gospel of Matthew often refers to Old Testament texts[14] and shares
literary and cultural conventions found in ancient romance novels[15]
and biographies.[16] These comparisons can help modern female readers
assess whether or not the experiences of the male characters in the
Matthean texts, which they have been taught to accept as normative
for them and male readers, will remain normative. At the same time,
this question of normativeness must be recognized as a modern one,
since in the ancient cultural milieu out of which Matthew was written,
the special protocols of male public speech would have led the author
to assume a male audience.[17]

As the selected writings are examined for conventional gender role
behavior, the question will be asked whether the four Matthean texts
could been have been told with female disciples or with both female and male disciples. This question enables female readers to begin
their reading with thinking about the effects of the text on them as
women and thus allows them to engage themselves both physically and
mentally with the text. Female readers can decide whether to accept,

challenge, or reject the text when they have evaluated the dynamics of the text and compared them to their own specific contexts.

Mt. 10:5–15 and 28:16–20

In Mt. 10:5–15, the narrator invites the audience to identify with the twelve disciples as Jesus commissions them to go out, heal the sick, and preach about God's kingdom. In Mt. 28:16–20, the narrator also urges the audience to identify with the eleven disciples as the risen Jesus commissions the disciples to go out and expands their work to include all nations, not just Jews.[18] This final scene looks backward as well as forward, since the audience must recall everything that Jesus has said and done and what the narrator has told them, as they identify with the disciples and receive Jesus' instructions to teach and win converts. These two texts will be examined together since both are commissioning scenes which emphasize the willingness to travel,[19] one of the values advocated in the overall construction of Matthew's gospel.

After reversing the male disciples to female disciples, modern readers need to know the ancient conventions about women's and men's gender roles in traveling in order to assess how unusual it would be to portray a commission to a group of women to go out and to what extent the author is attempting to make one kind of discipleship normative for all readers. Assessment will begin with a study of conventions found in the Hebrew Scriptures, then proceed with an analysis of those in ancient romance novels,[20] and end with a study of conventions in a sample of ancient biographies.[21] This step is not as enormous or as cumbersome as it first appears, since after a few investigations modern readers will be familiar with most of the ancient conventions used with respect to women's and men's gender roles, including those which pertain to travel.

Matthew's dependence upon the Hebrew Scriptures has often been recognized.[22] If the author of Matthew assumed that his audience was familiar with the Hebrew Scriptures, then he would have used its conventions to engage his audience in his narrative. Wolfgang Trilling and Benjamin Hubbard have argued that the literary form of the commissions in the Hebrew Scriptures influenced the shaping of the final scene in Matthew.[23] Hubbard examines the structure of the commissioning scenes more extensively than Trilling, finds seven components (introduction, confrontation, reaction, commission, protest, reassurance, and conclusion), and perceives a similar structure in Mt. 28:16–20.[24] Although the goal of Hubbard's form-critical research is to hypothesize how Mt. 28:16–20 evolved, his data can be utilized to describe the pattern of a commissioning type-scene; the variations in the seven components can be studied to explain the function of the scenes in their larger narratives.[25] Every time a commission occurred, the audience expected it to be narrated with distinctive components and would perceive divergences meant an emphasis on certain themes. Since I want to determine if the implied audience would have expected men and not women to be commissioned in Mt. 28:16–20, I will focus on how women's commissions differed from men's.

Only one of the twenty-seven commissioning scenes that Hubbard examines portrays a woman being commissioned. Sarah (Gen. 17:15–27), whom Hubbard cites,[26] Hagar (Gen. 16:7–15; 21:15–21), the widow of Zarephath (1 Kings 17:8–16), and Ruth and Orpah (Ruth 1:6–19a)[27] are the only women in the Hebrew Scriptures who are commissioned. What is noticeable about their commissions is their narrow scope in comparison to Abraham's. Sarah's and Hagar's commissions address the auspicious future of their sons. The widow of Zarephath is told to bake bread for Elijah. Ruth and Orpah are told to return home. Abraham's commission establishes God's covenant with him as well as with his son and directs him to an unfamiliar place.

The mission given to men usually focuses on something other than the birth of sons, baking bread, or going home. Of the twenty-six texts in Hubbard's study where men are commissioned, only seven include the promise of many descendants and three of these are equally concerned with directing the man to a certain location (Gen. 11:28–30, 12:1–4a; Gen. 26:1–6; Gen. 46:1–5a).[28] Thirteen more include commands to travel and do not mention the blessing of many descendants.[29] Seven texts combine the command to travel and speak.[30] Five others, concerned neither with travel or reproduction, focus on a specific job or task: Samuel as a prophet (1 Sam. 3–4:1a), Joseph as the Pharaoh's grand vizier (Gen. 41:37–45), Solomon's building of the Temple (1 Chr. 22:1–6), the Jews' rebuilding of the Temple under Cyrus (Ezra 1:1–5), and the Servant's mission (Isa. 49:1–6).

This brief study of the commissioning scenes in the Hebrew Scriptures suggests that, if a commissioning type-scene existed, the implied audience would have usually expected a commissioned person to be male. To reiterate, commissioning type-scenes have plot patterns where the gender role behavior expected was that of males. The audience might have expected the disciples in chapters 10 and 28 to be women if the commissions had involved childbirth or promoted their sons' and

husbands' commissions. Matthew, however, has no interest in a commission involving childbirth; in fact, Matthew advocates a relationship
with God based on the observance of God's commands rather than
biological descent (Mt. 3:8–9, 12:46–50).

Since all of the commissioning scenes except Ezra 1:1–5 address
individuals, scenes of traveling groups must be examined next. If Matthew's audience was familiar with the Hebrew Scriptures, they would
have had expectations not only about commissioning type-scenes but
also about the portrayals of women and men in plots that involve
travel. Some of these expectations may have led them to have certain assumptions about commissioned groups. The Hebrew Scriptures
especially need to be examined to see whether a group of traveling
women would have sounded commonplace enough that commissioning scenes could have been adapted to depict women as the recipients
of a commission.

When the narrative sections of the Hebrew Scriptures are examined for how the travel motif is used, a scene of a group of women
who travel without men is unusual. Jephthah's daughter travels with
her friends in the mountains (Judg. 11:38–39). Judith goes into the
Assyrian camp accompanied by her female servant. Only the friends
of Jephthah's daughter (Judg. 11:38) and Judith's slave (Jdt. 10:10) are
portrayed as traveling companions who support the other woman in her
goals and return home with her.[31] When women are depicted as traveling without men, they travel without other women too. For instance,
Tamar, a widow, bereft of the financial support of a husband and sons, is
portrayed as returning home alone (Gen. 38:11). Jereboam's wife travels alone to get help from the prophet Ahijah for her sick son and then
returns home (1 Kings 14:4, 17). The Levite's wife travels away from
a threatening situation and journeys to her father's house alone (Judg.
19:2, cf. 19:10). It is noteworthy that in none of these texts does traveling diminish the woman's virtue. Even in Gen. 34:1–2 where traveling
alone is the context for Dinah's rape, the narrator attributes the cause
of her rape to Shechem's violence and not to her solitary travel.

In the narrative sections, groups of traveling women usually venture
out with men or are accompanied by men, who usually (but not always)
belong to their household. Rebekah and her female attendants follow
the male slave to Isaac's house (Gen. 24:61). David leaves ten concubines behind but takes with him the rest of his household, which would
include his wives and children, when he flees from Absalom (2 Sam.
15:16). The women in Egypt travel with the men to the new land
under the leadership of Moses (cf. Ex. 15:20) and continue to travel

with the men when Joshua resumes the leadership. Sometimes two
women travel with a man. For example, Lot's two daughters go with
their father to the hills (Gen. 19:30). Leah and Rachel return with
Jacob and their children to his home (Gen. 31:17–18). Hannah and
Peninnah go with their husband Elkanah to Shiloh to offer sacrifices
(1 Sam. 1:1–8). Individual women also traveled with or were accompanied by men: Sarah (Gen. 12:5); Zipporah (Ex. 4:20); Deborah (Judg.
4:9); Naomi (Ruth 1:1–2); Abigail (1 Sam. 25:18–20); the Queen of
Sheba (1 Kings 10:2; 2 Chr. 9:1); and the Shunammite woman (2 Kings
4:24–25, 2 Kings 8:2).

Only a few texts therefore depict women traveling without men.
Several of them indicate that individual women could be described as
commissioned to perform tasks other than bear children, bake bread, or
return home. Jereboam entrusts his wife with the task of procuring help
for their sick son (1 Kings 14:2). Jephthah tells his daughter to go and
spend the next two months with her friends as she has requested (Judg.
11:38). Uzziah tells Judith to go and carry out her plans (Jdt. 8:35).
These few texts, however, would not have prepared the audience for
the portrayal of twelve women going out from town to town preaching
about God's kingdom or eleven women traveling and winning converts
in all the nations.

On the other hand, portrayals of men, embarking on a trip as well
as returning home, either alone or with a group of men, abound in
the Hebrew Scriptures. The journey motif forms the framework for nar-
rating the feats of such men as Jacob, Moses, Joshua, Elijah, David,
Jeremiah, and Jonah as well as the accomplishments of many less no-
table men. What is particularly significant is how often leaders send
out groups of men, usually to fight, spy, or deliver messages: Gen.
42:2; Ex. 17:9; Num. 13:1–24, 22:5–15, 31:1–12; Josh. 1:11–15, 7:2,
8:1–9; Judg. 18:2, 20:12, 21:20; 1 Sam. 25:5; 2 Sam. 10:1–5, 20:6–
7; 2 Kings 1:9–13, 2:17, 7:15, 20:12–14; 1 Chr. 19:1–5, 19:8, 21:1–6;
2 Chr. 16:4, 34:21; Neh. 2:5, 9; Isa. 36:2, 37:2, 39:1–4; (cf. Jdt. 2:4–13;
1 Macc. 3:38–39, 7:8–10, 7:27, 8:17, 12:49, 15:15–17, 16:1–4, 16:18–
20).[32] These accounts suggest that audiences would have understood
the commissioning of groups of men to travel as a common feature of
stories about male leaders and thus as gender role reinforcements for
behavior socially acceptable for men, but not for women.

The author of Matthew could have assumed that his audience was
familiar with writings other than the Hebrew Scriptures and developed
these expectations about plots involving women's and men's travels
from their acquaintance with them. If Matthew can be classified as

popular literature, then it would have shared the conventions of other popular literature, for instance, ancient romance novels. Xenophon's *An Ephesian Tale* and Chariton's *Chaereas and Callirhoe* utilize the travel motif in a way similar to that in the Hebrew Scriptures.[33] The heroines Anthia and Callirhoe and other female characters travel extensively, but always with a man. In both novels the heroine's capture and status as a slave initiates her journeys without her husband. She moves from place to place as she is passed from man to man and adjusts to that new place. Her traveling is never motivated by her own goals. She never chooses where she goes until she is reunited with her husband. Then she goes home.

The heroes in the two novels also become slaves, but they gain their freedom and resume their travels. In *An Ephesian Tale*, after Habrocomes regains his freedom, he works as Apsyrtus' manager, then decides to leave to search for Anthia, joins Hippothous and his robber band who help him in his search, and later embarks on his own again. In *Chaereas and Callirhoe*, when Chaereas' trial in Babylon is interrupted by a revolt, his constant companion Polycharmus urges him to join the Egyptians to avenge the Babylonian king. Chaereas becomes the commander of the Greek soldiers and later admiral of the Egyptian fleet. The plots involving the men's travels, therefore, could have conditioned the audience to expect a group of men rather than a group of women to receive a command to be sent out in Mt. 10:5–15 and Mt. 28:16–20. The men in the ancient novels have goals motivating their travels.

If Matthew is an ancient biography, as a number of scholars claim, then the genre itself would have led the audience to anticipate an emphasis on the men who traveled with Jesus. Ancient biographies often use a travel motif to plot a man's accomplishments, military feats, and popularity. Richard Burridge's study of ancient biographies reveals that major portions of Isocrates' *Evagoras*, Xenophon's *Agesilaus*, Philo's *Moses*, Tacitus' *Agricola*, Plutarch's *Cato Minor*, and Suetonius' *Augustus* are devoted to the man's war travels with other men.[34] Burridge claims that 68.8 percent of Philostratus' *Apollonius of Tyana* focuses on Apollonius' travels and dialogues.[35] Travel is not a major motif in Lucian's *Demonax.*

In these biographies women are rarely mentioned. Isocrates claims that Evagoras was blessed with many children (72), but tells nothing about his wife or any woman. Xenophon only mentions Agesilaus' sister Cynisca, whom he encouraged to breed chariot horses (9.6). Evidently, a biography could omit the man's wife, for Plutarch mentions in his biography of Agesilaus that he had a wife and two daughters

(*Age.* 19.4–6). Philo includes an account about the protective care of Moses' mother, sister, and the Egyptian princess in his childhood and tells about Moses' marriage (1.11), the accompaniment of his wife and children with him to Egypt to deliver the Hebrews (1.15), his sister's leadership of the women's choir (1.32, 2.46), and the accompaniment of the women with the men on their journey out of Egypt (1.27, 1.60, 2.27). The bulk of the book, however, is about Moses' interaction with men: the Egyptian king; his twelve spies; his soldiers as they fought against the Phoenicians, the Canaanites, and the Amorites; and his brother and his sons, whom he made priests.

Tacitus, Plutarch, Suetonius, and Philostratus also rarely mention women in their biographies. Tacitus tells about the influence of Agricola's mother on his character (4) and implies that his wife Domitia Decidiana moved with him to govern a province in Asia, where she bore him a daughter (6). Plutarch mentions that Cato left his wife, Atilia, at home when he and his friend went to Macedonia to join a military tribune (9.1); left his household and daughters with his second wife, Marcia, when he pursued Pompey (52.1–5); but took his sister Servilia with him to Asia, where he left her (54.1–2). In his account about Caesar Augustus, Suetonius refers to Augustus' grandmother, mother, daughter Julia, and three wives, but never depicts women as travelers with or without men. Philostratus does not portray women as travelers either. He writes about Apollonius' mother (1.4–5); his rejection of marriage (1.13); his discussions about Medea, Sappho, and Damophyle (1.28, 1.30); his encounter with the piebald woman (3.3); and his healings and exorcisms of women and their sons (3.38, 3.39, 4.25, 4.45). If the treatment of women in these biographies is typical and the Gospel of Matthew were read as a biography, the audience would have expected little to be said about the women in Jesus' life and their travels.

A study of commissioning scenes in the Hebrew Scriptures and scenes involving travel in the Hebrew Scriptures, two ancient romance novels, and several biographies suggests that a scene of eleven or twelve female protagonists traveling without men would have sounded odd. Regardless of whether or not real women traveled in groups, the story could not be told that way and be convincing, in light of the conventional ideas of appropriate gender role behavior. A commission to women in Matthew could not have been adapted by adding scenes similar to those in the Acts of Paul 7–43, where Thecla rejects her betrothed, refuses her mother's entreaty to be Thamyris' wife, and undergoes persecution for her refusal before Paul validates her call with a commission to preach. After all, marriage is upheld in Matthew (5:31–32, 19:1–12). Although Peter had a wife (Mt. 8:14; cf. 1 Cor. 9:5) and left her and all his household and possessions behind (Mt. 19:27), his traveling does not require that he divorce her. As already shown, narratives about men who travel without their families are common.

The oddness of a scene of eleven or twelve women traveling without men suggests that the commissions of the male disciples, which are presented to the implied audience as normative for both men and women, are not normative and probably would not have been viewed as normative for all by an ancient audience. If the commissions were truly considered ones that women could receive, then the reversal of traveling male disciples to traveling female disciples in the narrative would not sound strange. Given the types of traveling scenes available, perhaps the author could have expanded the commissions and addressed the women in his implied audience by adding women to those addressed by Jesus to go out. A portrayal of women who travel alone is unusual, but not of women who travel with men. This adjustment, however, would overlook other dynamics. Women do not travel with just any men; they usually travel with members of their household. Since a disciple expressed his loyalty through the renunciation of his household (parents, children, land, possessions; see Mt. 19:27–29, 10:37–38), the inclusion of women from his household might leave his loyalty in question. If the proof of loyalty had another basis, female characters could have been included as recipients of the commissions.

How women can be devoted, commissioned disciples is, therefore, not depicted in Mt. 10:5–15 and 28:16–20. Knowing this viewpoint, modern female readers, who come to these texts believing that women's words and leadership are valuable, ought to resist further identification with the disciples. Identification with them would mean accepting a kind of loyalty that is based on the exclusion of women. Identification with the male disciples would require these modern women to deny their female gender as they affirm the charges to heal, teach, and make disciples. Denial of one's female gender, as was mentioned in chapter 2, leads to self-hatred and self-doubt, feelings that will constrict these women as they speak and lead.

It could be argued that Matthew addressed in other texts the way in which women in his audience might participate with the men. That Jesus tells the two women in Mt. 28:10 to "go" tell his brothers, the disciples, to meet him in Galilee means that they receive a separate commission.[36] That women are said to have accompanied Jesus on his travels from Galilee in Mt. 27:55 means that even though they were absent when Jesus addressed the disciples in chapter 10, the audience in retrospect can know that these women had a role in Jesus' ministry.[37] If it is true that Mt. 27:55 and Mt. 28:1–10 address women's participation in Jesus' mission plans, then the author may not have been making Mt. 10:5–15 and Mt. 28:16–20 normative for men and women in his implied audience. He was simply not addressing women. As mentioned earlier in the chapter, the gender of the audience is a modern question. In the cultural milieu in which Matthew was written, the protocol of male speech would have taken a male audience for granted.[38]

Identification with the female characters in Mt. 27:55 and 28:10, however, would also lead those modern women who view their own words and leadership as vital as men's to hurt themselves. They would be cooperating with the narrator's subordination of women. The story line subordinates the roles of the two women at the tomb to those of the male disciples. The task of the two women is overshadowed by the global task of the male disciples. Those modern female readers who have a strong sense of call and service to God would undermine themselves in such an identification with the women.

Mt. 23:1–12

In this portion of chapter 23 in the Gospel of Matthew, the narra-tor invites the audience to identify with the disciples and the crowds and accept Jesus' position as Jesus instructs them to act differently from the scribes and the Pharisees and treat each other as brothers. In this text, after the male disciples[39] are reversed to female disci-ples, modern readers need to know the ancient conventions governing speeches to determine whether it would be unusual to portray a group of women and a crowd as the audience of a speech about self-conduct. The speeches in the Hebrew Scriptures, ancient romance novels, and ancient biographies will be analyzed to determine whether a female au-dience would be unusual. The speeches will include all addresses, long or short, delivered to two or more people.

Examination of the Hebrew Scriptures reveals speeches, regardless of the topic and the length, are seldom directed to a group of women. Naomi gives a brief speech to the women in Bethlehem about her des-titution (Ruth 1:20–21). Jeremiah addresses "all the people and all the women" when he denounces their offerings to the queen of heaven (Jer. 44:24–30). Except for these two instances, speeches are not directed to women, unless women are subsumed in the address "the people." Leaders, such as Moses and Joshua, are often portrayed as speaking to the people, all the people, all the congregation, all Israel, or the Israelites: Ex. 13:3–16, 35:4–19, 35:30–36:1; Num. 14:7–9, 14:41–43, 16:28–30, 34:13–15, 36:5–9; Deut. 1:6–4:40, 5:1–26:19, 27:1–8, 27:12–28:68, 29:2–30:20, 31:2–6, 32:46–47; Josh 3:9–13, 6:16–19, 18:2–7, 24:2–15. The inclusion of women in the above general categories cannot be assumed. Each text has to be studied to decide whether women are actually addressed. In Deut. 5:1, for example, Moses convenes "all Israel" and tells them God's commands. Since the wife is omitted in the list of those persons prohibited to work on the Sabbath in Deut. 5:14, Tikva Frymer-Kensky argues that the second person singular imperative directly addresses women as well as men, who would not allow their servants, children, or livestock to work.[40] Danna Nolan Fewell, on the other hand, claims that the circumcision of "all in the people" in Josh. 5:5 and "all the nation" in Josh. 5:8 and the specification of women, children, and resident aliens in addition to "all the assembly of the people" in Josh. 8:35 reveal that women are actually marginal members of "all the people."[41] Her observations suggest that "the people" whom Joshua addresses in his speeches may be all men.

Whereas speeches to groups of women are rare, speeches delivered to a group of men are frequent: Gen. 49; Ex. 12:21–27; Lev. 8:31–35, 9:2–4, 10:6–7, 10:12–15; Num. 13:17–20, 16:5–11, 16:16–17, 30:1–16, 31:15–20, 31:21–24, 32:6–15, 32:20–24, 32:29–31; Deut. 31:10–13, 31:26–29; Josh. 1:10–15, 4:5–7, 8:4–8. Sometimes a group of men and the people are addressed: Josh. 23:2–16; 2 Kings 18:26–37 (Isa. 36:11–22); 1 Chr. 28:2–10; 2 Chr. 13:4–12, 23:3–7; Jer. 26:12–15, 27:16–22, 28:5–9, 42:7–22. These texts must also be examined to determine whether "the people" actually includes women.[42]

In the ancient romance novels *An Ephesian Tale* and *Chaereas and Callirhoe*, speeches are not directed to groups of women either. In *An Ephesian Tale* there are no speeches. The narrator often conveys Anthia's and Habrocomes' thoughts and feelings in solitary laments or prayers. In *Chaereas and Callirhoe*, however, the hero Chaereas and several male characters do deliver speeches. These speeches are either directed to other men or to a crowd. In Book 3, after Chaereas enters Callirhoe's tomb and laments the theft of her body, the crowd with him mourns for her. When he returns from a search for his wife's body, he reports to the crowd about the funeral offerings and the stranger on the ship he found. Then in Book 7, he urges his three hundred soldiers to defeat the Persians. In Book 8, when he returns home with Callirhoe, he speaks before the crowd again and tells them what had happened since he had last seen them. Several other characters in *Chaereas and Callirhoe* deliver speeches. Two men, jealous of Chaereas' marriage to Callirhoe, give speeches before other envious suitors as they plan Chaereas' downfall (1.2). Two robbers present suggestions to the rest about what to do with Callirhoe (1.10). Dionysius and Mithridates both present their cases before Artaxerxes and the people in the courtroom (5.6–7). The Egyptian king addresses his council about whether or not to fight against Tyre (7.3). In the biographies in Burridge's study, speeches are also not directed to groups of women. In some of them, speeches play no part in the way the life of the man is told. Isocrates' *Evagoras*, Xenophon's *Agesilaus*, Suetonius' *Augustus*, and Lucian's *Demonax* contain no speeches. In those biographies that do contain speeches, these are directed to men or a crowd of people. Plutarch's *Cato Minor* contains one major speech given by Cato to a group of men (68–69). Tacitus' *Agricola* includes both Agricola's speech to his soldiers (33–34) and Calgacus' address to his army (30–32). Philo's *Moses* contains Moses' speeches to groups of men (1.10.54–57, 1.50.222–26, 1.56.307–9, 2.32.171–72, 2.49.273) or his people (1.31.173–75, 1.36.201–2, 1.59.322–27, 2.42.230–32, 2.50.280–82). Philostratus' *Apollonius of Tyana* also contains several speeches given by men to men (e.g., 3.42, 4.8, 4.21, 4.38, 5.26, 5.33–36, 5.43, 6.10–11, 6.16, 7.14, 8.7, 8.26).

This study of speeches in the Hebrew Scriptures, two romance novels, and several ancient biographies suggests that the audience would have expected speeches in a narrative to be delivered to (1) men, (2) a crowd, or (3) men and a crowd. A scene with a group of women and the crowds exhorted by Jesus would have sounded unusual. Even if groups of real women were instructed by Jesus, the story could not be told that way and be persuasive to the audience. This oddness can serve as a signal that the instructions to the male disciples, which are presented to the implied audience as normative for men and women, are not normative. If the instructions were truly considered stipulations that women could accept and implement, then the replacement of the male disciples by a group of female disciples in the narrative would not sound strange. It is possible that the author of Matthew was not attempting to influence or persuade women. In other words, the author of Matthew did not envision women in his audience who would identify with the disciples.

It could be argued that since Jesus also addressed the crowds in 23:1, the author did not neglect women as a part of his implied audience.

Because Jesus taught the crowds, the author is presenting Jesus' instructions about humility and service to both men and women. Women, therefore, can identify with the crowds. Closer examination of Mt. 23:1–12 reveals that the women in the crowds are ignored. Women appear to be addressed and included when Jesus warns the crowds about the adverse influence of scribes and Pharisees on them and when he tells them that they are one community with one teacher and one master, the Christ. It is Jesus' warning to the crowds about being called rabbi and master that discloses the gender of those in the crowds whom he is addressing. Jesus is speaking to men. If Jesus were also speaking to the women, the narrator would be portraying Jesus as assuming that women as well as men would aspire to be called rabbis and masters and need to be corrected. Women are rarely portrayed as desirous of power and status over others; more often they seek privileges for their sons or their people.[43]

That Jesus is not addressing women in the crowds reaffirms that the disciples whom he addresses with them are male. Everything that Jesus says is directed to both groups; there is no break in the twelve verses where Jesus turns to speak to the crowds and then the disciples or vice versa.[44] Women are marginal in this text. How they need to better relate to each other and men is not addressed. How men ought to relate to women is not addressed either.

Knowing that women are not addressed in the text, modern female readers who are concerned about mutual respect and power relations ought to resist any further identification with the disciples in this text. Identification means affirming a kind of egalitarianism that is based on the absence of women. Affirmation of the disciples' experience would require these modern female readers to deny their female identities as they accepted Jesus' words. Denial of one's female gender, as mentioned before, leads to self-hatred and self-doubt, feelings that will undermine the mutual respect and empowerment that these women value for themselves and the people they know.

As a final comment, I want to acknowledge that analysis of the text could have begun and ended with a study of the gender of the crowds instead of beginning with a study of scenes with speeches. Such a study could lead to the assumption that the text tells us what really happened. One implication of the use of gender reversal is that modern readers can see that women may be marginalized in this text because the author was limited by the kind of scenes he could use to write convincingly in view of widely held conventional ideas about acceptable gender role behavior. Groups of real women may have been exhorted by Jesus, but such scenes would not be not narrated in the special protocols of male public language.[45]

Mt. 26:20–29

Once more the audience is urged to identify with the male disciples as they eat the Passover meal with Jesus in Mt. 26:20–29. The meal is dominated by the disclosure of the traitor among the disciples and Jesus' interpretation of the significance of the bread and the cup. Jesus explains the purpose of his impending death in terms of the broken bread and the wine and invites them to share his suffering and death. The audience who identifies with the disciples can allow themselves to be addressed by Jesus' words and participate vicariously in the meal. After the male disciples are reversed to female disciples, modern readers need to know ancient conventions about scenes with meals in order to assess whether a meal with a group of women would sound unusual. The Hebrew Scriptures, the two ancient romance novels, and several ancient biographies will be analyzed to evaluate whether a scene with twelve women at a meal would be odd.

A study of Passover scenes and references to Passover in the Hebrew Scriptures indicates that the depiction of the attendance of a group of women at Passover without the presence of men would have been unusual. Groups of men, that is, the priests and the Levites, killed and roasted the lambs; but Passover is repeatedly described as a meal that all the people or the Israelites attended and enjoyed: Josh. 5:10–12; 2 Kings 23:21–23; 2 Chr. 30; 2 Chr. 35:1–19; Ezra 6:19–22. Scrutiny of these five texts suggests "the people" would include women.[46] Although each household is instructed to divide one lamb among its members and with another household, if they cannot eat all of it (Ex. 12:1–20), how the men and women would arrange themselves at the Passover dinner is not mentioned.

In other meal scenes, groups of women eating a meal together are not portrayed either. The only women who are explicitly mentioned are individual women. Ruth is invited by Boaz to sit with the reapers and eat (Ruth 2:14); the woman of Endor prepares the food for the meal, but does not eat with Saul and his servants (1 Sam. 28:24–25); and Esther hosts a banquet and reclines with her husband (Esth. 5:5, 6:14, 7:8).[47] The rest of the meal scenes also subsume women among the people: Gen. 29:22, 31:54; Ex. 32:1–6; 1 Sam. 9:13, 22–24; 1 Sam. 30:16–20; 1 Kings 8:62–66; 2 Kings 4:1, 38–41; 2 Chr. 7:8–10, Esth.

9:18.[48] Again, how the people arranged themselves at the meals is rarely mentioned. Only the meal which Samuel hosts for Saul portrays the seating arrangement: Saul sits in a prominent place among the guests (1 Sam. 9:13, 22–24).

Whereas groups of women are not portrayed in meal scenes, groups of two men or more eating together are. Men are the guests of a male host in Gen. 18:1–15, 19:3, 26:30 (37:25), 43:16–34; Judg. 14:10, 19:8, 21; 1 Sam. 20:24; 2 Sam. 11:13, 13:23–29; 1 Kings 1:9–10, 13:19; 1 Chr. 12:39–40; Esth. 1:3, 2:18.

In the two romance novels, groups of women are not depicted as attending feasts. Banquets are activities enjoyed by groups of men and sometimes by groups of men and women. In Book 4 of *Chaereas and Callirhoe*, after Mithridates learns who Chaereas and Polycharmus are, he holds a banquet and invites them and his friends. In the same book, another meal scene occurs where Dionysius hosts a feast for his prominent fellow citizens. There are no explicit references to the presence of women in these two scenes. Following Dionysius' banquet, however, the narrator tells about Pharnaces' frequent visits to Miletus to see Callirhoe and his invitations to both Dionysius and Callirhoe to banquet with him. In *An Ephesian Tale*, the narrator refers to three feasts. In Book 2, Hippothous and his robber band spend a night feasting. In Book 3, Perilaus is feasting with his friends while Anthia is attempting to commit suicide in a different room. The narrator does not explicitly refer to the presence of women in either scene. In Book 8, however, men and women banquet together. Before they return to Ephesus, Anthia, Habrocomes, Hippothous, Cleisthenes, Leucon, and Rhode offer sacrifices and feast together.

Of the ancient biographies in Burridge's study, Philo's *Moses*, Suetonius' *Augustus*, Plutarch's *Cato Minor*, and Philostratus' *Apollonius of Tyana* each include meal scenes. None of the meal scenes mention the presence of groups of women, although in some cases, their presence with men may be implied. Philo tells about Moses' ruling on the participation of the bereaved in the Passover feast and implies all the people, male and female, celebrated it (2.51–52).[49] The narrator in Suetonius' *Augustus* summarizes the manner in which Augustus hosted dinner parties, refers to two men that he invited, and does not specify the gender of the other guests (74–75).[50] At the end of Plutarch's *Cato Minor*, Cato eats supper with a group comprised only of men, that is, his "companions" (οἱ ἑταῖροι *hoi hetairoi*) and "the magistrates" (οἱ ἄρχοντες *hoi archontes*) of Utica (67). Apollonius attends four feasts, only one of which may have included women (*Apollonius of Tyana* 2.28–34,

3.27–33, 6.15, 6.27). According to the narrator, the Indian king and five relatives, which possibly included women, feasted while lying on a mattress whereas the rest sat in chairs to eat (2.28).

This study of meal scenes indicates that audiences would have expected meals to be depicted as events attended by (1) men, (2) female guests who are married or related to the male guests or the host, or (3) a group of people whose gender is unspecified. They may have also expected Passover to be celebrated by a group of men or a group of men and their wives instead of "the people," as designated in the Hebrew Scriptures. Scholars have claimed that Greco-Roman symposium literature influenced Christian and Jewish writings,[51] especially its division of the meals into two parts, the meal proper and the drinking party, the former which matrons (and sometimes their daughters) would attend with their husbands and the latter which, beginning with the pouring of wine, would be attended by the male guests and prostitutes, courtesans, and flute or harp girls. Some works, such as Plato's and Xenophon's *Symposia*, depict banquets with no women present at the meal or the drinking party. Following the conventions of the time, Passover could be described either as a feast attended by all men or as a meal attended by men with their wives reclining next to them.

A scene of a group of women attending a meal with a male host would have sounded unusual. The author of Matthew would not have persuaded his audience about the significance of Jesus' death, if the group to whom Jesus was talking about his death were women. This oddness can serve as a signal that the experiences of the disciples, which are presented to the audience as normative for men and women, are not normative. If the disciples' inquiry about betrayal and Jesus' invitation to share his suffering and death were experiences in which women in his implied audience could participate, then the reversal of the twelve male disciples to twelve female disciples would not sound so strange.

Perhaps the author of Matthew could have addressed the women in his implied audience if he had included women along with the twelve disciples at the Passover meal. A group of women with a male host is an unusual depiction, but not a group of men and women at a meal with a male host. Again, such an adjustment would be incompatible with other dynamics in the narrative. In meal scenes, women accompany their husbands or fathers. The presence of women from their households, wives and daughters, at the Passover meal might have sounded contradictory to Peter's claim in Mt. 19:27 that he and the other disciples had left everything, even though wives are not among the relationships they must leave behind.[52] In other words, their absence simplifies the narrative and enables the audience to focus on another facet of the disciples' loyalty: will they share Jesus' suffering and death? The alternative, the presence of unrelated women, that is, prostitutes, courtesans, and flute girls, would have festive connotations inappropriate for the solemnity of the meal.

How women can share Jesus' suffering and death is not depicted in Mt. 26:20–29. Modern female readers who come to the text with strong commitments to risk as they love others ought to resist further identification with the disciples. Identification means affirming a loyalty to Jesus that is expressed through the exclusion of women. Denial of one's female gender, as mentioned before, leads to self-hatred and self-doubt, feelings that will undermine these women's commitments as they care for others in their communities.

Summary: Usefulness for Sermon Preparation

The reversal of the male disciples to female disciples in each of the four texts and the comparison of each text to similar scenes has demonstrated that gender reversal creates a scene that sounds odd. To write convincingly, the author could not portray the disciples as female characters or add women to the commissioning scenes in Mt. 10 and 28:16–20 and the meal scene in Mt. 26. The concern for power indicates that the speech in Mt. 23 was directed to male disciples and the men in the crowds. These dynamics suggest that the author of Matthew probably envisioned a male audience. Modern feminist literary critics, such as Fetterley, have argued that women need to become more aware when the implied audience of texts is male. Gender reversal helps to see that these four texts are directed to men. If modern female readers accept the perspectives of these texts and continue to identify with the disciples, they will hurt themselves. They will undermine their belief in the importance of women's speech and leadership, their concern for mutual respect and empowerment in their communities, their commitments to risk caring for others, and their female identities.

Modern women, however, must not resort to identifying with the female characters in other pericopes. Recognition that the commissions could be depicted as ones that male protagonists receive but not female protagonists, that speeches were usually directed to groups of men or crowds and not to women, and that meals could be portrayed with male guests or male guests with female kinsfolk but not with groups of women offers a way to see that women are marginal in these texts because the author was limited by the kinds of scenes he could use to write convincingly to men. Recognition of the author's limitations can offer the possibility of acknowledging that other avenues for expressing loyalty to God were not available in that cultural milieu. The literary and cultural conventions for expressing them had not yet been established.

This limitation of gender role stereotypes, plot patterns, and plot motifs becomes highly noticeable when the gender of Jesus is reversed. In the studies of the four texts, the gender of the disciples with whom the narrator invites the audience to identify was reversed, but not the protagonist Jesus. Since what enables identification with the disciples is identification with Jesus' position, Jesus' gender can be reversed too. When the gender of Jesus is reversed, scenes of a woman commissioning a group of women, of a woman speaking to a group of women and a crowd, and of a woman hostessing a meal become even more unusual. Naomi commissions Ruth and Orpah to go home (Ruth 1:8–15). Several women are depicted as directing a speech to a man or a group of men or laments to the divine.[53] Of the narratives examined, only Vashti gives a banquet for a group of women (Esth. 1:9). These particular writings provide few conventions for writing about female protagonists in the way Jesus and his twelve disciples are described.

In light of these limitations, a reading strategy that focuses on gender reversal may not seem to offer women anything for the preparation of sermons. Its application on the four Matthean texts displays even more intensely how male-oriented these texts are. The application of the strategy on Mt. 10 and Mt. 28, for instance, reveals that their portrayals of the disciples do not encompass how women can be commissioned disciples. I am convinced, however, that women can respond positively to the void disclosed by the strategy in at least two ways as they write sermons.

First, women can use some of the data that is gathered from a study of a biblical text where the strategy has been applied. They can include the data in a sermon that reflects upon whether we have a full picture of what happened and what gender roles are being reinforced. For example, without going into too much detail, a sermon on Mt. 10 or Mt. 28 could address how the protocols of male public language limited the author's options in how he could sway his male audience to accept his perspective about commissioned discipleship. Although real women may have been traveling with Jesus, the author could not portray the scenes that way. He had to write about Jesus' disciples in a way that met his audience's expectations. The sermon might reflect upon whether men at the end of the twentieth century need to hear a scene that excludes women in order to be persuaded to be loyal commissioned disciples. The author of Matthew is so convinced that loyalty to family (as understood in the first century) keeps men from doing what they must do to obey God's will that his portrayal of Jesus is one where men express their loyalty by leaving family members, especially female members.

Secondly, women can view the absence of female protagonists as a clue to explore other writings. For instance, the religious journeys in women's biographies and autobiographies can be used to complement Mt. 10 and Mt. 28 (or as the basis of a portion of sermons in a series).[54] A sermon might begin with some illustrations or a story about the damaging effects of modern women's identification with male protagonists and then mention the detriments of women's identification with the disciples in Mt. 10 or Mt. 28 before proceeding with a treatment of discipleship from a woman's biography or autobiography. Men in the congregation might appreciate a sermon that deals with discipleship differently than Mt. 10 or Mt. 28. The experiences of the male biblical characters, which the strategy emphasizes are not transferrable to women, are probably not normative for all men either. Race, class, sexual preference, and other factors may alter a man's identification with the male characters.

What this strategy offers for sermon preparation is the opportunity to help church members understand how the Bible can be used today to reinforce the gender roles of ancient times and thus place destructive expectations on the expression of faith today. The strategy can also provide the occasion for church members to learn that reading and listening to the Scriptures is a gendered activity and that women are unable to read and affirm their female identities when the protagonists are male. By examining the gender role behavior in biblical texts, sermons can be developed that address the need to expand our ideas of what women and men can do, how women can participate in the leadership and community of the church, and how women and men can communicate and demonstrate their faith.

In closing this chapter, one drawback to the application of gender reversal to the reading process must be mentioned, especially since it provides a way to introduce the strategy that will be explored in the next chapter. My application of gender reversal leaves the impression that female readers cannot identify with a male character and his concerns but must always resist this identification unless there is a similar story about a woman. Some feminists argue that not all writings with male protagonists must be resisted because the dynamics of the reading process are more complex. Some male protagonists convey not "male" but "human" experiences and values with which woman can resonate.

Because of these observations, the next chapter will explore a reading strategy that focuses on analogy, a strategy which provides a way for women to identify with the male protagonist(s) in some texts.

Chapter 4

ANALOGY

In the previous chapter, the use of gender reversal clarified that Mt. 10:5–15, 23:1–12, 26:20–29, and 28:16–20 were written about men and to men to persuade them to adopt a particular kind of discipleship. Modern women can acknowledge that they have been taught that these texts are directed to them when actually they are not addressing women. Some feminist critics, such as Patrocinio Schweickart, offer another way to read these texts because they have observed that the immasculation process is more complex.[1] Schweickart argues that she learned to reverse unconsciously the roles of the characters and suppress objectionable aspects when the thrust of the story matched her own aspirations and desires.[2] Her analysis of the reading process indicates that women who recognize the patriarchal context of the Bible can still identify with the experiences of the male protagonist(s) in some biblical texts if these experiences contain aspirations that are common to women.

This chapter will focus on how women can read biblical narratives analogously and affirm their female identities and experiences. Since women have often read biblical texts analogously, a discussion of what a feminist analogous reading involves will be presented first. Then the strategy will be applied to each of the four texts. The four examples will demonstrate another way for clergywomen to read biblical texts so that they can write sermons that take seriously the patriarchal context of the biblical texts; however, as in the last chapter, I will conclude with a few ideas about the helpfulness of the strategy for sermon preparation.

Development of the Strategy

Women have learned to draw out the contemporary relevance of biblical texts, often by describing analogous situations. For instance, the account of Sarai and Hagar is seen as similar to the relations between black and white women in the U.S.[3] The lack of witnesses to verify Anita Hill's charge against Clarence Thomas is deemed similar to the absence of witnesses to validate the accusation of Potiphar's wife against Joseph.[4] The story of Ruth and Naomi's cooperative relationship is compared to the possibility of harmonious coexistence between modern Israelis and Palestinians.[5] The rivalry between Leah and Rachel is viewed as similar to the competitiveness among sisters in modern families.[6] Modern people can express faith as Abraham did in the sacrifice of his son Isaac when they do not withhold from God what is most precious to them.[7] A woman's departure from her church to seminary is compared to the movement of Adam and Eve from the Garden of Eden.[8] Jesus' third temptation (Lk. 4:1–13) is termed the "pinnacle complex," the attempt of men and women in the ministry to maintain authority by viewing themselves as above everyone else.[9] Jesus' contrast of the people in the synagogue to the lepers and the widows among the Gentiles is contemporized with a contrast of affluent church members to bag ladies and homeless people (Lk. 4:17–27).[10]

When women or men draw these analogies, they do not always acknowledge that they can only make these comparisons if they ignore certain parts of the biblical story and add contemporary elements.[11] Sometimes women formulate analogies without considering the implications of the masculine gender of the protagonist in the biblical text. For example, the struggle to write a poem about a woman who had conceived during a rape is compared to Jacob's wrestling with the angel in Gen. 32.[12] A long and difficult childbirth is compared to Jesus' ordeals in Gethsemane.[13] Jesus' promise to his disciples to go before them and prepare for their arrival at his house with many rooms becomes an Asian American woman's vision of community where every person has a place.[14] Just as Jesus debated with the religious leaders about divorce and distinguished between those Scriptures which reflect a response to a specific historical situation and those which uphold God's intentions (Mt. 19:3–9), modern women can make this distinction in their interpretations.[15]

The type of analogous reading that Patrocinio Schweickart suggests requires that readers notice the gender of the protagonist. She agrees with Judith Fetterley that if she identifies with a male protagonist, such as Birkin in *Women in Love*, a novel that she recognizes as sexist, then she continues to immasculate herself.[16] Affirming Birkin's desires for autonomy and intimate relationships as similar to her own feminist aspirations is in itself insufficient. Such a text arouses these human desires in her but conveys them in a way that will immasculate her.[17] Only by consciously reversing the roles of Birkin and Ursula and ignoring certain patriarchal elements can she read Birkin's experiences as analogous to her own and resist immasculation.[18] Schweickart's observations imply that the steps of role reversal of the characters and suppression of patriarchal elements are too weak to curtail the immasculation process when done unconsciously. The attraction to the experiences of the male protagonist overrides these steps.

A feminist analogous approach to reading patriarchal texts, therefore, recognizes that in order for women to affirm the experiences of the male protagonists as "human" ones rather than "male" ones, specific steps that they perform unconsciously must be done consciously. Literary theorists have often discussed unconscious influences on readers. According to Iser, the real reader's experiences form the background for comprehending the text; they guide the reader at least on an unconscious level and significantly shape the outcome of the reading.[19] However, Iser does not discuss this part of the reading process in detail.[20] Other literary theorists, such as Jonathan Culler and Stephen Mailloux, discuss how the experience of reading literary texts or of reading the extraliterary world affects people as they read a specific text.[21] Neither presumes that real readers are aware of these influences as they read.

I am proposing, therefore, that women need to use consciously some of the maneuvers that have developed from Schweickart's experiences of reading and have guided her and possibly many women to read patriarchal texts. The role(s) of the male protagonist(s) must be reversed so that the female reader can affirm her female identity and experiences. Patriarchal aspects of the story must be suppressed to affirm the central "human" thrust of the story and resist immasculation. The discarded patriarchal elements, which Schweickart leaves undefined, would need to include not just those that blatantly denigrate women but also those that favor one race or class over another, promote hierarchical relationships, and utilize dualistic categories that justify oppressive relationships,[22] because acceptance of these aspects would also diminish female readers.

In rereading the four texts, I will not attempt to recontextualize them with contemporary settings. After the roles of the characters are reversed, our attention will be on the thrust of the story with which female readers are urged to identify and develop their analogous readings. Examples of those elements that women must eliminate to maintain a positive reading experience will be given. Since readers are always using strategies which allow them to give greater significance to certain textual elements than others and to ignore some altogether, this approach is only highlighting what is done as a matter of course.[23] The problem of whether the patriarchal elements can be adequately separated from the thrust of the scene will also be addressed.

Mt. 10:5–15

In Mt. 10:5–15, Jesus sends out the twelve male disciples to preach about the nearness of the kingdom of God and heal the sick. The disciples will do what Jesus had done. In the previous chapters, Jesus was the kind of Messiah who removed people's suffering and challenged religious laws to demonstrate love to them. Through eliciting belief in Jesus' power and admiration of his teaching and healing of the sick, the narrator has aroused the audience to identify with the male disciples: the audience is urged to share Jesus' power, alleviate human suffering, and tell about the nearness of God's kingdom.

As modern women read this chapter, they are guided to accept the role of the implied audience and identify with the twelve male disciples. Modern women can read the text analogously as an invitation to share Jesus' power and the message of God's nearness and to care for their fellow human beings, especially the sick and the outcast. They can read the instructions to shake the dust off their feet as encouragement to move on to someone else when help is refused. When Mt. 10:5–15 is read in the context of the rest of the chapter, moving on must be understood as the means to deliver the message about the nearness of the Kingdom to as many people as possible before the End occurs. Moving on limits abuse but does not end it because in the remainder of the chapter Jesus speaks about the persecution that the disciples can expect wherever they go.[24]

Modern women can especially enjoy an analogous reading of Mt. 10:5–15 when they deliberately reverse the roles of Jesus and the twelve male disciples to a female Messiah and twelve female disciples. They can feel themselves validated in a way somewhat similar to the way male readers have identified with Jesus and the disciples. Implicit in the Gospel of Matthew, as in most literature where the implied audience is asked to identify with male protagonists, is the affirmation of the male reader's maleness.[25] If it seems outlandish to reverse the characters to a female Christ and female disciples, let me emphasize again that women would only be consciously doing what it has been suggested women have already done unconsciously in order to read some texts with male protagonists.[26] A deliberate reversal allows women to give themselves an explicit affirmation of their gender identities, which male readers have received implicitly by the text, and can help keep them aware that the perspectives and actions of the disciples must not be affirmed without eliminating those elements that diminish them as female readers.[27]

When modern women read Mt. 10:5–15 analogously as an invitation to share Jesus' power and the message of God's nearness to people in their own lives and the world, they must set aside or accommodate at least four aspects of the text. First, female readers must suppress Jesus' command to the disciples to limit ministry to their own race, since this demand conveys patriarchal preference for one race above all others. This omission, however, would be consistent with the thrust of the whole narrative. Since the disciples do not go out after they receive their commission in Mt. 10 and Jesus expands their commission in Mt. 28:16–20, disregard for the narrow focus of the disciples' ministry in Mt. 10:5–15 would mean reading it within its larger narrative context.[28] The absence of a report of the disciples' departure and return discourages the audience from accepting the disciples' missionary work prematurely.[29] Since the disciples have not yet seen how Jesus will face the situations he says they will face because of him, they are unprepared to go out.[30] When they are ready, their mission will be extended to other peoples.

The second element that a female reader must suppress is its promotion of hierarchical relationships. A few disciples are sent to a large number of people who are assumed to be lost and in need of the message of God's nearness and are not consulted about what they need and want to know about God. Since in previous and subsequent chapters Jesus demonstrates how dialogue can occur when he heals the sick (e.g., Mt. 8:5–13, 20:29–34), the suppression of hierarchical relationships may not significantly change the thrust of the text.[31] Commissioned disciples would engage in dialogue as Jesus did and would expect people to approach them as Jesus was approached. Also, they would not force their views on people; they would leave if unwelcomed.[32]

If women reverse the roles of Jesus and the disciples and suppress these two elements, they can more readily retain the thrust of Jesus' commands as human rather than male aspirations. Modern female readers can acknowledge it as a patriarchal text, affirm their female identities, and still accept its invitation. The third and fourth aspects are more integral to the portrayal of Jesus and the disciples. If women take into account the cultural context of Mt. 10, they can dismiss the third aspect as harmless, at least the way that they initially understood it. The fourth one poses more difficulties.

The third element is the notion of losing one's self to find it, the reason that Jesus gives the commissioned disciples later in the chapter that their mission and persecution will not be in vain (10:39). If modern female readers understand the demand to lose one's self as a requirement that perpetuates an oppressive self-denial, already enculturated in them,[33] and is insensitive to the different ways that women quest, then female readers may conclude that there is no way to affirm the disciples' quest. Women, however, can put this element aside as innocuous if they understand it in its cultural context. To demonstrate that women can set the element aside and retain the text, I must first explain why the disciples' quest might be viewed as a male quest.

Some feminists claim the pattern of losing one's self to find it typifies the quests of male heroes, but not those of female heroes.[34] In their opinion, contrary to Joseph Campbell's position that all heroes, male and female, separate from the familiar and face trials that require them to lose themselves and give themselves for the sake of others or for some higher purpose other than to seek self-preservation,[35] the quests of female heroes in literature display a reverse pattern. Whereas a male hero moves from a position of pride to one of humility, a female hero moves from a lack of self to the discovery and affirmation of the self.[36] A male hero stands on his own to face trials alone; a female hero searches to reconnect with her family and her past.[37] In her analysis of Madeleine L'Engle's A Wrinkle in Time, Marion Zimmer Bradley's The Mists of Avalon, Margaret Atwood's Surfacing, and Maxine Hong Kingston's The Woman Warrior, Mara Donaldson demonstrates that the female hero in each of these books has a quest where relationship to others is crucial for the hero to become a self.[38]

On the basis of these two patterns, it might be argued that Jesus models to the disciples and the audience the kind of quest typical of male heroes. He has left his family in Galilee and all that is familiar; for the sake of the forgiveness of many people, he will face the hostility of the religious leaders and his death, all of which he will overcome through his resurrection; and then he will return home to Galilee. The pattern of the male quest, however, does not fully explain the dynamics of Jesus' ministry. Jesus separates himself from his biological family, but he does not become an isolated self who alone confronts great trials. He defines himself in relation to God, whom he calls Father, and in relation to those who do God's will, whom he calls his family. The pattern of the male quest also does not adequately describe the dynamics of the disciples' ministry in Mt. 10. In demanding the disciples to love him more than mother, father, son, or daughter, Jesus assumes that their identity and self-worth rest in their familial relationships. Jesus urges them to seek their identity and self-worth in terms of their relationship to him. The disciples who are called to imitate him, therefore, change "families" and never become isolated individuals. Losing the self in this case does not mean the same thing as negating the self. Losing or denying the self for Jesus' sake means taking the risk to define one's self in relation to Jesus and those who do God's will (12:50) instead of in relation to one's biological family. The notion of affirming or negating a developed self or ego is a twentieth-century concern that the text does not address.[39] If modern women recognize this difference, then the notion of losing one's self in this commission might be unobjectionable. Losing one's self in this quest is an affirmation of interdependence with those who are responding to God's will.

The notion that is actually more problematic is Jesus' command that the disciples love him more than father, mother, daughter, or son (10:37). Although loving Jesus more would permit them to love their families some, except for Mt. 8:14–15, the narrator does not portray Jesus or the twelve disciples doing anything to care for their biological families.[40] The audience is given the impression throughout the gospel that the disciples must put aside all special feelings toward them, give exclusive attention to Jesus, and spend all their time with him and the other disciples as they learn from him.[41] This reattachment to Jesus and their group marks them as good, faithful disciples.[42]

This devotion to Jesus and their group to the exclusion of their parents and children may be the most troublesome aspect for some female readers to suppress. If love for father, mother, son, or daughter is understood as an expression of loyalty to family which threatens to diminish a loyalty to Jesus, then the quest of the disciples is based on a dualism, which, as in the case of other dualisms, perpetuates oppressive relationships. How does the Gospel of Matthew maintain that love for family is incompatible with love for Jesus? Since one of the purposes of Jesus' coming is the dissolution of family ties (10:34–36),[43] love for family members opposes Jesus' establishment of a family based on those who do God's will (12:50). Love for Jesus thus becomes associated with doing God's will and storing treasures in heaven whereas love for family becomes associated with those material things that hinder the doing of God's will: lands, houses, possessions (19:21, 29). Female readers, who do not want to polarize family and religious communities or materiality and the soul,[44] who recognize the potential for harm and good in both family and religious communities, would have to ignore Jesus' demand to love him more and focus on the thrust of the text: the quest which urges them to attend to both the needs of people's souls and bodies by telling about the nearness of God's Kingdom and healing their bodies.

Ignoring Jesus' demand, however, significantly alters the thrust of the text. It confounds a ranking of different kinds of love so that a different picture of discipleship emerges. A committed disciple can love both Jesus and family members. A disciple who loves Jesus can spend time with family. Identification with the group of disciples in Mt. 10 can thus become something intermittent for modern female readers rather than an ongoing way of life as depicted in the text. Female readers can analogize going back to their families at the end of the quest or calling home or taking their families with them on the quest. Unlike the disciples who are sent out to care about the material needs of others but give minimal attention to their own, modern women can attend to the material needs of themselves and their families as well as other people.

The deletion of Jesus' demand to love him more moves the text in such a different direction that were its omission continued throughout the Gospel of Matthew a new story would be created. Female readers cannot delete the demand without rewriting the gospel narrative. It might be asked why not dispense with this text and use a modern one that provides female readers a way to affirm familial relationships in their quests.[45] Reading a different text is one way to respond to Mt. 10:5–15 in a self-affirming manner. Another way is to accept its invitation and at the same time continue to criticize its polarization of family and religious communities. The value of this perhaps more conservative position is that it allows women to affirm those impulses that brought them to the text in the first place; it also encourages women to challenge its view of family and discipleship and bring about the rewriting of the text in human lives.

Mt. 23:1–12

The narrator invites the audience in this chapter to identify with the disciples and the crowds as Jesus instructs them about how to treat each other. Jesus begins by advising them to do what the scribes and the Pharisees say but not to imitate their actions. These people, according to Jesus, are very poor models. Their actions contradict their teachings. They call attention to themselves with their religious titles and their seats at banquets and in the synagogues. Jesus tells the disciples and the crowds that they must not be called "rabbi" or "master" or call anyone "father" because they have one teacher and are all brothers, they have their Father in heaven, and they have Christ as their master. Jesus teaches them that the one who is great among them will be their servant.

Modern women who have accepted the role of the implied audience are encouraged to identify with the disciples. When they identify with them, they accept the instructions that they must not emulate the arrogant behavior of the scribes and the Pharisees and must regard each other as "brothers" (ἀδελφοί adelphoi). Female readers have gravitated to this text and read it analogously, citing it as an instance where Jesus challenged patriarchal structures and promoted egalitarianism.[46] If modern women consciously reverse the roles of the disciples, Jesus, and the scribes and the Pharisees to female disciples, a female Messiah, and female scribes and Pharisees, then they can more fully enjoy identification with the disciples. They can affirm their gender identities as male readers already do.

Reversal of the disciples in Mt. 23:1–12 may seem unnecessary, since "disciples" (μαθηταί mathētai) could refer to a larger group than the twelve male disciples and thus would include female disciples.[47] The narrator, however, has given no indication that other disciples have been added since chapter 10, especially female disciples. Later in Mt. 27:55 the narrator refers to women who had followed Jesus from Galilee, but even here does not designate any of them as a disciple as Joseph of Arimathea is described.[48] The narrator therefore is probably using "disciples" synonymously with "the twelve disciples."[49] If modern women revise their reading of the disciples in Mt. 23:1 in light of Joseph of Arimathea in Mt. 27:57 to include more than the twelve, the disciples are still all male.

While reversing the roles of the characters and identifying with the thrust of Jesus' commands to them, female readers must suppress or accommodate at least two elements in Jesus' instructions in order to avoid perpetuating oppressive relationships. One element that female readers must set aside is their awareness that all the people whom Jesus addresses belong to the same race. For modern female readers who understand that the oppression of women cannot be separated from issues of race, an egalitarianism that does not address the relations among races is inadequate. They can ignore this element if they read ` the instructions in the context of the whole gospel. In Mt. 28:16–20 the mission will be extended to other ethnic groups.[50] This extension will require disciples to practice egalitarianism among races other than their own.

A second element that female readers must suppress in order to affirm its egalitarian perspective is its stereotypical view of the Jewish religious leaders. When the disciples and the religious leaders are reversed to female disciples and female religious leaders, female readers can become aware that the egalitarianism that appeals so much to them is defined by pitting them against other women.[51] The female disciples who must not seek public recognition and with whom female readers are urged to identify are pitted against the female religious leaders who do everything for recognition. Female readers, familiar with how women have been depicted stereotypically in literature, must recognize that the religious leaders are caricatured so that their attributes, which are actually compatible with egalitarianism, are deemed totally deplorable.[52] Self-respect, the need for recognition and respect from others, and expectations of responsible behavior in other people are described as arrogance, ostentatiousness, and overbearance. Such a caricature promotes a kind of egalitarianism in which female readers are encouraged to reject any aspirations for public recognition and respect, aspirations which women (and other oppressed groups) need to claim and express so that they do not leave their abilities undeveloped.[53]

The dualism underlying the comparison of the disciples and the religious leaders fosters a position that can lead female readers to denigrate themselves. Women cannot easily eliminate this comparison by ignoring verses 1–7 and concentrating on verses 8–12 because throughout the gospel discipleship is defined by urging the audience not to do what the religious leaders do.[54] Female readers are in a position similar to that discovered in the study of Mt. 10:5–15 where dualism shapes its perspective. In a similar way, women can still affirm the egalitarian thrust of Mt. 23:1–12 that appeals to them so much if at the same time they question the caricature of the religious leaders.

Mt. 26:20–29

In this text, the narrator invites the audience to identify with the twelve disciples as they sit at a table and eat the Passover meal with Jesus. The narrator focuses on a dialogue between Jesus and the disciples about his betrayal. While Jesus prepares the disciples for his betrayal and death, the audience, who already knows from chapter 10 that Judas will betray Jesus, also receives preparation for Jesus' imminent death. The audience can identify with the anxious disciples and distance themselves from the traitor.

The narrator also invites the audience to identify intimately with the disciples as Jesus offers them the bread and the cup and reinterprets the Passover meal in light of his impending death. With the disciples, they are invited to accept the forgiveness for their sins that Jesus' death in the remaining chapters will bring. With the disciples who drink the cup, they are urged to share his suffering and death and to recall Jesus' words. In Mt. 20:17–28 he had told the disciples about his impending death, refused James' and John's request, and promised that the disciples would drink his cup. The disciples will suffer and die because they will challenge traditions and speak out on behalf of the outcast, the sick, and the poor as Jesus did.

Modern female readers who accept the role of the implied audience are also led to identify with the twelve disciples. As they follow the story line of chapter 26, they can become the disciples and allow themselves to join the dialogue about the betrayer; they can listen to Jesus' reinterpretation of the Passover meal, his offer of forgiveness, and his invitation to share his suffering and death. Modern female readers can more fully enjoy identification with the disciples when they consciously reverse the twelve disciples and Jesus to twelve female disciples and a female Messiah. As in the analysis of the two previous texts, role reversal gives female readers a reading experience where they can affirm their gender identities. In particular they can receive the promise that the suffering of the Messiah who has a body like theirs will bring about a new relationship between God and humanity. Female readers can also consider the negative and positive implications of a suffering female Messiah.[55]

In order to read Mt. 26:20–29 analogously as an intimate meal in which they eat bread and drink the cup with the Messiah who is about to die, some female readers may need to suppress or accommodate two aspects. One aspect some female readers may need to ignore is the implication that Jesus' invitation to share the cup means that they must choose to live lives of sacrificial love. To those female readers who are aware of how women have deprived and subordinated themselves for the betterment of men's lives or have not had any choice but to serve others, acceptance of this invitation could mean the perpetuation of women's subordination to men.[56] This invitation may be accommodated rather than disregarded if women view sacrificial giving as speaking out and acting on behalf of those who lack basic needs, not always putting everyone else's needs before their own. Although Jesus continually challenged unjust traditions and attended to his people's needs, female readers can recall that Jesus also retreated from people and potential danger before resuming his ministry (e.g., 4:12, 12:15, 14:13, 14:23). This type of reading, of course, means giving Jesus' withdrawals more emphasis.

The second aspect that some female readers may need to accommodate is the implication that commitment to God requires physical suffering and death. Drinking Jesus' cup implies more than accepting the possibility of suffering and death; drinking Jesus' cup means expecting to suffer and die.[57] Such an expectation that physical suffering is an integral part of the disciples' commitment to God promotes a devaluation of the human body. The body can be abused and killed for the sake of a higher cause. Those female readers, for instance, who know women who have devalued their own bodies and remained in abusive relationships for the sake of keeping sacred marriage vows, are left in an uncomfortable situation. One response to the dilemma is to discard the text; another is to affirm the desire to advocate for the betterment of other people's lives as Jesus did and at the same time question in what ways other than physical suffering faithfulness to God can be expressed.[58]

Mt. 28:16–20

At the end of the gospel, the audience is once more invited to identify with the disciples as they meet Jesus on the mountain in Galilee as he had directed them. The disciples who had deserted Jesus when he was arrested in Gethsemane are now with him. Still wavering in their devotion to him, they are "learners"[59] and thus still need his teaching and his presence. Once more Jesus tells them what to do. He commissions them to go to all the Gentiles and make disciples, baptizing them and teaching them all that he had commanded them. He promises that he will always be with them. The audience who identifies with the disciples receives the assurance that the risen Jesus will be with them too as they execute the commission.

As modern women read this final scene, they too are guided by the narrator to accept the role of the implied audience and identify with the eleven disciples. They can read this text analogously that they too must enable everyone else to know Jesus' commands, commands which call for the expression of compassion, forgiveness, mercy, peace, justice, and generosity in human relationships. They too, as "learners," can depend on Jesus' risen presence to guide them as they tell others about Jesus' commands and incorporate them into God's family.

Modern women can more fully enjoy identification with the eleven disciples when they consciously reverse the roles of Jesus and the eleven male disciples to a female Messiah and eleven female disciples. As male readers have had their goals affirmed, women can receive validation for their aspirations. For the moment, undistracted by arguments about whether or not Jesus authorized only men to proclaim his commands, female readers can allow themselves to imagine themselves speaking to many people about Jesus' teachings. They can affirm themselves as "learners," who depend on Jesus' risen presence to help them when they fail and doubt.

While reversing the gender of Jesus and the eleven male disciples and identifying with the thrust of Jesus' commands to them, female readers who want to extend the benefits of Jesus' message without perpetuating the detriments of patriarchy must suppress some of the elements of the scene. In addition to some of the elements in the commission in chapter 10, women must ignore or accommodate at least three other aspects. First, the stereotypical portrayal of "the Gentiles" tends to promote a hierarchical relationship between the disciples and those among "the Gentiles" whom they will teach. If modern women want to keep this text and implement the commission without perpetuating hierarchical relationships, then they must suppress its stereotypical portrayal of "the Gentiles" by recalling earlier depictions of the Gentiles and acknowledging that identification with the disciples means that they are "learners."[60]

The Gentiles are portrayed stereotypically because implicit in the instructions to the disciples is the assumption that the Gentiles need to have Jesus' commands taught to them. That the Gentiles must be taught God's commands presumes that they do not know them. That the Gentiles need complete knowledge of God's commands overlooks and undermines what the narrator has already shown some Gentiles know and how firmly some Gentiles believe in God's power. The dialogues of Jesus with the centurion (8:5–13) and the Canaanite woman (15:21–28) affirm that they know God's commands. They understand that God had directed Jesus to minister to Israel alone[61] and challenge Jesus' adherence to that command. Other Gentiles are depicted as believing in Jesus' divine power (e.g., 2:1–12, 27:54). Recollection of these responses can counter notions that those to whom the commissioned go are ignorant and faithless.

Another aspect that some female readers must set aside is the subordination of the two women in Mt. 28:1–10, who see the empty tomb, tell the disciples to go to Galilee, but do not receive the commission with them. After the step of role reversal, they would temporarily become two men whose role is subordinated to the female disciples in Mt. 28:16–20. Ignoring the subordination and absence of the two men in the commissioned task in Mt. 28:16–20 can be either oppressive or liberating, depending on whether female readers think women's liberation must occur separately from men or with them.[62] Those female readers who reject a reversal of power as the goal of women's liberation may have to view the commission as a temporary experience and ignore much of the gospel that portrays discipleship as a community of one gender of people.

Perhaps even more critical for female readers is finding a way to adopt a commission that privileges tradition over experience. The experience of the two women at the tomb verifies that the disciples did not steal the body as the Jewish religious leaders suspected they would and the guards rumored they did.[63] At the same time, the narrator urges the audience, who cannot have the tomb experience, to know that their vicarious experience of reading about Jesus' death and the empty tomb is sufficient. The commissioned disciples also did not watch Jesus die or see the empty tomb and could only know about his death and the tomb because of the women's report. Much more important is the task entrusted to the commissioned disciples to hand down Jesus' teachings to others, a task also entrusted to the audience who identifies with them.[64] Female readers, aware of how easily tradition ossifies and becomes impervious to changing and immediate needs, might want to suppress this distinction between tradition and experience by emphasizing the promise of Jesus' presence. Jesus, who challenged traditions void of mercy and compassion, remains available among modern disciples, who are learning to challenge traditions as he did.

Summary: Usefulness for Sermon Preparation

In rereading the four texts, the question was never asked whether female readers could do what the male protagonists were doing. The question underlying the strategy was how modern women might do what the male protagonists are doing if they identify with them. The thrust of the text was examined, the roles of the characters were reversed, and then examples were given of elements that female readers might need to suppress or accommodate into their reading of the text. Focus was placed on how female readers who want to identify with the thrust of the text might affirm it without perpetuating patriarchal perspectives. In some cases, an element could be ignored because its omission barely changed the narrative. In some cases, the element could be held in check by emphasizing another element. In still other cases, an element required continued critique while the thrust of the text was affirmed. Women can have a more positive reading experience, neither totally rejecting the text nor wholeheartedly accepting it.

The strategy is compatible with some of the more traditional approaches to writing sermons. Women can claim the experience of a male character in some texts as a general human experience, one that women can have even if women have not been portrayed doing it, one that is worthy of recommending in a sermon for a congregation of women and men. The strategy, however, does not primarily attempt to provide a contemporary setting for the experience of the main character (male or female) to be used in a sermon. The development of a sermon must focus on the critical evaluation of the text that the strategy demands. This strategy requires women to think about the needs of the people in their community and scrutinize the patriarchal aspects of the text that accompany the central thrust with which they identify. These patriarchal elements might find their way into a sermon and promote oppressive relationships and various forms of bias if women do not consciously and conscientiously examine.

When women apply this strategy to biblical texts, they can use the data from the analysis to develop sermons that encourage their congregations to question and dialogue with the perspective of the texts. A sermon on Mt. 28, for instance, could guide a congregation to question its emphasis on the handing down of traditions and the subordination of experience to tradition. A sermon developed from a study of Mt. 26:20–29 could reflect upon the necessity of physical suffering as a mark of discipleship and imagine other expressions of faithfulness to God. Although a sermon need not always display the reversal of the roles that are used during the study of the text, there may be occasions where role reversal is the best way to encourage a congregation to dialogue with the text. For example, the reversal of Jesus, the disciples, and the religious leaders in Mt. 23:1–12 to all female characters may enable women in a congregation to reflect more easily upon the detriments of identification with the disciples. This identification would affirm a type of egalitarianism that pits them against other women and unfairly criticize these women for their arrogance, ostentatiousness, and overbearance.

This reading strategy, which focuses on reading the text analogously, is a dynamic one. It allows women to affirm the viewpoints and experiences of the male protagonist(s) to which they have been drawn and at the same time commits them to discern the oppressive aspects of these experiences and perspectives. Not all of the patriarchal aspects have been addressed in my study of the four Matthean texts. Even those examined need modification by real readers in their own contexts. The roles of the characters in the texts preceding Mt. 10:5–15, 23:1–12, and 26:20–29 were not reversed as the female characters were in Mt. 28:1–10; they could have been reversed to explore whether their roles are also subordinated to that of the disciples. There is another way to examine how female characters in preceding texts shape the dynamics of Mt. 10:5–15, 23:1–12, 26:20–29, and 28:16–20. Women readers can study how the author used female characters to foster bonds between male characters and to encourage the audience's identification with the disciples. I turn now to explain and apply a strategy that focuses on women as exchange objects.

Chapter 5

WOMEN AS EXCHANGE OBJECTS

Feminist literary critics, such as Patrocinio Schweickart and Florence Howe, have argued that when men identify with a male protagonist, the female characters become the means or the objects by which the male reader is bonded with the male author.[1] The reading experience for women is different. Women must often identify against themselves because the activities and perspectives of the male protagonist(s) are defined against the female characters.[2] It might seem that biblical texts without female characters would not present this problem of bifurcation for female readers. This position, however, overlooks how female characters in preceding texts continue to shape later texts. The two women in Mt. 28:1–10, as we have observed, affect the thrust of Mt. 28:16–20. Female characters in texts preceding Mt. 10:5–15, 23:1–12, and 26:20–29 have an impact on these texts.

This chapter will develop and apply to the four texts a reading strategy that focuses on women as exchange objects. Female readers can see how female characters enable the audience to identify with Jesus and the disciples and accept their perspectives. Rereading the four texts with this strategy also allows women to see how female characters are used to define discipleship. They can evaluate in what ways they want to challenge and redefine discipleship in the present. As in the case of the other two strategies, this one can help women use biblical texts in their preparation of sermons in a way that reflects and affirms their feminist perspectives.

Development of the Strategy

Both Patrocinio Schweickart and Eve Sedgwick use Levi-Strauss' sociological theory of women as exchange objects[3] to analyze some of the dynamics that can occur in the reading of literature. Schweickart draws from Levi-Strauss' theory to describe the bond that female characters foster between the author and the male reader. She is mainly concerned with how a female character is reduced to an object for the benefit of the male readers, for she equates the female character to the text that circulates between author and readers and forms a close relationship between them.[4] This dynamic in the reading process, the establishment of a bond between the author and readers through the identification against female characters, must be studied along with a consideration of how male and female characters interact with each other in the narrative world of texts, especially biblical texts. Female readers need to know how the characters interact with each other because examination of these relationships can help them decide whether they will challenge this reading dynamic or continue to identify against the female characters.

Sedgwick's study of several modern literary works offers this needed complement. She has used Gayle Rubin's critique of Levi-Strauss' theory to analyze the relationships between male characters and has demonstrated that male characters use relationships with women to form bonds with men and to show their dominance over other men.[5] What Sedgwick's analysis highlights is that men's relationships with other men are the primary ones, not their relationships with women. Although most readers know that the relationship between Jesus and the twelve male disciples is the primary one in the Gospel of Matthew, what role female characters have in this relationship has seldom been recognized. Her approach provides a way to explore their impact on Jesus' relationship with the disciples.

Sedgwick's approach can be adapted to an audience-oriented study of the relationships between male characters in biblical texts without female characters. Since in the reading process previous material prepares and guides the audience to accept the perspective in later material,[6] attention can be shifted back to this previous material to study how the female characters have been used to foster bonds between male characters. This analysis can be used to determine how the female characters continue to shape the relationships between male characters in the later material where no female characters are found. No female characters play a major continuing role throughout the Gospel of Matthew and so analysis of the function of female characters as exchange objects will be less involved than Sedgwick's study.[7]

This type of analysis differs from a study of the function of female characters as foils. The examination of female characters as foils in the

Gospel of Matthew has attempted to reveal what the women have done that the disciples ought to have done. When the woman who touched Jesus' cloak in Mt. 9:20–22, for example, is understood to function as a foil, her exemplary faith in Jesus is contrasted to the little faith of the disciples.[8] The woman (and other such minor characters) model to the audience one aspect of discipleship so that the audience can become better disciples than the character group of disciples.[9] However, when a female character is examined as an exchange object, the analysis focuses on how a male character relates to that woman to gain authority or superiority over another man (or men) and what ways the male character(s) and the audience must not emulate her.

As the question is asked how female characters strengthen the bonds between male characters, the question is also asked how female characters foster the reader's identification with the narrator's position. Female characters may have a more complex function in some texts than Schweickart and Howe have observed. Readers may be encouraged to identify with female characters and then subsequently urged to identify against them as they identify with the male characters. In scenes where readers are not encouraged to identify initially with female characters, these characters may be depicted quite positively to elicit a positive response to the male protagonist(s). Recognition that female characters might have more than one function could be helpful for understanding why most of the female characters in the Gospel of Matthew are viewed favorably but excluded from the character group of disciples.[10] It must be kept in mind that identification against female characters does not necessarily mean rejecting them out of revulsion for their behavior. In the Gospel of Matthew, identification against female characters usually occurs without animosity toward them.[11]

The next step after analyzing how female characters function as exchange objects and how they continue to influence the audience's response to the selected texts is deciding how to appropriate each text. Some biblical scholars, such as Susan Durber, would argue that since biblical texts construct their readers as male and since in the symbolic order of language the subject position is always male, women must either pretend to be male and read biblical texts or not read them at all.[12] As discussed in chapter 2, women can view language differently. They can recognize that those forms of discourse customarily designated as men's have been validated and favored over other forms and that women's uses of language, including spoken communication, can provide them a way to resist the perspective of a text and read it differently. Women might still want to dismiss a particular text, but this rejection would result from a judgment that it does not benefit people in their communities.

I turn now to each of the four texts. First I will study how female characters in material preceding the four texts function as exchange objects and how they continue to shape the narrative and the audience's response to the four texts. Some attention will be given to the function of minor male characters. Secondly, how female readers can respond to the four texts, which require them to identify against themselves because of the continuing impact of the female characters on these texts, will be addressed.

Mt. 10:5–15

In Mt. 10:5–15 the narrator reports that Jesus calls together his twelve disciples and sends them out to do what he has done: preach about the nearness of God's kingdom, heal the sick, and cast out demons. Although only five of the disciples' names were mentioned earlier (4:18–22; 9:9), the audience is allowed to assume in retrospect that Jesus called the others in a similar way during his ministry and that most of the disciples (5:1) would have heard Jesus' teaching on the mountain (chapters 5–7) and seen him heal the sick (chapters 8–9). The disciples are integral to Jesus' ministry, for at the very beginning of his ministry he calls his disciples (4:18–22) and shortly afterward he commissions them to share his ministry (9:36–10:42).[13] The narrator delays telling the audience about the disciples' commission because the audience needs to hear Jesus' teachings about the kingdom (chapters 5–7) and witness the demonstration of his teachings in his deeds (chapters 8–9).

In chapters 5–7 Jesus teaches the disciples along with the crowds. Female characters do not play a role in the disciples' education, although Jesus, addressing adultery and divorce, argues that lust for a woman is adulterous and divorce of one's wife is permissible only on the grounds of unchastity. In chapters 8–9 several female characters do play a role in establishing the teacher-pupil relationship between Jesus and the disciples: Peter's mother-in-law, the ruler's daughter, and the woman who touches Jesus' garment.[14] Although the gender of these three women has been noted as an example of how Jesus challenged customs of his day and interacted with women,[15] how their gender has been used to define discipleship is rarely discussed. This function of the three female characters will now be addressed.

The healing of Peter's mother-in-law (8:14–15) occurs after Jesus healed a leper (8:1–4) and from a distance cured the centurion's servant (8:5–13). All three stand on the fringes of Jewish religious life and thus have a marginal status.[16] What is different about Jesus' healing of the woman is her identity. She is Peter's mother-in-law. This reference to Peter reminds the audience that Peter and perhaps other disciples, who have not been explicitly mentioned, have been with Jesus. That Jesus next gives orders to go to the other side (8:18) and, when he gets into the boat, the disciples follow him (8:23) reinforces the impression that disciples other than Peter had also been with him as he healed the leper, the centurion's servant, Peter's mother-in-law, and the sick people brought to Peter's house.

The audience needs to be reminded of the disciples' presence during Jesus' healings because then the audience can more easily assume that the disciples have seen and learned how Jesus heals and will be ready to be sent out by Jesus in chapter 10. Peter's mother-in-law can be understood as an exchange object between Jesus and the disciples since her healing teaches them how to heal and thus strengthens the teacher-pupil bond between them. She, on the other hand, does not develop such a relationship with Jesus. Her subsequent service to Jesus affirms her cure and depicts her in a traditional woman's role.[17] She is never designated as a disciple.

The narrator mentions the disciples' presence only indirectly in Mt. 8:14–15 in order to focus the audience's attention primarily on Jesus and his power to heal the sick. Her cure strengthens the bond between the audience and the narrator. The narrator does not invite the audience to identify with her; instead the audience is urged to agree with the perspectives of Jesus and the narrator. Consequently, Peter's mother-in-law also functions as an exchange object between the audience and the narrator. The narrator uses the woman to gain power over the audience so that they will agree that Jesus is a powerful Messiah and his healing activity fulfills the words of the prophet Isaiah (8:17). After hearing several more healing accounts, the audience is ready at the beginning of chapter 10 to identify with the disciples and accept Jesus' assignment to preach and heal the sick as he had done. As Jesus associated with sick people, unclean people, and sinners and allowed himself to become unclean, they must do the same.[18]

It can be correctly argued that the leper and the centurion also serve as exchange objects. Their faith and the cures function to elicit the audience's belief in Jesus' messianic power and to teach the disciples how to heal. They are like Peter's mother-in-law; they do not become disciples. Consideration of these minor characters as exchange objects means that a factor other than gender prohibits her from becoming a disciple: she, like the leper and the centurion's servant, is the recipient of a healing.[19] Consistently throughout the Gospel of Matthew, recipients of a healing or exorcism do not become disciples.[20] When Jesus sends out the eleven disciples in Mt. 28:16–20, he does not tell them to make disciples by healing people; he commands them to make disciples by teaching them.[21]

The healing of Peter's mother-in-law along with the healings of the leper and the centurion's servant contributes toward defining the commission of the disciples in chapter 10. The disciples are given the task to heal others as Jesus had; they do not go out because they have been healed of a disease or a physical limitation. Discipleship is not based on the personal experience of a mighty deed of healing performed by Jesus. The audience is invited to identify with the disciples and distinguish themselves from those who are not disciples, namely, recipients of a healing. A disciple is above all a learner, one whom Jesus teaches. Later they will also be teachers and make disciples as Jesus has.

Jesus' announcement to the religious leaders that he has come to call sinners may give the impression that recipients of a healing do become disciples, especially since he has just pronounced the sins of the paralytic forgiven. His announcement, however, must be seen as a response to the religious leaders' question of why he was eating with tax collectors and sinners and as an explanation to the audience of why he commissioned a man with Matthew's status as his disciple. The narrator tells about Jesus' comparison of his association with tax collectors and sinners to that of a physician with sick people in order to convince the audience that Jesus again ignores customs for a purpose: he must attend to human needs. His commissioned disciples must be comprised of sinners because these are the people whom Jesus came to call and serve. The calling of Matthew emphasizes that the commissioned disciples are comprised of sinners, not recipients of a healing.[22]

The three healings each have their own emphases as well. The healing of Peter's mother-in-law differs from the other two in that, in addition to providing the audience a reminder of the disciples' presence during Jesus' mighty deeds, the audience is given some information about Peter. The reference to Peter's house and the identification of the woman as his mother-in-law means that he has or has had a wife and could have children, servants, and lands. In reading Mt. 10:37–

39, the audience knows that Peter has had to make (or will have to make) some serious choices to remain one of Jesus' disciples. Peter's mother-in-law represents what he and the others must consider less important than their relationship to Jesus: houses, children, lands, possessions. She also represents what a disciple must not be. After she is healed of her fever, she remains in the house. Her encounter with Jesus does not lead her out of the house. A disciple, on the other hand, leaves everything (4:18–22) and must not remain concerned with household matters (8:19–22). In Mt. 10:9–13 the disciples depend on others to provide food and shelter and devote themselves to preaching and healing.

After the healing of Peter's mother-in-law, Jesus calms a storm and performs three exorcisms and five healings: the two demoniacs at Gadarene, the paralytic, the ruler's daughter, the woman who touched his cloak, two blind men, and another demoniac. These deeds also function to convince the audience of Jesus' messianic power and emphasize certain aspects of discipleship. The dynamics in the healings of the ruler's daughter and the woman who touched Jesus' cloak (9:18–26) will occupy our attention now.

The ruler's daughter can be understood as an exchange object between the ruler and Jesus and between Jesus and the disciples. The ruler recognizes Jesus' healing power and entrusts his daughter to him. The girl becomes Jesus' "daughter" as he goes with the ruler and the ruler drops out of the story. This transition accentuates Jesus' authority and power to heal. The girl functions as an exchange object between Jesus and the disciples because they learn from his actions. Here, the disciples who follow Jesus to the ruler's house learn that they must respond to those who want them to heal their daughters. The girl, dependent on her father to intercede for her healing, is contrasted to the woman who must rely upon Jesus to announce publicly her cure.[23] That Jesus becomes a father to both is not usually noticed. The woman, who has no father or brother to intercede for her in a society where men were considered responsible for the women in their households,[24] receives Jesus as her surrogate father when he calls her "daughter" and affirms her faith.[25] The twelve disciples also have a responsibility to accept as daughters those women who have no kinsmen and need their help.

The healings of the girl and the woman have strengthened the teacher-pupil bond between Jesus and his disciples. The girl and the woman, like the other recipients of a healing, do not develop such a bond with Jesus. They do not become disciples. The girl and the woman represent those persons who need the disciples' protection. The audience is not encouraged to identify with the girl. Instead, the narrator invites the audience to identify first with the ruler and then with Jesus, both men who protect the girl. The narrator initially guides the audience to identify with the woman who touches Jesus' cloak. This initial identification with the woman allows the audience to affirm more directly Jesus' messianic power.[26] Quickly the audience is required to reverse this identification. Jesus, who heals and restores the woman to society, and his disciples who are with him (9:19) are the ones whom the audience must aspire to emulate. This reversal in identification has implications. Disciples protect such women but do not seek security for themselves; they must face dangerous, precarious situations (8:23– 27) and persecution as they go out to heal the sick (10:14, 17–23). The willingness to face persecution and death was one of the recurring values listed in the Introduction.

When the three female characters are treated as exchange objects, modern female readers can see that the three characters have contributed toward defining the mission which the twelve male disciples are sent to do in chapter 10. The three female characters (along with several male characters in chapters 8–9) have been used to convey to the audience that commissioned disciples are those who have been taught by Jesus and not those who have personally experienced Jesus' power through the cure of an illness. Peter's mother-in-law has emphasized that disciples are those who have left everything and are unconcerned with household matters. The girl and the woman have stressed that disciples are those who face persecution and are not those who need protection.

The role of the three women in the reading of chapter 10 has implications for modern female readers. When women identify with the twelve male disciples in Mt. 10:5–15, they have already agreed that the three women could not be commissioned disciples because they represent concerns that do not characterize discipleship. By identifying with the male disciples, they have also allowed themselves to deny their female identities. Once more female readers are told in a literary work that who they must not be has female gender and who they must be has male gender so that they cannot affirm their female identities and reality as they read.

If some women had been included among the commissioned disciples, then female readers would have had the option to identify with them.[27] The absence of women among the twelve disciples in Mt. 10:1– 15 leaves the impression that women are excluded because all women are like the three women. All women must be healed or protected or concerned with household duties. They cannot be imagined as healing and protecting others or leaving their households to preach and heal. Men, however, can be imagined in both ways. Identification with the disciples would, therefore, mean consenting to stereotypical views of all women and their subordinate status. Female readers can, of course, refuse to perpetuate these stereotypes by refraining from identifying with the commissioned disciples. This response in certain contexts may be the best one. It is not without problems, however, because refusal to identify with the disciples can also express consent to the stereotypes, since it does not actively propose how women can be different. The point in reading a text such as Mt. 10:5–15 is not just to make sense of it, although comprehension is necessary, but to evaluate and change its negative influence on women's lives.

Another way female readers can respond to the text is to choose to embrace rather than reject the women's concerns[28] and thus challenge the exclusion of women from commissioned discipleship. Women, for instance, might question why mission can be based on what you do for others because of what you have seen and been taught but not on an experience of renewed health. Women might ask why disciples who are willing to face dangerous situations and minister to others cannot at the same time strive to make their own lives secure.[29] If female readers broaden discipleship to include the values associated with the female characters, then women cannot be excluded from commissioned discipleship and female readers can affirm their female identities. What this inquiry also opens up is the lifting up of male supplicants from their subordinate status (e.g., the leper in 8:1–4 who is not designated as a disciple) and greater appreciation for what they and women as commissioned disciples can contribute to others.

Of course, such questioning of the definition of discipleship means reading the text in a direction different from the one that the text had guided us to accept as we read the text using the type of literary criticism discussed in the Introduction. This kind of questioning also means that women must not feel compelled to affirm healing experiences, household responsibilities, and the protection of women just because female characters represent them. The female character may reflect more what the author thought about women than what real women experienced. Female readers must affirm the concerns associated with these three female characters on the basis of their compatibility with what they believe is beneficial for them and the people they know in their own contexts.

Mt. 23:1–12

In Mt. 23:1–12, the audience is invited to identify with the disciples
and the crowds whom Jesus instructs. Jesus urges that they refuse to
be addressed with prestigious titles like those of the scribes and the
Pharisees. He tells them that they are all brothers with one Father, one
teacher, and one master. This instruction has followed two controversies initiated by the religious leaders and his own question to them,
where he proved himself more skillful than they in the interpretation of
the Scriptures. The crowds, whose presence is mentioned in Mt. 22:33,
have overheard Jesus' responses. The disciples, whose presence has not
been explicitly mentioned since Mt. 21:20, are on the sidelines too as
Jesus demonstrates his ability to interpret the Scriptures.[30] Jesus has directed his responses to the religious leaders; but the crowds and his
disciples who are nearby have benefited from the discussions. They are
prepared to hear that Jesus ought to be their sole teacher, for he has
shown them that his understanding of the Scriptures is better than that
of all the other religious leaders.

The two controversies and Jesus' question have also shown the audience that Jesus is the most astute interpreter of the Scriptures. He has
answered the Sadducees' question about the resurrection and the Phar-
isee's inquiry about the greatest commandment. He left the Sadducees
speechless; but in addition, he has left the Pharisees unable to answer
how David could call the Christ Lord. Of the three debates, only one
has a female character, that of the Sadducees' discussion about the resurrection (22:23–33). The woman who marries the seven brothers in
this controversy can be examined as an exchange object to see how
she affects the relationships between male characters and between the
narrator and the audience.

The woman becomes the center of the discussion between Jesus
and the Sadducees. The Sadducees, who according to the narrator do
not believe in the resurrection, use the woman and her marriages to
ridicule the idea of resurrection and to challenge Jesus.[31] By marrying
her, the six younger brothers had observed the Mosaic law of levirate
marriage (Dt. 25:5–10, Gen. 38:8–11), which functioned to insure that
the name of the deceased brother would live on in the offspring of a liv-
ing brother.[32] Implicit in the Sadducees' question about whose wife she
would be in the resurrection is their assumption that resurrected life
would be no different from the life they know. Implicit in their question
is also their assumption that Jesus can give only one answer: she would
be married to all of the brothers. That the woman would have to be

married simultaneously to seven men in the resurrection is so ridiculous to them that there must not be any such thing as the resurrection. The woman is supposed to be the means by which the Sadducees and her first husband gain mastery over other men. The Sadducees do not succeed in displaying their superior knowledge. Jesus counters their position and wins the debate with an argument they will take seriously since he bases it on a text from the Pentateuch.[33] In the story itself, the woman does not enable the eldest brother posthumously to gain mastery over his brothers because she does not bear his child through marriage to any of them. All the brothers die without a child born to perpetuate the eldest brother's name and to inherit his possessions as the law of levirate marriage provided. The law of levirate marriage, which in this case functioned to privilege the deceased eldest brother over the younger brothers because his wife's offspring would receive the "double" inheritance of the eldest brother (Dt. 21:15–17), had failed. From the Sadducees' perspective, all seven brothers would be unfortunate because none of them had offspring to live on for them.

It is intriguing how Jesus uses the woman in the Sadducees' example to gain mastery over them. When Jesus says that marriage does not exist in the resurrection, he implies that none of the brothers would be married to her in the resurrection. He also implies in his interpretation of Ex. 3:6, 15–16 that the woman is inessential for the eldest brother's name to live on. Abraham, Isaac, and Jacob are alive because God raised them up to resurrected life, not because their wives bore them children.[34] The woman represents the futile attempts to perpetuate the eldest brother's life through children and to secure his privileges over his brothers. The woman's death especially shows this futility.[35] Her death means that the eldest brother's situation is the same as the younger ones: no progeny. The brothers are alike. From Jesus' perspective, that they are alike in this way is not unfortunate, since God can extend their lives.

As Jesus responds to the Sadducees, the crowds and the disciples also learn on the sidelines that marriage does not occur in the resurrection and that God, not children, perpetuates a man's life. Jesus' response conveys to the crowds and the disciples the uselessness of the woman's marriages. Although she had no other choice except to marry the six younger brothers, by marrying them, she had confirmed the prominence of the eldest brother's name and had fostered hierarchical bonds between the seven brothers.[36] Since God, not children, extends life after death, this way of relating is unnecessary and more than that it is fruitless.

The audience has been urged to accept Jesus' perspective about the resurrection and his critique of the law of levirate marriage.[37] Although Mt. 22:24–28 has implied how brothers ought not to relate to each other, not until Mt. 23:1–12 is the audience told how brothers must interact with each other. When Jesus turns to instruct the crowds and his disciples in Mt. 23:1–12, he urges them to treat each other in an egalitarian manner, neither desiring status over others as the Pharisees and the scribes do, nor acknowledging the status of men over them. Only God must they acknowledge as father. Only the Christ must they recognize as their leader and teacher. Among themselves, they are to treat each other as brothers.

The audience knows that this way of treating each other as brothers is different from the kind of interaction the woman fostered among the seven brothers. Just as the disciples and the crowds must not allow themselves to be called rabbi or master or call anyone father, they must not ascribe to themselves more status as an eldest brother would or defer to a brother as a younger brother would. Unlike the woman, however, the disciples can actively choose. In fact, the disciples have already chosen to remove themselves from households that perpetuate hierarchical relationships. The disciples can treat each other as "brothers" who are equals, since they have left everything (4:18–22; 19:27) and have no possessions to divide or bequeath, and since the law of levirate marriage would not apply to a group of men, most of whom are not blood relations. The audience is assured that the disciples who have left their parents, children, lands, houses, and possessions are not deprived of anything. Children are not necessary for extending life after death or for becoming great. Being a servant makes a person great.

When the woman is examined as an exchange object, modern female readers can see that she continues to shape the audience's response in chapter 23 where Jesus instructs the disciples and the crowds. The audience must not passively participate in hierarchical relationships as the woman appears to have done; they must treat other people as their equals as Jesus advises the disciples and the crowds. However, if modern female readers allow themselves to identify with the disciples and the crowds in Mt. 23:1, they are identifying against themselves since they must also identify against the woman. Women must deny their female identities.

It might be argued that, since female readers are urged to identify against male characters too, that is, the seven brothers, the reading process is less abusive. That conclusion might be true if women had been explicitly mentioned among the crowds and the disciples whom Jesus addressed in Mt. 23:1. Unlike male readers who are told that they must not be like some men, the seven brothers, and then told what men they must be like, the disciples, female readers are told they must not be like the woman, yet are never explicitly told what women they are supposed to be like. Male readers know men are disciples, but female readers are left to guess that women are among the disciples and the crowds in Mt. 23:1.[38] This ambiguity leaves the impression that men can choose to participate in or disengage themselves from hierarchical relationships, but women, like the wife of the seven brothers, may be unable.

When female readers identify with the crowds and the disciples in Mt. 23:1–12, they are, therefore, denied a firm affirmation of their female identities. One way women can affirm their female identities more strongly is to challenge the notion that discipleship must exclude the concerns that the woman represents. They can reconsider whether a passive participation in hierarchical relationships and the goal to perpetuate life through children must *always* be understood as incompatible with discipleship. They can ask, when the woman is granted her own motive, whether basic survival, in this case, through marriage, the economic means available to her,[39] must be understood as antithetical to Jesus' command to lose one's self for his sake. Such inquiry allows female readers to consider the complexities of real life where hierarchical structures may be productive and where children may extend the influence and benefits of their progenitors in positive ways. If female readers challenge how discipleship is defined in the text, then they can interject a female presence into discipleship so that they have firmer female identities.

Again, such questioning means reading the text in a different direction. This inquiry must not obligate women to affirm what the woman in Mt. 22:24–28 represents merely because she is a woman.[40] That a woman passively engages herself in hierarchical structures and perpetuates life through children may reflect more what the author thought about women than what real women experienced. Although affirmation of the woman in at least one way would diffuse the bifurcation in the reading of Mt. 23:1–12, female readers must be granted the choice to reject the woman's concerns. None of the values linked with the woman may be compatible with what some women believe will enhance life in their particular communities.

If female readers conclude that none of what the woman represents can be included in discipleship, then they are left with the uncertainty that women are among the disciples in Mt. 23:1–12. Identification with the disciples in spite of this ambiguity becomes a defiant decision to imagine that women as well as men can disengage themselves from hierarchical relationships and treat others in an egalitarian manner.

Mt. 26:20–29

In Mt. 26:20–29 the audience is invited to identify with the twelve disciples as Jesus reveals the identity of his betrayer to his disciples and reinterprets the Passover meal in light of his impending death. The events prior to this scene have prepared the audience for Jesus' discussion about his death with his disciples. Jesus has predicted his death for the fourth time (26:1–2), the religious leaders have plotted his death (26:3–5), the woman has anointed Jesus' body for burial (26:6–13), and Judas has met with the religious leaders to assist them in their plans (26:14–16). Each character has prepared for Jesus' death in a particular way, but Jesus is mainly concerned with preparing the disciples to understand the significance of his death.

Before Jesus provides its significance, the audience learns with the disciples the time of Jesus' death and witnesses the preparation for his burial. Jesus had already predicted his death three times, but he had not said until now that it would occur during Passover. The religious leaders' plans to delay Jesus' death until after Passover will be thwarted. It is the next scene that contains a female character who can be examined as an exchange object. This study will explore how she affects the relationships between Jesus and the disciples and between the audience and the narrator.

The woman who anoints Jesus in this scene has often been viewed as a foil whose insight exposes the disciples' denseness,[41] whose generosity reveals Judas' greed,[42] and whose devotion highlights the religious leaders' treachery.[43] When she is examined as an exchange object, her action of anointing Jesus can be understood not as something that the disciples should have done for Jesus to express their love for him or their knowledge of his impending death but as another occasion in which Jesus teaches them.[44] Jesus corrects the disciples' perspective that the perfumed oil should have been sold and the money given to the poor. Jesus defends the woman's action with the argument that special deeds, such as preparation for burial, take precedence over almsgiving that can occur any time.

The woman's action is the focus of Jesus' teaching to the disciples. They criticize her use of the perfume and are corrected so that their perspective is similar to Jesus'. They thought they knew what the woman's action meant, but they do not. Their attack on the woman's deed could be understood as an attempt to gain mastery over Jesus. If the anthropological categories of honor and shame are used to understand the dynamics among the characters, then the disciples had challenged Jesus' honor by attacking the woman whom Jesus had taken under his tutelage when he accepted her gift.[45] One way to challenge a man's honor was to criticize those under his tutelage.[46] Jesus accepted the disciples' challenge and treated them as his equals; however, in winning the challenge he proved himself their superior.[47]

Jesus succeeds in using the woman's action to assert his superior interpretive skills. His interpretation of her act as a beautiful thing and preparation for burial triumphs over the disciples' assessment of it as a waste. As he reestablishes his position as the disciples' teacher, he praises the woman but does not regard her in the same way he does the twelve disciples. He does not teach her. She must be defended and protected; they can be rebuked and learn. The disciples are put back into their role as learners because of her. They continue to learn from Jesus during the Passover meal; they learn the identity of his betrayer and the significance of his death.

As the disciples criticize the woman's deed, the narrator allows the audience to identify with them, and then shifts this identification to Jesus so that they learn that the disciples have incorrectly interpreted the woman's action. The audience as well as the disciples needs Jesus to interpret the action for them. The audience is encouraged to view the woman's deed favorably, but they are not urged to identify with her or emulate her. Instead, they are invited to identify against her as they accept Jesus as the one who can tell the disciples the significance of her deed. Although it appears that the audience is asked to identify with her because Jesus commends her action, it must not be overlooked that the woman does not talk about what her action means. Her silence leads the audience to believe Jesus' assessment is also the woman's and to ignore what hers might be.[48] The audience identifies foremost with Jesus.

Here is an instance where the audience is asked to identify against a very positively portrayed female character. A favorable view of her is needed to accentuate a positive view toward Jesus and to counter the disciples' attack. What is not usually recognized is that Jesus' profuse praise of the woman's action is actually what leads the audience to identify against her. The praise characterizes her as someone only concerned with burial rites. In order for the audience to adopt Jesus' perspective that actions and events must be interpreted, they must identify against her and continue to learn with the disciples.

In summary, whereas the disciples represent those whom the audience must be like, that is, pupils who must learn the significance of events and actions, the woman represents those whom they must not be like. She is concerned with burial rites, the physical body, the death of Jesus, but not the significance of his death. Although her deed is praiseworthy, it does not characterize all of discipleship. The audience must be concerned with the purpose of Jesus' death and the risen Jesus, not with the Jesus whose earthly life ends.

Although the woman's action is directed to the earthly Jesus, her action can influence the audience to become focused on the risen Jesus. When the woman prepares Jesus for burial, she enables the audience to experience Jesus as the risen Jesus at this point in the narrative. Since corpses, not live bodies, are prepared for burial, then in a sense he is already dead. If the ancient belief that anointing a corpse would transform the dead person's deterioration into a state of preservation is taken into account,[49] then the woman's anointing of Jesus allows the audience to view him as already passing from death to life, that is, as risen. During the next scenes where the disciples prepare the room for the meal and Jesus eats the Passover with them, the audience can relate to Jesus as the risen Jesus and learn with them the significance of his death.

The woman, therefore, functions in two ways as an exchange object. First, she is used by Jesus to reestablish his place as the disciples' teacher. He interprets her action, showing the disciples that their understanding of her action is wrong and that they must interpret correctly the significance of actions and events. The disciples continue to learn from Jesus. In the meal, Jesus interprets for them the bread and the cup as his body and blood. His death is no ordinary death; it has a particular significance. Secondly, the audience learns to interpret correctly the woman's action and the meaning of Jesus' impending death. At the same time, the woman's action allows the audience to experience Jesus as the risen Jesus during the meal. If the audience's experience of Jesus has already been that of the risen Jesus, then the woman's action also permits them to feel they are actually at the meal.

When the woman is examined as an exchange object, modern female readers can see how she reestablishes the teacher-pupil bond between Jesus and the disciples and continues to affect the audience's identification with the disciples in the Passover scene. The role of the woman in the reading of Mt. 26:20–30 has implications for female readers. As women identify with the twelve male disciples in the Passover scene, they have already agreed that the woman who anointed Jesus could not possibly be a disciple and attend the meal because she represents concerns that do not characterize discipleship. When female readers identify with the male disciples, they have also agreed to deny their female identities.

If women had been included in the meal, then female readers could have identified with them.[50] The implication of women's absence is that all women are like the woman who anointed Jesus. They are concerned with physical needs and burial rites and cannot engage themselves in the interpretation of events as the twelve men can. As with Mt. 10:5–15, identification with the disciples would mean consenting to this stereotypical treatment of women. Female readers can avoid this subordination of women by refusing to identify with the twelve male disciples. Again, depending on the context, this response may be the best one whereas in other contexts it means perpetuating the stereotypes because alternative views of women are not expressed.

One way female readers can read the text is to choose to accept rather than discard the woman's attentiveness to Jesus' body, the burial rite, and his death as worthy concerns and challenge the exclusion of women from the Passover meal with Jesus. Women might question why the twelve disciples must be more focused on learning the meaning of the woman's action and Jesus' death than on recognizing that Jesus' life was ending. Attention to the end of Jesus' earthly life could mean a greater appreciation for what he had done in his life for so many people.[51] If female readers broaden discipleship to include her interests, then women can no longer be excluded and female readers can affirm their female identities.

Once more, this kind of challenge means reading the text in a direction other than what the text encourages. This attempt to redefine discipleship does not mean that female readers must feel forced to accept the concerns of the woman just because she shares the same gender. As in the analysis of the other female characters, the woman who anointed Jesus may reflect the author's concerns more than those of real women. Modern female readers must affirm the values associated with the woman on the basis of their congruence with what they consider beneficial and life-giving for themselves and other people.

Mt. 28:16–20

At the end of the Gospel of Matthew, the narrator urges the audience
to identify with the eleven disciples who, as learners, worship and doubt
the risen Jesus whom they meet on the mountain in Galilee. Jesus commands them to go out, make disciples of all the Gentiles, teach them
all his commandments, and baptize them. The audience who identifies
with the disciples knows more than they, not only because the audience has heard the narrator's perspective and those of all the other
characters, but also because the disciples as a character group have not
witnessed all that has happened since his arrest (Mt. 26:56). The audience knows the details of his trial and crucifixion and the events at
his tomb. Except for Peter's denial in Mt. 26:69–74 and Judas' suicide
in Mt. 27:3–10, the group of disciples is not mentioned until Mt. 28:7,
where the angel urges the two women to tell the disciples to meet Jesus
in Galilee. When these two women are examined as exchange objects,
modern female readers can see how they affect the relationship between Jesus and the disciples in the final scene and how they shape the
audience's relationship with the narrator.

The two women at the tomb play a more complicated role than
Peter's mother-in-law, the ruler's daughter, the woman who married
seven brothers, or the woman who anointed Jesus. The narrator encourages identification with these two women whereas the narrator
does not with the other women. The narrator had already led the
audience to identify with the women as they watched Jesus die on
the cross (Mt. 27:55–56) and Joseph bury him (Mt. 27:61). In Mt.
28:1–8 the audience identifies with them as they experience the unusual events at the tomb and the angel sends them to tell the disciples
to meet Jesus in Galilee. As they are going, the resurrected Jesus
meets them and, repeating the angel's words, confirms them. At this
point, when the narrator reintroduces Jesus, the role of the women
changes.

The audience, who has become accustomed to Jesus' actions and
words as indications of which characters with whom they ought to
identify, is redirected by Jesus' words to the women to identify with
the disciples. He tells the women to tell "his brothers"[52] to go to
Galilee and does not ask the women to accompany the eleven. The
audience assumes that the women are going to the disciples while the
guards are reporting to the religious leaders. In the next scene, where
the disciples meet Jesus and are commissioned, the audience identifies with the disciples and no longer with the two women. Jesus has

not treated the two women the same way that he has the eleven male disciples. He commissions the women for only one specific purpose, the reestablishment of his relationship with the disciples. The women are not needed for anything else. The eleven men will have an ongoing task. As commentators have noted, the women at the tomb have enabled the disciples to meet Jesus in Galilee.[53] The women can be understood as exchange objects between Jesus and the disciples even though the audience has initially identified with them in Mt. 28:1–7. By allowing the audience to identify with the women as they watched Joseph bury Jesus and the angel unseal the tomb, the narrator proves to the audience without any doubt that the disciples could not have stolen the body as the religious leaders had feared (Mt. 27:62–66). The women went to the tomb, not the disciples. The positive behavior of the women, that is, their obedient response to the angel and their unqualified worship of the risen Jesus, assures the audience that the disciples will receive the message to go to Galilee.[54]

By shifting the audience's identification from the women to the eleven male disciples, the narrator also communicates to the audience that the disciples did not need to experience the events at the tomb and the cross as the women did.[55] All they needed was a reminder to go to Galilee as Jesus had already told them (Mt. 26:32). More important than witnessing Jesus' death and seeing the empty tomb is the acceptance of the commission to make new disciples and Jesus' promise to be with them always. The task of discipleship is to teach others, a task not given until now.[56] As Jesus' scriptural quote had softened the disciples' desertion, their absence at his death and the tomb is also made to be inconsequential.[57]

The audience who, along with the eleven disciples, have not had and cannot have the experiences of the two women at the cross and the tomb can readily identify with the disciples, since the commission is something they can implement in their own lives. The women, therefore, also function as exchange objects between the audience and the narrator to facilitate the audience's identification with the disciples. This way of reading has two consequences. The audience identifies against the two women in the final scene.[58] They represent those who are concerned with Jesus' death, the physical body, corpses, gravesites, and concrete proof of his death. The audience identifies with the disciples who are concerned with the risen Jesus, the making of new disciples, and the teaching of Jesus' commands which Jesus had taught them.

When the two women are examined as exchange objects, modern female readers can see that they continue to shape the final scene and the audience's response to it. The role of the two women in the reading of Mt. 28:16–20 has implications for female readers. When female readers identify with the eleven male disciples in the final scene, they have already agreed that the two women could not be commissioned disciples because they represent interests and values that do not characterize commissioned discipleship. By identifying with the male disciples, female readers have also allowed themselves to deny their female identities.

If women had been included among those whom Jesus commissioned, then female readers could have identified with them. The absence of women from commissioned discipleship leaves the impression that women are omitted because all women are like the two women. They are all preoccupied with physical needs, death, corpses, and burial sites and unequipped to teach and make disciples. Since identification with the male disciples would involve a confirmation of these stereotypical views of women and their subordination, women can decline from identifying with them. This response, appropriate in some contexts, may not be enough in others, since ways in which women can be different need to be formulated.

Instead, women can decide to value rather than dismiss the women's concerns for Jesus' death, his body, and the tomb and challenge the exclusion of women from commissioned discipleship. Tending to the dead Jesus need not necessarily mean that attention is not being paid to the risen Jesus. By attending to Jesus' body, the women had encountered the angel and then the risen Jesus. If women redefine discipleship to include these interests, then women cannot be excluded from commissioned discipleship and women can affirm their female identities.

As in the study of the other three texts, such an attempt to broaden the definition of commissioned discipleship almost means completely rewriting the final scene. Female readers must not, however, feel compelled to affirm the interests connected with the two women at the tomb only because they are women. In this case, the exclusion of Joseph, who places Jesus in the tomb, from commissioned discipleship helps female readers see that these concerns are not just those of female characters. Female readers must affirm the two women's attention to Jesus' crucifixion, death, and the tomb on the basis of how similar concerns can better the life of their communities.

Summary: Usefulness for Sermon Preparation

In each of the four texts, preceding material was examined to explore how female characters could function as exchange objects and shape the audience's response to the four texts. When female characters are viewed as exchange objects, female readers are required to identify against themselves as they read the four texts, since female characters continue to affect the reading of these texts. To divert this denial of female identity, two responses were suggested: (1) women can refuse to identify with the male disciples or (2) they can identify with the concerns of the female characters and transform discipleship. The second response would benefit from an evaluation of the patriarchal elements of the texts as demonstrated in the last chapter.

Women can use this strategy for individual or group Bible study. Women can also prepare sermons from the analysis of how female characters function as exchange objects in biblical narrative. That female characters continue to influence readers' responses to the male characters in subsequent passages without female characters means that women who use texts without female characters for sermons must take into account the gender dynamics of previous texts. Female characters are often used to portray the values and the perspectives that the audience ought not to have. Sermons could disclose these attributes and challenge their rejection.

Consideration of the gender dynamics, for instance, in Mt. 8–9 could lead to a sermon that discusses how the three female characters in Mt. 8–9 contribute toward defining commissioned discipleship in Mt. 10:5–15 and how and whether discipleship could be broadened to include their views. In a similar way, a sermon on Mt 26:20–29 could discuss why women are absent and whether and in what ways what the woman in Mt. 26:6–13 represents should be included in the view of discipleship in Mt. 26:20–29. A sermon could also explore why a female character can be treated in a very positive manner and yet remain a marginal character in the narrative. What this strategy can also provide is a method for evaluating the effects of sermon illustrations with female characters.

This strategy which focuses on women as exchange objects offers female readers another way to read biblical narrative texts with male characters and another resource for preparing sermons. Unlike the other two strategies, it provides at the same time a way to read texts with female characters. The strategies that focus on gender reversal and analogy, however, as mentioned in chapter 2, can be applied to

most biblical narrative texts. I have applied the three strategies on texts
without female characters to be sure that they fit most biblical narratives. To demonstrate how these strategies can be used to examine a
text with female characters, I turn now in the next chapter to apply
them to Mt. 1:18–25.

Chapter 6

APPLICATION OF THE STRATEGIES TO MT. 1:18–25

In the application of the reading strategies to the four Matthean texts, I have attempted to develop several ways to read biblical narrative texts which would enable women to analyze as fully as possible the androcentric or misogynous tenor of the texts and help them decide whether to accept, dismiss, or challenge them. Texts without female characters were chosen as special test cases to show the general applicability of the strategies. These approaches, however, are also valuable in reread-ing texts that contain female characters and preparing sermons on these texts. To demonstrate how they can be used to analyze a text with fe-male characters, I will apply them to Mt. 1:18–25, one of the first texts in the gospel that employs female characters.

Summary of Mt. 1:18–25

Mt. 10:5–15, 23:1–12, 26:20–29, and 28:16–20 all center on the small group of Jesus' disciples and, having been included in lectionaries for at least the past ten years,[1] have been read and reflected upon fre-quently by groups of worshiping Christians. Mt. 1:18–25, also included in lectionaries,[2] does not focus on Jesus' disciples; yet its placement at the beginning of the gospel makes it an excellent choice of those texts with female characters on which to apply the three strategies. In the early chapters of the gospel, the narrator wins the audience's confi-dence in telling the rest of the narrative and shapes their identification with Jesus and the disciples.

A summary of the context and the flow of Mt. 1:18–25 provides a good prologue to the application of the strategies. At the beginning of Mt. 1:18–25, the audience, having just heard the genealogy, knows that

Jesus' descent from David means that Joseph will take Mary as his wife. The narrator invites the audience to identify with Joseph and learn how he decides to complete his marriage and accept Jesus who is not his biological son.[3] Joseph, who first decides to divorce Mary quietly, changes his mind through divine guidance about Jesus' future.[4] Joseph knows the law and is responsive to God's will. The entire account centers on his dilemma: how he can respond to Mary's pregnancy. Nowhere in the account are Mary's views expressed. Although Joseph is not assured of Mary's chastity, the audience is.[5] The narrator urges the audience to agree with him that Mary's conception of Jesus has occurred to fulfill the prophecy of Isaiah.

Gender Reversal

As the audience hears Mt. 1:18–25, they are asked to empathize with Joseph. Since the observation has often been made that Matthew's birth account concentrates on Joseph,[6] it might seem unnecessary to reread Mt. 1:18–25 by reversing the gender of the characters. Modern women, however, may be aware that Mt. 1:18–25 is told from Joseph's point of view, but not that identification with his perspective means accepting his experience as equally relevant to women and men. Gender reversal provides a way to reveal that the narrator is not addressing women in this text. Gender reversal is also useful for analyzing some of the ways that literary conventions have been used to marginalize Mary.

After the gender of the characters is reversed, the scene becomes one where a woman judges her husband's adulterous behavior, decides to divorce him, and then reverses this decision when she receives an authoritative message about the child. Modern readers need to know the ancient conventions about annunciation scenes and scenes concerned with illicit relationships in order to assess in what ways this reversed scene would sound odd to Matthew's ancient audience.[7] A study of similar scenes in the Hebrew Scriptures, two Greek romance novels, and several ancient biographies is needed.

When the Hebrew Scriptures are examined for how women respond to the knowledge of the conception of another woman's child by their husband, no scenes are found where wives plan to divorce their husbands. The one instance where a wife is unhappy with her husband's involvement with another woman results in a plea to him for that woman's dismissal. This incident is the continuing account of Sarah, Abraham, and Hagar in Gen. 16 and 21. Abraham's relationship with Hagar would not be considered adulterous or illicit, since Sarah had given her slave Hagar to her husband Abraham to bear a child for her. Sarah, therefore, not because she wants Abraham to end an adulterous relationship, but because she feels Hagar's son threatens her son's status and her own, asks Abraham to send them away.[8] She cannot make the decision on her own, for Abraham is the one who must determine who will receive his inheritance.[9] Because of divine guidance, Abraham agrees with Sarah's request.

If the dynamics are adjusted somewhat so that the woman considering divorce is pregnant herself, the scene is still unusual. Wives are not depicted in the Hebrew Scriptures as seeking divorce from their husbands when they are pregnant with another man's child. The only married woman who is portrayed as conceiving a child from relations with someone other than her husband is Bathsheba. Bathsheba, however, plays a passive role, leaving David to resolve the dilemma.[10] The story in 2 Sam. 11–12 focuses on David's response to the problem. He responds first with deception and then with violence. He urges Uriah to go to Bathsheba; and, after failing to pass the child off as Uriah's, he has Uriah murdered. Then Bathsheba becomes his wife. Perhaps Tamar is another example, since Judah gives the impression that Tamar is betrothed to Shelah and will allow the marriage to be completed when Shelah matures.[11] The people who report Tamar's pregnancy to Judah view her as betrothed to Shelah, for they call her his daughter-in-law. Although Tamar is not passive in resolving the charges against her, Judah is the one who must judge whether she committed adultery, since he is responsible for the reputation of his family (Gen. 38).

Thus, a scene where a wife judges the sexual behavior of her husband and another woman would have sounded odd. In the Hebrew Scriptures men are the ones who are depicted as judging adulterous or other kinds of illicit relationships, although the woman is not always the wife, is not necessarily viewed as the guilty party, and does not always become pregnant. When Potiphar hears his wife's accusations that Joseph made sexual advances toward her, he decides Joseph is guilty and puts him in prison (Gen. 39). Ishbosheth, responsible for his father's concubine Rizpah after his death, accuses Abner of sexual intercourse with her (2 Sam. 3:6–10). David puts aside his ten concubines with whom his son Absalom, now dead, had sexual relations (2 Sam. 20:3). Although David provides for them, they no longer have any conjugal rights. Ishbosheth's and David's responses have specific implications. Ishbosheth is charging Abner with attempting to be a successor to his father Saul whereas David is rejecting Absalom's attempt to usurp his throne.[12] In three additional cases, men address the situation because they view themselves as the ones who have been violated. Dinah's and Tamar's brothers avenge their sisters' rapes (Gen. 34; 2 Sam. 13). The Levite seeks revenge against the Benjaminites who raped and killed his wife (Judg. 19–20).

Two Greek romance novels, *An Ephesian Tale* and *Chaereas and Callirhoe,* display a pattern similar to that found in the Hebrew Scriptures. No scenes are found where wives plan to divorce their husbands after they have discovered the conception of another woman's child with their husband. In *An Ephesian Tale* there are two scenes somewhat similar to the one about Sarah, Abraham, and Hagar where the wife is jealous of her husband's involvement with a female slave. Manto is jealous of her husband's affection for Anthia and tells her servant Lampon to kill her, but instead he sells her to merchants sailing to Cilicia (2.11). Rhenaea sends her male servant Clytis to put Anthia on a ship sailing to Italy to get her away from her husband (5.5). As Abraham's relationship with Hagar is not portrayed as adulterous or illicit, but as a threat to Sarah's status and her son's, the husbands' relationships with Anthia are viewed as threats to Manto's and Rhenaea's status as their wives. Also, as Sarah is dependent on Abraham to dismiss Hagar, these women are dependent on men to drive away their female rivals, although the men are their male servants and not their husbands.

Men are the ones who resolve complaints about adulterous and illicit relationships, either acting violently because the law permitted it or settling the matter in court. In *Chaereas and Callirhoe,* Chaereas, acting within his legal rights, attempts to catch and kill the man whom he has been led to believe has become sexually involved with Callirhoe (1.4).[13] Dionysius charges Mithridates of adulterous intentions with his wife Callirhoe and takes him to court (5.4–8).[14] In *An Ephesian Tale,* Apsyrtus flogs and imprisons his slave Habrocomes when his daughter Manto convinces him that Habrocomes tried to seduce her (2.5–6).

Even though ancient biographies rarely mention women, they probably would have played a significant role in shaping ancient audiences' expectations about scenes concerning divorce, adultery, or illicit relationships. In the biographies in Burridge's study, three of them refer to these situations.[15] Men are the ones who initiate the divorce or address the illicit relationship in these biographies. Plutarch mentions that Cato the Minor divorced his first wife, Atilia, because of improper behavior (*Cato the Minor* 24.2–3); gave his second wife, Marcia, to Hortensia, although she was pregnant with his child (25.1); and later took Marcia back (52.1–5). He also mentions that Lucullus sent away his wife, Servilia, one of Cato's sisters, because of her unchastity (24.2–

3). He mentions that Caesar disparaged Cato's relationship with his sister Servilia (54). Suetonius writes about Augustus' divorces (*Augustus* 62) and his delight in "deflowering" maidens, whom even his wife Livia brought to him (71). Augustus took his fourth wife, Livia, from her husband while she was already pregnant (62). Mark Antony criticized Augustus for divorcing his third wife, Scribonia, because she complained too much about a rival (69.1). Philostratus writes about Apollonius' advice to a king who wanted to execute a eunuch who had committed adultery with one of his concubines. The king wanted him killed because his action signified usurpation of his throne, but Apollonius told him the eunuch's impotence was punishment enough (*Apollonius of Tyana* 1.36).

To gain a sense of how divorce and adultery were portrayed in ancient biographies, additional ones will be considered. Four more biographies by Plutarch mention divorce and adultery. Only one narrates that a woman sought a divorce. Alcibiades' wife, Hipparete, left him because she disliked his consorting with courtesans; she went in person as required to submit her plea for a divorce (*Alc.* 8.2–4). Alcibiades picked her up and carried her home before she could submit her request. In the other biographies, men initiate divorce or assess a relationship. Plutarch writes that Sulla divorced his third wife because of barrenness and then married Metella, whom he later divorced (*Sulla* 6.11, 35.2). Pericles divorced his wife and with her consent gave her to another man (*Per.* 24). Caesar divorced his wife Pompeia because he believed his wife ought to be above suspicion (*Caes.* 9–10). A senator charged Clodius with committing adultery with his sister (*Caes.* 10).

Seven more biographies by Suetonius mention divorce and adulterous relationships where men are the ones who address the situation. Suetonius records that Caesar divorced Pompeia because he thought that she ought to be devoid of suspicion as well as of guilt (*Julius* 6.2, 74.2), and that he executed a freedman for adultery with the wife of a knight (48). Nero divorced Octavia on grounds of barrenness, sent her away, and then put her to death on grounds of adultery (*Nero* 35.2). Titus divorced his second wife (*Titus* 4.2). Domitian married a woman already married, divorced her because of her love for the actor Paris, and shortly afterward reclaimed her (*Dom.* 1.3, 3.1). Tiberius was forced to divorce Agrippina and marry Julia, Augustus' daughter (*Tib.* 7.2). She was sent away later because of immorality and adultery. Augustus sent her a bill of divorce in Tiberius' name (11.4). Caligula married Livia Orestilla and then divorced her (*Cal.* 25.1), separated Lollia Paulina from her husband and then divorced her (25.2), and sometimes sent bills of divorce to women in the name of their husbands (36.2). Claudius divorced his first wife because her parents offended Augustus, divorced his third wife for frivolous reasons and his fourth wife for unseemly behavior and suspicion of murder, and had his fifth wife killed after he discovered she was already married (*Claud.* 26).

A study of scenes from the Hebrew Scriptures, two Greek romance novels, and several ancient biographies suggests Matthew's audience would not have expected a scene where a woman suspects her husband of adultery and considers a divorce. They would have expected a male character to be given this kind of portrayal. The initiation of divorce and the assessment of adulterous or illicit relationships are gender role behaviors usually expected of men, not of women. That a female character cannot be placed in such a scene suggests that Joseph's experience, which is presented to the implied audience as normative for men and women, is not normative. If his situation was truly considered one that women could experience, then a reversed scene would not sound strange. The author is not really addressing women in his audience.[16]

The author, however, could have addressed women in his implied audience, if he had presented the angel's message differently.[17] A scene about a woman's decision to divorce an adulterous husband would sound unusual to Matthew's ancient audience, but not a scene where a woman hears a message about the future of the unborn child, especially if the woman is the child's mother and the child is a son.[18] The announcement of an unborn son's future to his mother is included in a few biblical annunciation type-scenes. A study of the biblical annunciation type-scenes can suggest how the author could have presented the angel's message to Mary and thus allowed women in the audience to identify with her. To facilitate this exploration, the first part of Mt. 1:18-25, Joseph's suspicions of adultery, will be ignored temporarily. Focus will be placed on scenes where a woman, who has conceived or will conceive, receives an authoritative message about her son.

Eleven scenes in the Hebrew Scriptures can be classified as annunciation type-scenes. According to Robert Alter, the development of the three components of annunciation type-scenes (the barrenness of the wife, a promise of future conception, and the birth of a son) could vary to foreshadow future events in the life of the unborn child.[19] He argues, for example, that the mother's failure to tell her husband Manoah part of the angel's promise about Samson's birth foreshadows Samson's uneven military career.[20] Esther Fuchs demonstrates that variations among the development of the components also affect the way the mother and father are characterized.[21] Since the concern here is how the angel's message could have been directed to Mary or to Mary and Joseph, Fuchs' observations must be examined.

Fuchs notes that, except for Isaac's birth, women play a key role in the biblical annunciation type-scenes.[22] This observation immediately confirms that Mary could have been addressed. Abraham, who is faithful to God, receives the promise of a son by his barren wife, names him at birth, and then circumcises him (Gen. 18:1–15; 21:1–7). Sarah's primary role is that of giving birth, but even in this scene she hears the promise from inside the tent.[23] In Gen. 25, Rebekah, who is barren and granted a child in response to Isaac's prayer, has a role more equal to Isaac's. Although her conception is attributed to Isaac's upstanding relationship to God, she alone receives the Lord's message about the future of her twin sons. Along with Isaac, she names them. Rachel's role is emphasized by the narrator's statement that God responded to her plight of barrenness and enabled her to conceive (Gen. 30). The woman's role gradually becomes more prominent. In the first scene the narrator reports that God fulfilled the promise of a son to Abraham; in the second scene, that God answered Isaac's prayer; and in the third, that God responds to Rachel.

Manoah's wife (Judg. 13), Hannah (1 Sam. 1), and the Shunammite woman (2 Kings 4:8–17) have even larger roles in the accounts of their sons' births. In the absence of her husband, Manoah's wife receives the promise of a son, information about his future, and instructions to follow during her pregnancy. When the messenger reappears, she recognizes far better than her husband that the man is a divine messenger. She names their son. In the annunciation scenes where Hannah and the Shunammite woman are promised sons, their husbands are peripheral characters. Hannah pleads to God to help her conceive a child rather than to her husband or the priest Eli. As with Rachel, the narrator reports that God responds to her plea. She bears a child and names him. The Shunammite woman receives the promise of a child from Elisha not in response to a condition of barrenness but in response to her hospitality to him. The woman's husband does not participate in the dialogue.

Fuchs and Alter examine only six annunciation type-scenes. Schaberg cites five more annunciation type-scenes.[24] Hagar, who has already conceived on behalf of Sarah, receives a message from an angel about the future of her son and is told to name him Ishmael.[25] When he is born, Abraham names him (Gen. 16:7–15). In Gen. 17:1–21, the Lord appears to Abram and establishes a covenant with him and Sarai, changes their names, promises a child to him and Sarah, whom Abraham will name Isaac, and blesses Ishmael. The problem of barrenness, which Hagar overcomes for Sarah in Gen. 16:7–15, is included in Gen. 17:1–21; but barrenness is not a problem for the women in the three remaining scenes in which the birth is a response to the inadequacy of a king to govern his people. A man of God proclaims the promise of a son to the house of David, a son named Josiah, who will begin the needed reforms (1 Kings 13:1–6). David tells Solomon, as he commissions him to build the Temple, that the Lord had come to him and told him that a son named Solomon would be born to him and build the Temple (1 Chr. 22:7–10). Isaiah exhorts King Ahaz to rely on God alone and not on foreign alliances. As a sign that God was Judah's ally, he prophesies that a young woman would bear a son and call him Immanuel (Isa. 7:10–17).

Before suggesting how the author of Matthew could have employed the annunciation type-scene differently, I must review other literature. Matthew's audience could have developed expectations about annunciation scenes from the narration of events in ancient biographies and Greek romance novels. There is one scene in *Chaereas and Callirhoe* which has some similarities to the biblical annunciation scenes. Callirhoe, who believes her husband Chaereas is dead, agonizes over whether she should kill herself and her unborn child or marry Dionysius (2.8–11). She imagines that she will have a son who will eventually rescue her and take her home; then she falls asleep. After seeing Chaereas in a dream, who tells her "I entrust our son to you," she awakens, deliberates more, decides to marry Dionysius, and, with Plangon's help, plans to pass her son off as Dionysius'. This scene reaffirms that Matthew's audience could have expected a scene where a woman receives a message about her unborn son. In this case, it is not a divine message, but it is an authoritative one. Her husband's approval of her course of action, which she receives in a dream, is what she needs to act decisively.

The ancient biographies sometimes refer to the man's birth and its unusual circumstances. Isocrates' *Evagoras* mentions that Evagoras' descent could be traced to the god Zeus. He claims that his birth was exceptional but refuses to recount the legends. Philo recounts the rescue of the infant Moses by Pharaoh's daughter. Suetonius records that Augustus' mother and father had dreams about him before his birth (*Aug.* 94.4). Cato's birth was not unusual, but Plutarch claims that Cicero's nurse saw an apparition who told her that he would be a great blessing to all the Romans (*Cicero* 2). He also mentions that Alexander's mother and father had dreams about him before his birth (*Alex.* 2). Philostratus reports that Apollonius's mother saw Proteus appear and tell her that she would give birth to him (*Apollonius of Tyana* I.4). In the scenes from *Chaereas and Callirhoe* and the ancient biographies, every woman is married. In the biblical annunciation type-scenes, the woman is usually married and has been married to her husband for a period of time.[26] Nonetheless, the author of Matthew could have adapted the type-scene to portray the promise of a son to a woman such as Mary, who is married but also in the process of completing her marriage, in order to emphasize a certain aspect of that son's future.[27] This modification would mean omitting the first component of type-scenes, the wife's barrenness. Barrenness, however, is not a condition of the Shunammite woman, Hagar, Immanuel's mother, or the mothers of Josiah and Solomon (or Callirhoe, or the mothers of Augustus, Cicero, Alexander, and Apollonius). The woman in an annunciation type-scene, therefore, does not always have to be a barren wife; rather her pregnancy must be specified as the result of God's will. Probably if the author had used the type-scene to depict the promise of a son to Mary who is betrothed, her marital status would have alerted the audience to Mary's special motherhood and Jesus' distinctive future. According to Alter, ancient audiences noticed changes in the type-scenes and interpreted their implications.[28] The author could have also emphasized that Mary received a promise of a *future* conception, a declaration of his deliverance of his people, and a command to name him, since these three elements, although not found in all eleven scenes, are in some of them.[29] The promise of a future conception, the second major component of type-scenes, would have eliminated the need to depict Joseph's consideration of divorce or the angel's command to complete the marriage.

The author of Matthew does not use the type-scene to emphasize a future conception. Because the authoritative message is given after Mary conceives (cf. Rebekah, Ishmael, and Callirhoe) and yet before she completes her marriage, the message must address the issue of marriage in some way. Remember that gender reversal and then adjustment of the dynamics produced a scene where Mary is contemplating divorce because she is pregnant with another mans' child. A command to Mary to continue the marriage would mean that Mary can allow Joseph to believe the child is his. She can justify her deception on the ground that her son has a special vocation. It would, however, be incongruent with the rest of the narrative to urge the audience to identify with a Messiah whose mother deceived her husband.[30] Since Mary does not deceive him, Joseph is the one who must resolve the dilemma.[31] Because the decision is in Joseph's hands, the angel's message must be directed to him. The intertwining of the issue of punishment for adulterous behavior or illicit relationships (an issue which reinforces gender role behavior for men) into the annunciation of Jesus' birth accentuates that the angel's message had to be directed to Joseph.

It can be argued that the author of Matthew still had a way to address the women in his implied audience. He could have included Mary along with Joseph as a recipient of the angel's words. The second component, the promise of future conception, could have been altered to include her. Since the second component is developed so that Manoah joins his wife to hear the angel's promise the second time, perhaps the angel could have appeared a second time so that Mary heard about Jesus' vocation in a dream.[32] Since Sarah, located inside the tent, hears the message to Abraham, perhaps Mary could have been positioned nearby as the message was given to Joseph.[33] Of course, with this revision Joseph would not have received the message in a dream.

That Mary could have been included in some manner means there are reasons why she is completely excluded. According to Fuchs, the more prominent a woman's role in annunciation type-scenes, the more motherhood within patriarchal structures is affirmed.[34] Mary's presence during the angel's message would have emphasized her maternal role. The author needs to marginalize her to the extreme to insure that the audience will not in any way affirm familial relationships based on biology. The audience instead must be led to claim loyalty to familial, nonbiological relationships as Joseph has and as Jesus later does in his ministry by calling his disciples, his family. The audience must identify with the disciples, who are mostly unrelated and who make disciples by teaching, not by conceiving and giving birth. Men, of course, cannot give birth; but they can mold others through teaching.[35]

Since Mary had to be excluded as a recipient of the angel's message, modern women ought to resist identification with Joseph. Joseph's dilemma, which is implicitly presented to female readers as a character role that all readers can experience, is not one in which women can participate. If his struggle were truly one that women could experience, then a reversed scene about a woman who considered divorcing her husband would not sound so strange. If his encounter with the angel were considered one that women could share in some way, then the scene would have included Mary as a recipient of the angel's message about Jesus. How women can respond to the angel's words is not encompassed within Joseph's experience. The narrator is actually addressing men, encouraging them to identify with Joseph, and preparing them to identify with Jesus and the disciples.

Analogy

Some women may decide that, even though Matthew's account of Jesus' birth is directed to a male audience, they still want to identify with Joseph. His efforts to do what is just and be receptive to God's will reflect a similar undertaking in their own lives. They want to accept the narrator's invitation to participate in Joseph's struggle to appropriate the law and respond to God's will. When they assume the role of the implied audience, they hear the angel's words as though they were addressed to them. They share the belief that the adult Jesus will play a distinctive role in the life of his people. They will not reject Jesus. They will assume a familial, although nonbiological, tie with Jesus just as Joseph had.

When women read Mt. 1:18–25 analogously as an invitation to establish a familial relationship with Jesus based on a responsiveness to God's will, they are accepting a position central to the Gospel of Matthew. This kind of relationship is expected of them when they later identify with the disciples. In Mt. 12:46–50, for instance, the narrator urges the audience to accept Jesus' address to his disciples that whoever does the will of God is his brother, sister, and mother. Modern women can more fully enjoy this analogous reading of Mt. 1:18–25 and evaluate its impact on them if they reverse the roles of Joseph and Mary. Reversing the roles gives them an explicit affirmation of their gender identities and can help keep them aware that they must not affirm Joseph's position without addressing those elements that could diminish them as female readers.[36]

The dynamics of role reversal are somewhat different in this text. When the roles are reversed, Mary becomes the one who is determined to divorce Joseph and then changes her decision. Joseph assumes Mary's role. Jesus' role remains unchanged. While rereading the other four Matthean texts, Jesus' role was reversed to that of a female Messiah because the narrator uses Jesus' words and actions to persuade the audience to identify with or against other characters in those texts. Since the narrator cannot use the words and actions of the infant Jesus to persuade the audience, there is no need to change his role.[37]

Women must suppress or accommodate aspects of the text as they reverse the roles of Mary and Joseph and read the text analogously. Four examples will be given that will require further reevaluation in

women's particular contexts. One element that they must accommodate is the impossibility of a man conceiving a child, an element which
strains the reversal. This impossibility forces female readers to adjust
the role reversal by imagining that Joseph's relationship with another
woman led to the child's conception. This type of adjustment actually
fits the thrust of the text quite well, since the narrator implies that
Joseph suspects that Mary has had a relationship with another man.
While using role reversal, female readers are spared the necessity of
trying to explain how Mary could take care of another woman's child
because, although Mary is not assured of how the conception occurred,
female readers who identify with the implied audience are led to believe
that the child's conception fulfills the Scriptures and occurred mirac-
ulously.[38] This assurance leads female readers to shift their thinking
again and imagine that Joseph himself somehow conceived. Joseph's
conception of a child seems preposterous, more fantastic than Mary's
conception of a child.[39] Role reversal in this instance exposes how central but subordinated Mary's anatomy for conceiving and giving birth
to Jesus is in Matthew's gospel narrative.[40]

Women can choose simply to ignore the impossibility of a man giving birth as they reverse the roles of Mary and Joseph and establish
a familial relationship with Jesus based on obedience to God. However,
female readers who do not want a relationship with Jesus that discounts
the role of women can read the text differently. They can question the
necessity of a relationship based only on obedience and consciously affirm the female anatomy that is needed to bear Jesus. In this way, they
can also refuse to perpetuate patriarchal history that traces generations
primarily through fathers.

Three more elements that could reinforce patriarchal relationships
need to be studied. One element some women may need to suppress
as they establish a familial relationship with Jesus is the allusion to one
race of people as the focus of Jesus' mission (1:21), an allusion that
could be used to justify the promotion of the interests of one race above
all others. Since in the rest of the gospel references are made to the extension of his mission to the Gentiles and this mission is announced
in Mt. 28:16–20, omission of this element would mean reading the account within its larger narrative context and recognizing the extension
of his mission. Some women, on the other hand, may find the element unobjectionable because in their particular contexts they need
and want to focus on how Jesus can promote liberation for their race.

A second element that women may find troublesome is the disregard for hearing the views, needs, and desires of the one who is

almost divorced. The law is considered and divine guidance is heard, but the perspective of the other marriage partner is not consulted.[41] Action is based only on doing the will of God as embodied in the law and revealed by the angel. The obedience that arises from this situation tends to polarize attentiveness to God's commands and responsiveness to humans. This dualism is deplorable because, as in the case of other dualisms, it justifies oppressive relationships: the views of human beings need not be heard if God's law and revelation are already known.

Women can decide to ignore this dualism by taking into account other texts where obedience to God is not separated from attentiveness to human requests. Jesus as a son of David displays obedience similar to that of Joseph's and also listens to the petitions and questions of human beings and reinterprets the Scriptures to address human needs. He even modifies his position about the restriction of his mission to Israel alone when he is pressured to tend to human need, as in the cases of the centurion's servant (Mt. 8:5–13) and the Canaanite woman's daughter (Mt. 15:21–28). When women read those texts where Jesus speaks for people (e.g., Mt. 26:6–13) or helps them without their initiative (e.g., Mt. 8:14–15), thus conveying a paternalistic attitude, women can bear in mind that these dynamics may function more to bolster Jesus' divinity and power than to model a way for the audience to interact with people.[42]

A third element which is more difficult to accommodate is the patriarchal manner in which Jesus is designated as the Messiah. When the roles are reversed, modern female readers as they identify with Mary would still be dependent on men to validate Jesus' messiahship, since Mt. 1:16 would be reread as "and Jacob the father of Mary, the wife of Joseph, of whom Jesus was born, who is called the Christ.[43] It is not merely a familial, nonbiological relationship to Jesus and recognition of his adult vocation that validates Jesus' messiahship. Jesus must also have the ancestral tie to the house of David that in turn goes back to Abraham. The narrator has told the audience about these relationships in the genealogy which precedes the birth narrative. This genealogy is a patrilineal one and the men are not ordinary men but those whose ancestry can be traced to King David and the great patriarch Abraham. Only four women's names are included. When women identify with Mary after role reversal, they have responded to God and are establishing a relationship with a messiah whose identity is associated with those who are powerful, wealthy, prestigious, and male.

It might seem that women could ignore this aspect if they kept in mind that the primary function of the genealogy does not have to be understood as the legitimation of Jesus as a Davidic Messiah. Instead, the genealogy provides an explanation of what kind of messiah he will be.[44] While keeping the roles of Mary and Joseph reversed, women could read the four women in the genealogy and Mary as figures who foreshadow the kind of leader Jesus will be. Each woman responds to the situation before her in a way that addresses not just her own needs but also the needs of her family and in some fashion the needs of the Jewish people.[45] The young widow Tamar, who had been denied Judah's son Shelah, plays the role of the harlot and secures what she needs to shield herself from poverty and what the law of levirate marriage entitled her deceased husband: an heir. Ruth, another young widow, who could have returned to her own home in Moab, instead, accompanies Naomi home to Bethlehem and, through her marriage to Boaz, secures what Naomi wants: a male heir for her deceased son, also Ruth's deceased husband.

Tamar's and Ruth's actions, indeed, have an impact upon all the people of Israel, although it is not yet apparent. Bathsheba's and Rahab's actions immediately affect all the Israelites. Bathsheba, formerly the wife of Uriah, a Hittite, acts on behalf of her son Solomon and moves David to name him as his legal heir to the throne rather than one of his other wives' sons. The people now have a new king. The prostitute Rahab, persuaded that the God of Israel was powerful, risks her own life when she hides the two scouts in her house and enables them to escape unharmed. The Israelites' conquest and occupation of the land can now begin. Mary, convinced that the child will have an important vocation among the Jews, decides to marry Joseph and protects the child from Herod. Jesus, too, will respond to the situations before him, thinking about not just his own survival but also the needs of his people.

Rereading the genealogy in this manner affirms that Jesus' background includes the marginal and the powerless. Women can ignore the implications that their relationship with Jesus means that they are accepting a messiah only associated with the elite. This reading does not however adequately counter the dominance of men's concerns over women's. As Tamar, Uriah's wife, Rahab, Ruth, and Mary (from role reversal) take into account the needs of those around them as well as their own, in each case the interests of a son, a husband, or some other man motivate their actions. Except for Ruth's consideration of Naomi's needs, which are nonetheless related to the loss of her two sons, none of the women focus on the needs of other women in their society. Even

Jesus, whom the women foreshadow in this rereading of the genealogy, will focus most of his attention on twelve male disciples.[46]

Modern women who identify with Joseph could perpetuate a concern for men's goals and well-being over women's. The genealogy and the birth narrative encourage this kind of empathy. Female readers who want to identify with Joseph are left in an uncomfortable position. They can overcome this situation and still accept the invitation of the text to establish a relationship with Jesus if at the same time they question and criticize its support of men's interests over those of women.

Women as Exchange Objects

Mary has often been compared and contrasted to the four women in the genealogy as a way to understand her role in the birth of Jesus. Janice Capel Anderson, for instance, has argued that the four women foreshadow Mary and prepare the audience to expect Mary's irregular conception.[47] This type of analysis views Mt. 1:18–25 as a shift away from an emphasis on Mary's role to an emphasis on Joseph's role in Jesus' birth.[48] When Mary is examined as an exchange object, the focus becomes how she is used in Mt. 1:18–25 to establish a bond between Joseph and Jesus and between the narrator and the audience. These bonds influence the audience's assessment of the genealogy in retrospect.

Joseph uses his relationship with Mary as the means to establish a relationship between himself and Jesus, although only after he has reevaluated his marriage to her and learns about Jesus' future. Mary has become pregnant during (or before[49]) the first stage of marriage, the period of betrothal, rather than after the second stage, the time when a woman would be brought to her husband's house and her marriage would then be completed. Joseph, who knows the child is not his, must reconsider his marriage to Mary, since he is diligent in his observance of the law. For him, adherence to the law is the means to do what is righteous in God's eyes. He decides to divorce her, since continuance of his marriage with her would mean association with a woman who, as an adulteress, had violated the law. Evidently, Joseph had other options, since the narrator states that Joseph decided to divorce her quietly and does not convey that he was forced to accept this course of action.[50]

Mary's pregnancy also forces Joseph to reevaluate his attitude toward the law. As he is considering a divorce, he receives God's guidance from the angel, which counters what the law has guided him to do. He must take Mary as his wife and name her son Jesus. Joseph's response to the angel's command may still have been within the bounds of what the law permitted him to do.[51] Nothing in the account suggests that Joseph's action was lawless, especially since the narrator has already implied that he had other options. What is striking is that he needed insight to choose this other option. His knowledge of the law is insufficient to do what is righteous. The angel's promise that the child would save his people from their sins convinces Joseph that he must change his mind. Joseph, a just man, is concerned with doing God's will and receptive to God's guidance to observe the law.

Mary's pregnancy has led Joseph to reevaluate his appropriation of the law. Now he can respond differently because his obedience to the law is based both on his knowledge of the law and a receptivity to God's guidance. He takes Mary as his wife. Because of this marital relationship, he becomes the one responsible for protecting the young Jesus from Herod's threats to kill him. Although Mary is protected too, Joseph's dreams are primarily instructions about how to guard Jesus. Joseph's relationship to Jesus becomes more important than his marriage to Mary in the second chapter. Mary has fulfilled her function of providing a relationship between Joseph and Jesus. Jesus becomes son of David.[52]

Mary also functions to draw the audience into the narrative so that they struggle with Joseph and empathize with his position. Mary's pregnancy threatens and challenges Joseph in his observation of the law. The audience joins Joseph in the resolution of his dilemma and establishes a familial, nonbiological tie to Jesus based on a responsive obedience to God's will. At the same time a specific relationship is established between the audience and Jesus' ancestors. Although Joseph's acceptance of Jesus allows Jesus' descent to be traced back to David, when the audience identifies with Joseph's relationship with Jesus, they cannot trace this relationship back to David and Abraham on the basis of Jesus' biological kinship ties. They can trace it back only on the basis of Joseph's obedience to God's will.[53] Identification with Joseph, in other words, precludes any notion that biological descent from Abraham guarantees membership in Jesus' family, which later in the gospel is presented as God's family too, since God is Father.[54]

As the audience identifies with Joseph and the narrator uses Mary to foster this identification, the audience is also encouraged to identify against Mary. Mary is not depicted as someone the audience must reject because she has done something horrendous.[55] Joseph's suspicions about adultery, which are dispelled for the audience in the quotation from Isaiah, are the only marks against her. Mary must be rejected because she represents what the audience must not affirm for themselves: a physical tie to Jesus. A physical bond (or birthright) is the kind of relationship that the audience ought not to maintain as the way to guarantee their place in God's family.[56] This conclusion might seem an overstatement of the dynamics in Mt. 1:18–25 if it were not for the fact that another scene supports it. In Mt. 12:46–50 Jesus rejects Mary and his brothers as his family, turns to his disciples, and claims those who do God's will as his true family. Once more the audience must identify against Mary and align themselves with those who do God's will in order to belong to Jesus' family.[57]

Analysis of Mary as an exchange object displays how she contributes toward shaping the audience's response to Joseph and prepares them to identify with the adult Jesus and his disciples. Mary's role has specific implications for female readers. When they identify with Joseph, they allow themselves to deny their female identities. They have also begun the process of agreeing that women cannot be disciples because all women are like Mary. Mary has a physical tie to Jesus and thus cannot struggle with the law, gain insight about God's will, and accept Jesus on the basis of this insight as Joseph has. Jesus' rejection of her in Mt. 12:46–50 reaffirms that Mary has only a physical tie to him. Although it would seem that other women could establish a familial relationship with Jesus based on obedience to God's will, since Jesus says whoever does the will of God is his brother and sister and mother, the narrator does not give a portrayal of female disciples so that female readers are provided a firm affirmation of their female gender as they identify with the disciples.

One way female readers can affirm their female identities is to choose to accept rather than reject Mary's physical tie to Jesus and thus challenge the exclusion of women from discipleship. If female readers broaden discipleship to include an affirmation of Mary's physical relationship to Jesus, then women cannot be excluded and female readers can affirm their female identities. Women, for instance, could question why discipleship and membership in God's family must always be based on doing God's will. Mary, who did not do anything, would be a part of Jesus' family simply because she was chosen. Affirmation of the notion of chosenness along with doing God's will, of course, could renew some of the problems that the author of Matthew desired to end. Mary, however, was not chosen because her descent could be traced back to Abraham. Affirmation of Mary's chosenness could mean learning that God has other ways to include people in Jesus's family, which is also God's family, than through knowing and learning God's commands.

As with the other four texts, this challenge leads to reading the text in a direction other than what the text invites its audience to do (when they assume the role of the implied audience as discussed in the Introduction). Female readers must not feel compelled to identify with Mary just because she is a female character. The communities in which women live must be considered as they affirm or reject Mary and what she represents.

Summary

The previous chapters developed and demonstrated how women might reread biblical narrative texts without female characters by using strategies that focus on gender reversal, analogy, and viewing women as exchange objects. The application of these three strategies on Mt. 1:18–25 has now demonstrated that the strategies are also useful for understanding the dynamics of texts with female characters and their impact on female readers.

Needless to say, women can also prepare sermons from the data gained when the three strategies are applied to biblical texts with female characters. The strategy that focuses on gender reversal, particularly when it is applied to Mt. 1:18–25, can enable women to recognize that gender roles for women can sometimes be extensively manipulated in biblical texts to privilege men's roles and responsibilities over women's. A sermon could address this dynamic, the detriments of identifying with the male protagonist or character, or the limitations of gender stereotypes. Sermons which utilize data from analogous readings and readings that focus on women as exchange objects could be developed in ways similar to what I have suggested in chapters 4 and 5. The strategy that focuses on women as exchange objects could lead to a sermon that contemplates both the function of the female character in the selected passage where she appears and her impact in the following chapters.

CONCLUSION

Feminist biblical scholars have used various approaches to read and appropriate the Bible which they recognize has a patriarchal context and contains denigrating views of women. In chapter 1, I reviewed some of the books and essays of feminist biblical scholars to show the need for additional reading strategies. In chapter 2, I discussed some of the research of feminist literary scholars to demonstrate that they have also struggled with how to read misogynous, patriarchal texts. Some of their findings provided me ways to develop reading strategies. Reading strategies that focus on gender reversal, analogy, and women as exchange objects, I proposed, could be applied to biblical narratives to assess the effect of their values on female readers and to help women decide whether to accept, challenge, or reject these pericopes.

The next three chapters (3, 4, and 5) developed the three strategies and applied them to four texts from Matthew. To ensure that the strategies fit most biblical narrative, I selected texts without female characters. The application of the strategies on the four texts has demonstrated how women might reread biblical narrative texts without female characters. In chapter 6, I demonstrated with a study of Mt. 1:18–25 that the three strategies are also useful for understanding the dynamics of texts with female characters and for evaluating the impact of these texts on female readers.

At the end of chapters 3, 4, 5, and 6, I briefly commented on the usefulness of the strategies for writing sermons. The three strategies offer clergywomen several ways to read, analyze, and respond to biblical narrative texts as they prepare their sermons. It is urgent to address the usefulness of the strategies for sermon preparation, since the worship service is the only occasion in which some people reflect upon biblical texts and it is one in which they can gain a different way of understanding and reading biblical narratives. Christine Smith claims that homiletics has responded inadequately to feminist biblical scholarship; yet feminist biblical scholars have too infrequently suggested how their approaches to reading the Bible can be used to develop sermons for worship services.[1] The chapter summaries and the Appendix are small steps in that direction.

The application of these strategies has provoked several pertinent questions that need to be addressed in order to assure that the purposes of the strategies are understood. For example, are these strategies merely attempts to rescue biblical texts from patriarchy? How is the authority of the Scriptures viewed when women use these strategies? Could men also use the three strategies to read biblical narrative texts? I will begin with the question about whether the strategies function to rescue the Bible from patriarchy and then proceed with the questions about the authority of the Scriptures and male readers' implementation of the strategies.

Theological and Ideological Implications

As women use these strategies to read biblical texts and evaluate the impact of the texts on them and the women they know, their affirmation of certain values in the texts and the broadening of perspectives in the texts might appear to be attempts to rescue the Bible from patriarchy and make the texts more palatable. Liberating biblical texts from their patriarchal contexts is not at all the goal of the application of the strategies. Providing several ways to reinterpret biblical texts and affirm certain parts of them is an attempt to allow women to follow the story line and identify with those characters whose values and perspectives they think resemble theirs and would promote life among women in their communities. As discussed in chapter 2, realistic narrative, which includes biblical narrative texts, can play an important role in the transformation of women's self-images and must be retained.

Providing women strategies to affirm or challenge certain aspects of biblical texts is also an attempt to enable female readers to acknowledge the Bible as an authoritative text and remain in dialogue with their ecclesiastical traditions and organizations. Whereas feminist literary critics and their students can reject misogynous literature and read literature more affirming of women, feminist biblical scholars and female readers of the Bible cannot as easily dismiss the Bible and move on to other literature. The Bible is a special text, special in a way that the Constitution of the United States is, although the Constitution can be amended and the Bible cannot. Just as U.S. citizens continue to believe that the Constitution has continuing relevance, churches and their members believe that the Bible has continuing relevance for present and future generations of people. If feminists dismiss the Bible completely and move on to other religious and theological writings, the Bible will nonetheless continue to influence people in more far-reaching ways than the misogynous literature dismissed by feminist literary critics will. Feminist biblical scholars have persisted in their reinterpretations of the Bible to lessen its destructive impact on women and other groups of people. These strategies are offered as a part of this ongoing enterprise.

The three strategies also relieve female readers from thinking that they have compromised themselves by continuing to read and enjoy the Bible. Female readers need not adopt a simplistic, dualistic solution to the appropriation of the Bible. The Bible is not a text that women must either reject or accept. The Bible is a text that women must and can read critically.[2] Women still have the option to dismiss specific biblical texts; but they can make this judgment after applying the strategies, following the story line of the narrative, and assessing the values in the text in light of their own experiences and those of the women they know.

The use of these strategies requires a different understanding of the authority of the Scriptures. Female readers consent to the authority of the biblical text as they read the story line to comprehend its perspective. They accept its authority as they examine whether the narrative context or the ancient cultural milieu will support an interpretation that affirms women. Female readers, however, withhold their consent or part of it at the point when they have evaluated the specific text and find they must reject or challenge its perspective. Female readers resist the text or give partial consent to the authority of the biblical text because total acceptance of the values in the text and identification with the protagonists would perpetuate oppressive situations in their communities. In other words, when female readers use the three strategies, they place authority in (1) the biblical texts, (2) studies of the ancient cultural milieu, (3) their communities, and (4) their own experiences, and accord themselves a moderating position (when possible) among these four sources of power and authority.

Throughout my discussion and application of the three reading strategies, I have focused primarily on how female readers can use them. Men who recognize the patriarchal context of the Bible could also use the strategies to assess the effects of the values of specific texts on them and other men. The strategies could help them decide whether to reject, accept, or challenge these texts. Clergymen could utilize these strategies as they prepare sermons. These strategies cannot, however, enable men to assess the effects of the values in biblical texts on women unless they are engaged in dialogue with women about these texts. One of the important components of the three strategies is that women be aware of their gender identities as they read. The use of the strategies by male readers would involve the same dynamic. Male readers must approach reading as a gendered activity that involves them both physically and mentally. They too are being persuaded to adopt and reproduce specific gender role behavior. Although they can imagine how biblical texts might affect women, they cannot presume to know their effects. They must discuss the texts with women.

Summary

These strategies offer possible ways to read and interpret biblical narrative texts, not solutions that restore integral roles for female characters in the narratives. Whether these strategies are applied to biblical narrative texts with female characters or with only male characters, in either case the marginalization of female characters and the patriarchal perspective of the text that promotes the marginalization of women are not eliminated or easily overcome. In the application of gender reversal, the marginalization of female characters is intensified. Its application on the five Matthean texts raises the question whether modern women can be disciples, since the five texts are directed to a male audience and the narrator does not attempt to engage women to participate in its narrative world. That the author was using plot patterns and motifs available in the protocols of male public language, which do not necessarily reflect what real women and men were doing, suggests that perhaps women can be commissioned disciples, although not like those in Matthew's gospel. Modern women can look elsewhere, believing God is also among those people who lack a written history.

On the other hand, the strategies that focus on analogy and women as exchange objects permit modern women to identify with male protagonists, such as the commissioned disciples in the Gospel of Matthew. The application of the strategy that focuses on analogy even allows modern women to forget about the marginalization of female characters when they apply it to texts without female characters. This disregard for the minor female characters does not, however, provide women an automatic acceptance of the perspective of the text. Women must proceed with an analysis of those aspects of the text that could promote attitudes and actions that would marginalize women and ethnic groups today. This analysis often leads to a complicated position where women affirm certain parts of the text and challenge other parts that could marginalize them. Women can affirm, for instance, their desire to advocate for the betterment of other people's lives as Jesus did but challenge the necessity of physical suffering as the means to do this.

The strategy that focuses on women as exchange objects, which also allows women to identify with male protagonists, provides a way to see the impact that female characters have on male protagonists and readers. The marginalization of the female character(s) can be overcome if the text is read differently than it has been written and the perspective of the male protagonist(s) is expanded. Discipleship in the Gospel of Matthew, for example, could be broadened to include the perspectives of the female characters, which often conflict with the views of the male disciples and Jesus.

These strategies offer several ways to read biblical narrative texts, ways that challenge a traditional understanding of the authority of the Bible. The strategies could be viewed as ones that uproot women from tradition and orthodoxy. I will not deny that the application of the strategies, while taking into account what the author is communicating to his audience, places much responsibility on female readers to assess how the text affirms or negates what would be the just and loving deed for them to do in their communities. At least with respect to the Gospel of Matthew, these strategies echo in some sense what the author was encouraging his audience to do: to discern the will of God from tradition, the Scriptures, the needs of human beings, and human experiences and to be disciples who are always learning.

Appendix

SAMPLE SERMON

This sermon is an example of how the strategy of gender reversal might be used in the preparation of a sermon. I preached the sermon at Calabash Presbyterian Church in Calabash, North Carolina, on July 2, 1995.

Where Is the Spirit?

Scriptures Readings: Joel 3:21–29; Mt. 28:16–20

Preliminary Remarks and Prayer:

When I was quite young, I thought that God dwelled in the front of the church with the minister and the choir. As I grew older, I learned that wasn't true; but I do have this feeling, whenever I step into a pulpit, of walking on holy ground. It's a privilege to be with you today and I thank you. Let us pray. Almighty God, open our hearts and souls to Your word. May the words of my mouth and the meditations of our hearts be acceptable in Your sight, O Lord, our rock and our redeemer. Amen.

In a small New England town, a Methodist church of about a hundred members was assigned a new minister at its June annual conference. The minister studied the roster of the congregation and noted that almost all of his members were retired or near retirement. These folks have worked hard, Rev. Jones thought to himself, and deserve to enjoy their golden years. I won't preach on any controversial subjects. At their age, they don't have the energy to study the latest information on the topics, so I'd be wasting my time. Besides, there's no need to raise their blood pressure and threaten their health. I certainly won't preach any stewardship sermons because they're all on fixed incomes and giving what they can. I'll preach pastoral sermons, sermons that make them feel good. I'll tell them stories and jokes and make them laugh. And so that's what he did.

During the next two months two people died. During the next month six people died. During the next three months twenty people died. At the end of eleven months, fifty people, half the congregation, had died. Rev. Jones was quite sad and consoled himself, "Well, all of them were quite happy during their last days, especially Mrs. Smith. She said she was so glad she didn't have to move to a nursing home."

One Sunday afternoon the district superintendent, after looking at the annual statistical reports, came to see him and said, "I want to take you to a nearby church." The two of them drove about an hour away to a church similar to his, one with mostly older adults. Some of the members were inside planning a churchwide stewardship event. Some of the members were getting ready to leave to hear a lecture on race relations. Another group was raking leaves and planting bulbs. Still another group was rehearsing a play about Paul in the fellowship hall. Rev. Jones was impressed. He said, "Wow! What a community! This congregation really has spirit!" The district superintendent said, "It surely does. Where's the Spirit in your congregation?"

Maybe you're thinking, "This story couldn't be true. There had to have been at least one feisty member in that minister's church who would have stopped that minister from preaching and leading in such a manner that half the congregation died. Besides, the way he viewed his members couldn't have caused their deaths. They were probably going to die soon anyway. Fifty people dead? Maybe ten, but not fifty. This story is absurd, unrealistic, never could have happened."

The story is easy to see through. You can tell it's not describing a real group of people. You and I both know that older members of congregations can be physically active and alert, capable of learning about and discussing controversial subjects, interested in a variety of activities, and concerned about church stewardship, which, of course, involves more than money. All that you need to do is look at yourselves or at other congregations and you can easily see that older people's interests are diverse, not all alike.

Not all stories are as easy to see through as the one I've told. If the story had said only ten people had died, would you have believed it? Would you have been just as annoyed and concerned about the minister's approach to ministering to older adults?

Not all stories are easy to see through. People are often unaware of the stories, the stereotypes, and the generalizations that influence what they do, what they say, and what they think. Many people *do* think that older adults are unproductive, uninterested in current events, only want to talk about the good old days, and ready to keel over any moment. Or people think all teenagers are destructive, all black men are criminals, all Jews are rich, all Asian Americans are good in math and science, all mothers are only interested in talking about their children, all college students in universities like Vanderbilt and Duke are rich spoiled brats, all white men are power hungry.

These generalizations, these stories do not instantly kill people's bodies; but they are deadly. These stories are deadly because they continually frustrate the aspirations and dreams of real people and cut off the possibility of friendships and relationships. The stories are deadly because they make it difficult for God's Spirit to move among people so that people establish a community rather than tear it down.

A few weeks ago in the Sunday paper there appeared a column about the treatment of a successful black businessman. When he is in elevators, white people back away from him. When he hails a cab with a white driver, the cab driver won't respond. So he stands there waving his hand over and over and over. When he is making business transactions, his clients can't believe that he has a business that is not connected at least in its beginnings with something shady like drugs. Black men, after all, are all crooks. He said that his success is constantly questioned, and at the very least correcting this disbelief is exhausting. I want you to think of all the wasted energy and all the relationships that never evolve in this situation. I want you to ask where is the Spirit?

In a panel about teaching religion courses, a seminary professor said that after she had a child, her male colleagues always asked about her child, about whom she loved to brag, but rarely about her work, which she also wanted to discuss. She had continued her research and had an article about to be published in a reputable journal. I want you to try to imagine the conversations and projects that could have emerged if her male colleagues had viewed her as a colleague. Where is the Spirit in this situation?

We have stories, too, that influence our actions, our thoughts, and our conversations. Most of our stories are ones we've been taught since we were babies. These stories are so deeply ingrained in our souls that we often cannot see through them without the help of another person. Somewhere along the way, Rev. Jones had been taught that older people are incapable of dealing with painful, controversial issues and are slow-witted, behind the times, and fragile. He needed the superintendent to show him that his story did not fit reality and his members were capable of a lot more.

Some of the stories we cannot see through are in the Bible. The ending of the Gospel of Matthew is one of those passages we need to help each other read so that we are not making it difficult for God's Spirit to move among us. For generations, this passage has been read and taught to girls and boys as the way Jesus' ministry will continue. Should it surprise us then that women as well as men are identifying with the eleven male disciples, feel called to the ordained ministry, and are going to seminary, sometimes with their families' approval and sometimes without it?

Almost 50 percent of the students at Louisville Seminary and Columbia Seminary are women. Women are being called by God, are studying and preparing themselves, and are pastoring churches and serving as chaplains. In spite of how many more female pastors there are now compared to twenty years ago, only a month and a half ago, one of my students who is preparing herself to attend a Methodist seminary, said, "My son-in-law told my daughter to tell me that I couldn't be a minister because all of Jesus' disciples were male." Despite the reality that women are leading and ministering in various positions, this Bible passage still influences people to discount and stifle women's calls to leadership roles in the church.

As one of those girls who grew up identifying with the male disciples, I read the gospels and rejoiced over the disciples' successful comprehension of Jesus' teachings. I lamented their failures, empathized with Peter's denial, feared implication, fled with them, and accepted the commission with them. Their story was my story. Over the past few years, however, I have wondered why the women at the cross in the Gospel of Matthew are not specifically recorded as Jesus' disciples too. Why did this gospel, written somewhere between 85 and 90 c.e., refuse to mention women along with men? Is that really the way it happened? Rather a bold question you might think; but not if you consider Paul's letters, written in the late 50s and the early 60s, which tell us women worked alongside Paul.

Can we allow God's Spirit to move among us today and consider women did more than what the Gospel of Matthew tells us? Can we allow God's Spirit to lead us to understand why women are not named among the commissioned disciples? I hope with all my being that my thoughts and reflections will open up this passage and we will sense God's Spirit with us.

As I have contemplated the question why the Gospel of Matthew tells only about the commission of male disciples, several explanations have surfaced. One explanation: The twelve male disciples represent the twelve tribes of Israel that we read about in the Old Testament. They are the New Israel which will include Gentiles. So, the male disciples are to be read symbolically, not literally. Another explanation: Writing in the first century was primarily a male activity. Men wrote to men. The Gospel of Matthew doesn't mention female disciples because it was written to men, telling them how to be faithful disciples of Jesus. Just as Joseph's view of Jesus' conception is told and not Mary's, only male disciples are mentioned.

Still reading, praying, and reflecting on what others had concluded, I discovered another purpose for emphasizing a commission to male disciples. According to a good portion of writings in the first century, whenever women traveled they were expected to travel with a male member of their household, either their husband, their father, their son, or a male servant. Jesus, as you know, demanded that his male disciples leave their lands, their houses, their parents, their brothers and sisters, and their children. They have obeyed him. They are committed disciples even though they've made mistakes. The presence of women from their households would make them look as though they weren't fully committed, wouldn't it? To make it perfectly clear that they are faithful and have left their households, women who only travel with their households must not be commissioned along with them.

Now, think a moment about the committed Christians you know, friends, neighbors, elders, deacons, ministers, not Mother Teresa, someone you know. Have they expressed their Christian commitment by leaving everything — children, parents, houses, lands, brothers and sisters? Have they? No. Have you? No. Even our missionaries take their children with them overseas. So how does this demand affect us?

This demand of discipleship can lead people and has led some people to devalue themselves and their contributions because they cannot be so committed that they are willing to leave everything. Even the designation of this kind of discipleship as one for ministers and not ordinary Christians is demeaning because it is saying a minister's commitment is better than that of lay people. Actually, ministers don't leave everything either.

Of course, you could say I'm treating the command to leave everything too literally because it's not meant to be fully implemented. It's just an ideal, a yardstick to measure faithfulness, a way to motivate people to share at least some of their possessions. But we need to remember Jesus is talking about leaving behind more than possessions; he's talking about leaving family behind. In this day and age when men are trying hard to care for their families and not be distant or absent or neglectful, do we really want this as a standard to measure our Christian commitment? Loyalty to both church and family is possible. Where is God's Spirit when committed discipleship is understood as including the demand to leave behind family? Where is the Spirit that is supposed to inspire us to affirm life and community, not separation and death? The Spirit is here, waiting, ready to break through as we affirm and try to discover other ways of demonstrating commitment, for commitment is what Mt. 28:16–20 is primarily about. Jesus' words to the disciples are about commitment, commitment to communicate the love of God to many, many people.

Are we being too cavalier when we overturn Jesus' demand and say in our day we don't have to leave everything to be committed disciples? Not if we realize that the commission is not just about a commitment to carry on *what* Jesus said but also a commitment to continue the *way* Jesus spoke and ministered. Jesus challenged customs and religious traditions again and again. Even though he wasn't supposed to, he ate with tax collectors, touched lepers, overturned the tables in the Temple, allowed sick people to enter the Temple, and talked with women. He even changed his mind about his mission and decided to include Gentiles. Jesus was always turning things around so that human needs could be met and people could be restored to their communities.

Where is the Spirit? In this room, in all of this room. Christ's Spirit is here as we help each other turn our stories around. Christ's Spirit is here, ready to move among us and give us new hopes, new dreams, new visions.

NOTES

Introduction

1. The term "patriarchy" refers to the whole system of cultural values that gives preference to men, the upper class, and the dominant race. "Androcentrism" refers more narrowly to a male perspective that excludes a female one.

2. When women used different conventions to read "The Yellow Wallpaper" (as I will discuss in chapter 2), textual elements also guided them. The reading theory which I am using is primarily that of Wolfgang Iser (*The Act of Reading: A Theory of Aesthetic Response* [Baltimore: Johns Hopkins University Press, 1978]). His theory emphasizes a reader who creatively assembles and experiences the meaning of a text in a temporal process of anticipation and retrospection but who is guided by strategies in the text to find the intentions underlying the author's choice of conventions. Nelly Furman ("Textual Feminism," in *Women and Language in Literature*, ed. Sally McConnell-Ginet, Ruth Borker, and Nelly Furman [New York: Praeger, 1980], 45–54) argues for a similar position between the total subjectivity and passivity of the reader. Iser, of course, has been criticized for privileging the text over the reader when he applies his theory; therefore, I will be expanding his notion of conventions so that I can pay attention to both the text and readers.

3. The term "point of view," as used here, refers to the dynamic relationship between author and audience and thus includes all the narrative strategies used to structure this relationship and shape the audience's response to the story. See Susan Sniader Lanser, *The Narrative Act: Point of View in Prose Fiction* (Princeton: Princeton University Press, 1981), 13–14.

4. Iser, *Act of Reading*, 59–61, 152. By "conventions," I am referring to a set of interpretive standards that guide the reader, some of which are embedded in the text, such as its genre and stylistic features, and some of which are derived from the reader's interpretive communities.

5. See Mary Ann Tolbert, "Protestant Feminists and the Bible: On the Horns of a Dilemma," *USQR* 43 (1989): 12–13.

6. Iser assumes, as most male theorists do, that the ideal reader is male; however, his recognition of the creative role of the reader and an expansion of his view of cultural conventions to include interpretive strategies mean his reading theory allows room for female readers to use the interpretive strategies that I suggest. J. de J. R. Jackson's *Historical Criticism and the Meaning of Texts* (New York: Routledge, 1989), P. J. Rabinowitz's *Before Reading: Narrative Conventions and the Politics of Conventions* (Ithaca, N.Y.: Cornell University Press,

1987), Steven Mailloux's *Interpretive Conventions: The Reader in the Study of American Fiction* (Ithaca, N.Y.: Cornell University Press, 1982), and Jonathan Culler's *Structuralist Poetics: Structuralism, Linguistics, and the Study of Literature* (Ithaca, N.Y.: Cornell University Press, 1975) are helpful for expanding Iser's notion of conventions. John Darr provides an insightful study of reading conventions in ancient contexts in *On Character Building: The Reader and the Rhetoric of Characterization in Luke-Acts* (Louisville: Westminster/John Knox Press, 1992).

7. The implied audience (or reader) is the role offered by the text that the real audience (or reader) plays when listening to (or reading) that text. Iser, *Act of Reading*, 34–38.

8. John Paul Heil, *The Death and Resurrection of Jesus: A Narrative-Critical Reading of Matthew 26–28* (Minneapolis: Fortress Press, 1991), 107. See also Keith Howard Reeves, *The Resurrection Narrative in Matthew: A Literary Critical Examination* (Lewiston, N.Y.: Mellen Biblical Press, 1993), 79–80, n. 70.

9. J. Andrew Overman, *Matthew's Gospel and Formative Judaism: The Social World of the Matthean Community* (Minneapolis: Fortress Press, 1990), 135–36.

10. Janice Capel Anderson, "Matthew: Gender and Reading," *Semeia* 28 (1983): 24.

11. Robert Harry Smith, "Matthew 28:16–20, Anticlimax or Key to the Gospel?" in *SBL Seminar Papers 1993*, ed. Eugene H. Lovering, Jr. (SBLSP 32; Atlanta: Scholars Press, 1993), 601–2; Michael J. Wilkins, "Named and Unnamed Disciples in Matthew: A Literary-Theological Study," in *SBL Seminar Papers 1991*, ed. Eugene H. Lovering, Jr. (SBLSP 30; Atlanta: Scholars Press, 1991), 438–39; David B. Howell, *Matthew's Inclusive Story* (Sheffield: JSOT Press, 1990), 248; Jack Dean Kingsbury, *Matthew as Story*, 2d ed. (Philadelphia: Fortress Press, 1988), 13–14, 33–37. Kingsbury asserts that readers learn the values of discipleship as they follow the narrator's and Jesus' evaluation of the twelve disciples; however, he leaves the impression in his discussion of the point of view in Matthew that readers must evaluate all the characters in order to acquire these values. These four scholars disagree about which characters can be categorized as disciples.

12. Daniel Patte, *The Gospel According to Matthew: A Structural Commentary on Matthew's Faith* (Philadelphia: Fortress Press, 1987), 205, n. 106.

13. Andrew T. Lincoln, "Matthew — A Story for Teachers?" in *The Bible in Three Dimensions: Essays in Celebration of Biblical Studies in the University of Sheffield*, ed. David J. A. Clines et al. (JSOTSup 87; Sheffield: JSOT Press, 1990), 105–6.

14. Richard A. Edwards, "Uncertain Faith: Matthew's Portrait of the Disciples," *Discipleship in the New Testament*, ed. Fernando F. Segovia (Philadelphia: Fortress Press, 1985), 59.

15. See Mary Ann Tolbert, *Sowing the Gospel: Mark's World in Literary-Historical Perspective* (Minneapolis: Fortress Press, 1989), 32, 46; Kenneth Sacks, "Rhetorical Approaches to Greek History Writing in the Hellenistic Period," in *SBL Seminar Papers 1984*, ed. K. Richards (SBLSP 23; Chico, Calif.: Scholars

Press, 1984), 123–33; P. Sigal, "Manifestations of Hellenistic Historiography in Select Judaic Literature," in ibid., 161–85.

16. For a discussion of the aural character of ancient writings, see Tolbert, *Sowing the Gospel*, 41–46, 70–79.

17. Lanser, *The Narrative Act*, 108–48. My discussion of her model is based on these pages.

18. The implied author is the presence or the "second self" that the author creates for the audience to know and experience. This "second self" is conveyed through all the choices that the real author made while creating the text. See Wayne Booth, *The Rhetoric of Fiction*, 2d ed. (Chicago: University of Chicago Press, 1983), 70–77, 151.

19. The implied author rarely speaks with a distinctive voice. Jack Dean Kingsbury cites three texts (Mt. 24:15, 27:8, 28:15) which indicate that the implied author placed himself after Jesus' resurrection (*Matthew as Story*, 33).

20. This type of narrator is defined by M. H. Abrams in *A Glossary of Literary Terms*, 6th ed. (New York: Holt, Rinehart, and Winston, 1993), 166.

21. Kingsbury (*Matthew as Story*, 34) implies that readers decide to accept Jesus' point of view and the narrator's because the implied author "places his voice in the service of" God's point of view. Kingsbury overlooks that the implied author of Matthew is persuading his audience to believe that his understanding of God's way is the one they must implement.

22. E. M. Forster designates "flat characters" as those with a few traits and predictable behavior and "round characters" as those with a number of traits, possibly conflicting, and with unpredictable actions and attitudes (*Aspects of the Novel* [New York: Harcourt, Brace, & World, 1927], 103–18. See also Abrams, *Glossary of Literary Terms*, 23–25). I am distinguishing the religious leaders from the disciples in this analysis in a way that Forster probably would not; he would call all ancient characters "flat." (For a similar position, see Robert Scholes and Robert Kellogg, *The Nature of Narrative* [New York: Oxford University Press, 1966], 164.) Since modern readers bring conventions to their reading of biblical texts that would lead them to view certain biblical characters as "flat" and others as "round" and since my focus is primarily on modern readers, I find it helpful to use these terms with Lanser's model. Frank Kermode refers to modern readers' construction of characters as full figures in *The Genesis of Secrecy: On the Interpretation of Narrative* (Cambridge: Harvard University Press, 1977), 76–78.

23. Kingsbury (*Matthew as Story*, 13–14) notes a similar dynamic in the readers' identification with the disciples, but does not comment that this dynamic of viewing the disciples as "round characters" is typical for modern readers. Fred Burnett argues that "textual indicators" in ancient writings allow for some characters (e.g., Peter) to be altered momentarily into round characters. He goes on to assert that these textual indicators along with a modern style of reading can lead modern readers to construct characters as "persons" ("Characterization and Reader Construction of Characters," *Semeia* 63 [1993]: 18–23.)

24. Kingsbury (*Matthew as Story*, 17) claims that Jesus reconciles the disciples to himself in Mt. 28:16–20 and implies that this gesture primarily influences the readers' view of the disciples. However, the disciples' failures had been softened prior to the final scene. Mark Alan Powell discusses the audience's identification with or distancing from the disciples with the terms empathy, sympathy, and antipathy in *What Is Narrative Criticism?* (Minneapolis: Fortress Press, 1990), 56–57.

25. I agree with Howell that the narrator does not encourage a simple identification with the eleven disciples in chapter 28 (*Matthew's Inclusive Story*, 233, 247–48), but I also think that the narrator does not encourage a simple identification with Jesus' position. Howell claims that the disciples function in Matthew almost the same way they do in Mark: the audience learns from the disciples' failures to be more obedient. This position works well for Mark, since the eleven disciples do not return in chapter 16; but it only partially addresses the function of the disciples in Matthew, who do reappear after their desertion.

26. Richard A. Edwards correctly argues that the disciples are consistently portrayed as "vacillating followers," a description which forces the audience to see that discipleship is always unfinished ("Uncertain Faith," 52, 59). In a more positive light, discipleship means being a "learner" and continuing to gain insight from Jesus. See Tolbert, *Sowing the Gospel*, 155, n. 44; Kingsbury, *Matthew as Story*, 14; Michael J. Wilkins, *The Concept of Disciple in Matthew's Gospel*, NovTestSup 59 (New York: E. J. Brill, 1988), 162–63, 217–24.

27. For a fuller treatment of the traits of Jesus and the disciples, see Kingsbury, *Matthew as Story*, 11–17. Other literary-critical studies include Howell, *Matthew's Inclusive Story*; Edwards, "Uncertain Faith" and *Matthew's Story of Jesus* (Philadelphia: Fortress Press, 1985).

28. As I study Matthew's point of view in the selected pericopes, I will pay attention to the textual elements and acknowledge divergences among readers; but, of course, my own values will shape this interpretation.

1. The Need for Reading Strategies

1. Biblical scholars who have utilized this approach are Sharon H. Ringe ("Luke 9:28–36: The Beginning of an Exodus," *Semeia* 28 [1983]: 83–99); Susan Brooks Thistlethwaite ("Every Two Minutes: Battered Women and Feminist Interpretation," in *Feminist Interpretation of the Bible*, ed. Letty M. Russell [Philadelphia: Westminster Press, 1985], 96–107); Elsa Tamez ("Women's Rereading of the Bible," in *Feminist Theology from the Third World: A Reader*, ed. Ursula King [Maryknoll, N.Y.: Orbis Books, 1994], 194–95); Ada María Isasi-Díaz ("The Bible and *Mujerista* Theology," in *Lift Every Voice: Constructing Christian Theologies from the Underside*, ed. Susan Brooks Thistlethwaite and Mary Potter Engel [New York: HarperCollins, 1990], 267–68). Sharon H. Ringe claims that many African American and Latin American women use the prophetic traditions to interpret the rest of the Bible in "When Women Interpret the Bible,"

in *WBC*, ed. Carol A. Newsom and Sharon H. Ringe (Louisville: Westminster/ John Knox Press, 1992), 4.

2. Rosemary Radford Ruether, *Sexism and God-Talk: Toward a Feminist Theology* (Boston: Beacon Press, 1983), 22–33.

3. Rosemary Radford Ruether, "Feminist Interpretation: A Method of Correlation," in *Feminist Interpretation of the Bible*, ed. Letty M. Russell (Philadelphia: Westminster Press, 1985), 117–18.

4. Ruether, *Sexism and God-Talk*, 32. She maintains her position in *Women-Church: Theology and Practice* (New York: Harper & Row, 1985), 41; "Recontextualizing Theology," *ThTo* 43 (1986): 26–27; and "Christian Quest for Redemptive Community," *CrossCur* 38 (1988): 13–14.

5. Ruether, *Sexism and God-Talk*, 32–33. See also Ruether, "Feminist Interpretation," 119–20.

6. Ruether, *Women-Church*, 42–49. See also Ruether, "Feminist Interpretation," 122–23.

7. Renita Weems, "Gomer: Victim of Violence or Victim of Metaphor?" *Semeia* 47 (1989): 87–104.

8. Thistlethwaite, "Every Two Minutes," 102.

9. Tina Pippin, "Eros and the End: Reading for Gender in the Apocalypse of John," *Semeia* 59 (1992): 195, 200.

10. Ruether, *Sexism and God-Talk*, 30.

11. Ibid.

12. Kwok Pui-Lan criticizes Ruether for assuming that the prophetic critical process can be removed from the original context and transferred to other contexts ("Discovering the Bible in the Non-Biblical World," in *Lift Every Voice: Constructing Christian Theologies from the Underside*, 280).

13. Katharine Doob Sakenfeld, "Feminist Uses of Biblical Materials," in *Feminist Interpretation of the Bible*, 61.

14. Elisabeth Schüssler Fiorenza, *In Memory of Her: A Feminist Theological Reconstruction of Christian Origins* (New York: Crossroad, 1983), 21.

15. Work has continued on reconstructing women's history and women's participation in religious communities. For example, Bernadette Brooten, "Early Christian Women and Their Cultural Context: Issues of Method in Historical Reconstruction," in *Feminist Perspectives on Biblical Scholarship*, ed. Adela Yarbro Collins (Chico, Calif.: Scholars Press, 1985), 65–91; Carol Meyers, *Discovering Eve: Ancient Israelite Women in Context* (New York: Oxford University Press, 1988); Susan Ackerman, " 'And the Women Knead Dough': The Worship of the Queen of Heaven in Sixth-Century Judah," in *Gender and Difference in Ancient Israel*, ed. Peggy L. Day (Minneapolis: Fortress Press, 1989), 109–24; Bonnie Bowman Thurston, *The Widows: A Women's Ministry in the Early Church* (Minneapolis: Fortress Press, 1989); Antoinette Clark Wire, *The Corinthian Women Prophets: A Reconstruction through Paul's Rhetoric* (Minneapolis: Fortress Press, 1990); Karen Jo Torjesen, *When Women Were Priests* (San Francisco: Harper-Collins, 1993); Elizabeth A. Castelli, *Visions and Voyeurism: Holy Women and the*

Politics of Sight in Early Christianity, ed. Christopher Ocker (Berkeley: Center for Hermeneutical Studies, 1995).

16. Schüssler Fiorenza, *In Memory of Her*, 48–53. See also her article, "Text and Reality — Reality as Text: The Problem of a Feminist Historical and Social Reconstruction Based on Texts," *StTh* 43 (1989): 28–31.

17. Schüssler Fiorenza, *In Memory of Her*, 44–46. See also "The Quilting of Women's History: Phoebe of Cenchreae," in *Embodied Love: Sensuality and Relationship as Feminist Values*, ed. Paula M. Cooey et al. (San Francisco: Harper & Row, 1987), 35–49.

18. Ibid., 45, 52.

19. Schüssler Fiorenza, *In Memory of Her*, xxiii.

20. Cf. Mary Ann Tolbert, "Defining the Problem: The Bible and Feminist Hermeneutics," *Semeia* 28 (1983): 124.

21. Schüssler Fiorenza, *In Memory of Her*, 92.

22. Elisabeth Schüssler Fiorenza, "A Feminist Critical Interpretation for Liberation: Martha and Mary: Lk. 10:38–42," *RIL* 3 (1986): 29–33. See also her book *But She Said: Feminist Practices of Biblical Interpretation* (Boston: Beacon Press, 1992), 67–69.

23. Ibid. In footnote 12 of the article, Schüssler Fiorenza admits that she has not examined John 11–12 with a hermeneutics of suspicion; in *But She Said*, she drops this footnote.

24. Schüssler Fiorenza, *Bread Not Stone: The Challenge of Feminist Biblical Interpretation* (Boston: Beacon Press, 1984), 18–19.

25. Phyllis Trible, "Depatriarchalizing in Biblical Interpretation," *JAAR* 41 (1973): 31.

26. Ibid., 47–48.

27. Phyllis Trible, "The Pilgrim Bible on a Feminist Journey," *The Daughters of Sarah* 15, no. 3 (1989): 6.

28. Trible, "Depatriarchalizing," 48.

29. Phyllis Trible, *God and the Rhetoric of Sexuality* (Philadelphia: Fortress Press, 1978), 202.

30. Ibid., 11.

31. Anderson, "Gender and Reading," 23, 25. See also Janice Capel Anderson, "Mary's Difference: Gender and Patriarchy in the Birth Narratives," *JR* 67 (1987): 199–200.

32. Anderson, "Mary's Difference," 199–202.

33. Anderson, "Gender and Reading," 25–26.

34. Ibid., 23.

35. Ibid.

36. Ibid., 24.

37. Ibid., 25.

38. Mary Ann Tolbert, "Protestant Feminists," 13; Kerry M. Craig and Margret A. Kristjansson, "Women Reading as Men/Women Reading as Women: A Structural Analysis for the Historical Project," *Semeia* 51 (1990): 131–32; Joanna Dewey, "Feminist Readings, Gospel Narrative, and Critical Theory,"

BTB 22 (1992): 170–71; Pippin, "Eros and the End," 195, 200; Mary Stewart Van Leeuwen, ed., *After Eden: Facing the Challenge of Gender Reconciliation* (Grand Rapids: Eerdmans, 1993), 196.

39. Craig and Kristjansson, "Women Reading," 132.

40. Joanna Dewey, Peggy Hutaff, and Jane Schaberg, "Respondents to Elizabeth A. Castelli's and Clarice J. Martin's articles," *JFSR* 6, no. 2 (1990): 64–66.

41. Ibid., 64–65.

42. Ibid., 64. See also Sandra M. Schneiders, "Feminist Ideology Criticism and Biblical Hermeneutics," *BTB* 19 (1989): 8; and *The Revelatory Text: Interpreting the New Testament as Sacred Scripture* (New York: HarperCollins, 1991).

43. Dewey, Hutaff, and Schaberg, "Respondents," 65.

44. Ibid., 70–73.

45. Mary Ann Tolbert, *Sowing the Gospel*, 296–97; "Mark," in *WBC*, ed. Carol A. Newsom and Sharon H. Ringe (Louisville: Westminster/John Knox Press, 1992), 273–74.

46. Janice Capel Anderson, "Feminist Criticism: The Dancing Daughter," in *Mark and Method: New Approaches in Biblical Studies*, ed. Janice Capel Anderson and Stephen D. Moore (Philadelphia: Fortress Press, 1992), 111.

47. Joanna Dewey, "The Gospel of Mark," *Searching the Scriptures: A Feminist Commentary*, ed. Elisabeth Schüssler Fiorenza, vol. 2 (New York: Crossroad, 1994), 508.

48. Schüssler Fiorenza, *But She Said*, 36, 39–48, 205.

49. Phyllis Trible, *Texts of Terror: Literary-Feminist Reading of Biblical Narratives* (Philadelphia: Fortress Press, 1984).

50. Schüssler Fiorenza, *But She Said*, 57–62, 209–10. For a critique of Trible, see Esther Fuchs, "The Literary Characterization of Mothers and Sexual Politics in the Hebrew Bible," in *Feminist Perspectives on Biblical Scholarship*, ed. Adela Yarbro Collins (Chico, Calif.: Scholars Press, 1985), 117–18.

51. Schüssler Fiorenza, *But She Said*, 205–9. Schüssler Fiorenza prefers the term "kyriarchal" over "patriarchal" because patriarchy has often been used to denote gender dualism (*But She Said*, 7, 8, 117; *Jesus: Miriam's Child, Sophia's Prophet* [New York: Continuum, 1994], 14). Since I defined "patriarchy" broadly in the Introduction, I will continue to use this term.

52. Schüssler Fiorenza, *But She Said*, 37. For a fuller discussion, see her more recent book *Jesus: Miriam's Child, Sophia's Prophet*, 97–106.

53. Schüssler Fiorenza, *But She Said*, 43–44. In *Jesus: Miriam's Child, Sophia's Prophet* (56), she admits that women's identification with Jesus' "masculine" qualities can be "humanizing."

54. Schüssler Fiorenza, *But She Said*, 43–44.

55. Schüssler Fiorenza, *Bread Not Stone*, 16–22; *But She Said*, 52–76.

56. Schüssler Fiorenza, *But She Said*, 73–74.

57. Katheryn Pfisterer Darr, *Far More Precious than Jewels: Perspectives on Biblical Women* (Louisville: Westminster/John Knox Press, 1991), 193.

58. Alice L. Laffey, An Introduction to the Old Testament: A Feminist Perspective (Philadelphia: Fortress Press, 1988).

59. See these essays in WBC, ed. Carol A. Newsom and Sharon H. Ringe (Louisville: Westminster/John Knox Press, 1992): Amy-Jill Levine, "Matthew," 252–62; Mary Ann Tolbert, "Mark," 263–74; Gail R. O'Day, "John," 293–304; Susan Niditch, "Genesis," 10–25; Drorah O'Donnell Setel, "Exodus," 26–35; Danna Nolan Fewell, "Joshua," 63–66; Sidnie Ann White, "Esther," 124–29. In Searching the Scriptures: A Feminist Commentary, ed. Elisabeth Schüssler Fiorenza, vol. 2 (New York: Crossroad, 1994), see Adele Reinhartz, "The Gospel of John," 561–600; and Elaine Wainwright, "The Gospel of Matthew," 635–77.

60. Levine, "Matthew," 253.

61. Tolbert, "Mark," 266.

62. Amy-Jill Levine, The Social and Ethnic Dimensions of Matthean Salvation History (Lewiston, N.Y.: Edwin Mellen Press, 1988); Tolbert, Sowing the Gospel.

63. Susan Tower Hollis, "The Woman in Ancient Examples of the Potiphar's Wife Motif, K2111," in Gender and Difference in Ancient Israel, ed. Peggy L. Day (Minneapolis: Fortress Press, 1989), 28–42.

64. Laffey, An Introduction to the Old Testament, 214–16.

65. Ibid.

66. Sidnie Ann White, "Esther: A Feminine Model for Jewish Diaspora," in Gender and Difference in Ancient Israel, ed. Peggy L. Day (Minneapolis: Fortress Press, 1989), 173.

67. J. Cheryl Exum, Fragmented Women: Feminist (Sub)versions of Biblical Narrative (Valley Forge, Pa.: Trinity Press International, 1993), 92. See also her study of gender roles in "Feminist Criticism: Whose Interests Are Being Served?" in Judges and Method: New Approaches in Biblical Studies, ed. Gale A. Yee (Minneapolis: Fortress Press, 1995), 65–90.

68. Ibid., 140.

69. Mieke Bal, Lethal Love: Feminist Literary Readings of Biblical Love Stories (Bloomington: Indiana University Press, 1987); Murder and Difference: Gender, Genre, and Scholarship on Sisera's Death (Bloomington: Indiana University Press, 1988); Death and Dissymmetry: The Politics of Coherence in the Book of Judges (Chicago: University of Chicago Press, 1988).

70. Mieke Bal, "Murder and Difference: Uncanny Sites in an Uncanny World," JLT 5, no. 1 (1991): 15; Lethal Love, 69–73; Murder and Difference, 130.

71. Bal, Lethal Love, 132.

72. Ibid.

73. Esther Fuchs, "The Literary Characterization of Mothers," 117–36; "Structure and Patriarchal Functions in the Biblical Betrothal Type-Scene," JFSR 3 (1987): 7–13; "'For I Have the Way of Women': Deception, Gender, and Ideology in Biblical Narrative," Semeia 42 (1988): 68–83; "Marginalization, Ambiguity, Silencing: The Story of Jephthah's Daughter," JFSR 5 (1989): 35–45.

74. Pamela J. Milne, "The Patriarchal Stamp of Scripture: The Implications of Structuralist Analyses for Feminist Hermeneutics," *JFSR* 5, no. 1 (1989): 34.

75. Ibid.

76. Susan Durber, "The Female Reader of the Parables of the Lost," *JSNT* 45 (1992): 59–60.

2. Scholarship of Feminist Literary Critics

1. Elaine Showalter, "Women and the Literary Curriculum," *College English* 32 (1971): 855–56.

2. Lee Edwards' reflections about her educational experiences illustrate Showalter's position ("Women, Energy, and *Middlemarch*," *Massachusetts Review* 13 [1972]: 226–27).

3. Judith Fetterley, *The Resisting Reader: A Feminist Approach to American Fiction* (Bloomington: Indiana University Press, 1978), xii, xxi–xxii.

4. Pascal A. Ifri in "Proust's Male Narratee," *Style* 22 (1988): 524–32, concurs with Fetterley's position and demonstrates that the same holds true for one the most important works in French literature, Marcel Proust's *A la recherche du tempes perdue*.

5. Fetterley, *The Resisting Reader*, xx.

6. Ibid., xxii.

7. Ibid.

8. Elaine Showalter, "Towards a Feminist Poetics," in *The New Feminist Criticism: Essays on Women, Literature, and Theory*, ed. Elaine Showalter (New York: Pantheon Books, 1985), 125–43; "Feminist Criticism in the Wilderness," in Ibid., 243–70.

9. Showalter, "Women and the Literary Curriculum," 857–58. A sample of her syllabi includes black women writers and the issues of racism in literature. Showalter and other white feminists have been criticized for not adequately addressing issues of race and sexuality. See Maggie Humm, *Feminist Criticism: Women as Contemporary Critics* (New York: St. Martin's Press, 1986), 16; Elly Bulkin, *Lesbian Fiction* (Watertown, Mass.: Persephone Press, 1981), 276.

10. Judith Fetterley, ed., *Provisions: A Reader from 19th-Century American Women* (Bloomington: Indiana University Press, 1985), 36.

11. Paul J. Achtemeier, *Mark* (Proclamation Commentaries; Philadelphia: Fortress Press, 1975), 111; Leonard Swidler, *Biblical Affirmations of Woman* (Philadelphia: Westminster, 1979), 261–62; Ruth Hoppin, *Priscilla: The Author of the Epistle to the Hebrews* (New York: Exposition Press, 1969); Stevan L. Davies, *The Revolt of the Widows: The Social World of the Apocryphal Acts* (Carbondale: Southern Illinois University Press, 1980), 95–109.

12. Gayle Greene and Coppélia Kahn, "Feminist Scholarship and the Social Construction of Woman," in *Making a Difference: Feminist Literary Criticism*, ed. Gayle Greene and Coppélia Kahn (New York: Routledge, 1985), 24.

13. Toril Moi, *Sexual/Textual Politics: Feminist Literary Theory* (New York: Routledge, 1985), 76–79.

14. Schüssler Fiorenza, *But She Said*, 29; *In Memory of Her*, 60–61.

15. Luce Irigaray, *Je, Tu, Nous: Toward a Culture of Difference*, trans. Alison Martin (New York: Routledge, 1993), 25.

16. Pam Morris, *Literature and Feminism: An Introduction* (Cambridge: Blackwell, 1993), 164–89. See also Mary Helen Washington, "Foreword," in *Their Eyes Were Watching God*, by Zora Neale Hurston (New York: Harper & Row, 1990), ix–x, xiii; Gayle Greene, "Looking at History," in *Changing Subjects: The Making of Feminist Literary Criticism*, ed. Gayle Greene and Coppélia Khan (New York: Routledge, 1993), 11.

17. Edwards ("Women, Energy, and *Middlemarch*," 230) offers a good example of how the female-authored work *Middlemarch* retains male perspectives. Much of the discussion of popular female-authored romance novels stresses how these books portray independent, courageous women whose lives are contained within traditional marriages.

18. This summary is based on Jacques Lacan, *Ecrits: A Selection* (London: Tavistock, 1977). Cf. Ann Rosalind Jones, "Inscribing Femininity: French Theories of the Feminine," in *Making a Difference*, ed. Gayle Greene and Coppélia Khan (New York: Routledge, 1985), 82–83; Moi, *Sexual/Textual Politics*, 99–101.

19. Julia Kristeva, "Woman Can Never Be Defined," in *New French Feminisms*, ed. Elaine Marks and Isabelle de Courtivron (New York: Schocken, 1981), 137, as cited by Linda Alcoff, "Cultural Feminism Versus Post-Structuralism: The Identity Crisis in Feminist Theory," *Signs* 13, no. 3 (1988): 418.

20. Luce Irigaray, *This Sex Which Is Not One*, trans. Catherine Porter (Ithaca, N.Y.: Cornell University Press, 1985), 148–49. Irigaray proposes that women create their own embodied language and discourse.

21. Durber, "The Female Reader," 77.

22. Moi, *Sexual/Textual Politics*, 56, 76; Greene and Khan, "Feminist Scholarship," 25; Nelly Furman, "The Politics of Language: Beyond the Gender Principle?" in *Making a Difference: Feminist Literary Criticism*, ed. Gayle Greene and Coppélia Khan (New York: Routledge, 1985), 62–64.

23. Nelly Furman, "The Politics of Language," 64.

24. Ibid.

25. Ibid., 71.

26. Greene and Khan, "Feminist Scholarship," 2–5, 18; Chris Weedon, *Feminist Practice and Poststructuralist Theory* (New York: Basil Blackwell, 1987), 25–32; Moi, *Sexual/Textual Politics*, 92–94.

27. Jane Collier and Michelle Rosaldo, "Politics and Gender in Simple Societies," in *Sexual Meanings: The Cultural Construction of Gender and Sexuality*, ed. Sherry Ortner and Harriet Whitehead (Cambridge: Cambridge University Press, 1981), 275–329; Henrietta Moore, *Space, Text and Gender: An Anthropological Study of the Marakwet of Kenya* (Cambridge: Cambridge University Press, 1986), 64–71; and Henrietta Moore, *Feminism and Anthropology* (Minneapolis: University of Minnesota Press, 1988), 37. See also Sherry Ortner, "Is Female to

Male as Nature Is to Culture?" in *Woman, Culture and Society*, ed. M. Rosaldo and L. Lamphere (Stanford: Stanford University Press, 1974), 67–88.

28. Weedon, *Feminist Practice*, 25–26.

29. Ibid., 72, 151. See also Deborah Cameron, *Feminism and Linguistic Theory* (London: Macmillan, 1985), 134–61, and Rita Felski, *Beyond Feminist Aesthetics: Feminist Literature and Social Change* (Cambridge: Harvard University Press, 1989), 51–85. Cameron and Felski discuss the role that institutional power structures have in excluding women from certain forms of discourse but not all forms of discourse.

30. Weedon, *Feminist Practice*, 33, 85.

31. Ibid., 124.

32. Linda Alcoff, "Cultural Feminism," 419.

33. Ibid., 420. Elizabeth A. Meese also notes this problem in *Crossing the Double-Cross: The Practice of Feminist Criticism* (Chapel Hill: University of North Carolina Press, 1986), 83. Diane Fuss argues that the one "essence" that most feminists refuse to relinquish is politics in "Reading Like a Feminist," *Differences* 1, no. 2 (1989): 89–90.

34. Alcoff, "Cultural Feminism," 420.

35. Tolbert, "Protestant Feminists," 13.

36. Weedon, *Feminist Practice*, 33.

37. Susan Schibanoff notices in Christine de Pisan's *Book of the City of Women* that intimate conversation with other women provided Christine knowledge about women and confidence in her own knowledge about women so that she was transformed from an immasculated reader to a woman reader ("Taking the Gold Out of Egypt: The Art of Reading as a Woman," in *Gender and Reading: Essays on Readers, Texts, and Contexts*, ed. E. A. Flynn and P. P. Schweickart [Baltimore: Johns Hopkins University Press, 1986], 101).

38. Jean E. Kennard, "Convention Coverage or How to Read Your Own Life," *New Literary History* 13 (1981): 69–88.

39. Ibid., 74–78.

40. See, for example, Caroline Lucas, *Writing for Women: The Example of Women as Reader in Elizabethan Romance* (Philadelphia: Open University Press, 1989), 18–36. Lucas argues that women can read Elizabethan romances written by men subversively and to their advantage.

41. Kennard, "Convention Coverage," 83–84.

42. Kate Cooper argues that female protagonists in *The Apocryphal Acts* function to instruct a male audience; however, in those writings, the women deviate from accepted gender role behavior. ("Apostles, Ascetic Women, and Questions of Audience: New Reflections on the Rhetoric of Gender in the Apocryphal Acts," in *SBL Seminar Papers 1992*, ed. Eugene H. Lovering [SBLSP 31; Atlanta: Scholars Press, 1992], 147–53).

43. I have not fully tested the strategies on these two texts; my comments are meant to be suggestive.

44. Patrocinio Schweickart, "Reading Ourselves: Toward a Feminist Theory of Reading," in *Speaking of Gender*, ed. Elaine Showalter (New York: Rout-

ledge, 1989), 27–28. She refers to Fredric Jameson's thesis that "the effectively ideological is also at the same time necessarily utopian" to argue that female readers' attraction to some male-oriented texts comes from authentic desires. See Jameson, *The Political Unconscious: Narrative as a Socially Symbolic Act* (Ithaca, N.Y.: Cornell University Press, 1981), 286.

45. Schweickart, "Reading Ourselves," 27–28. Feminist literary critics have also explored why romance novels appeal to so many women. Helen Taylor in "Romantic Readers," *From My Guy to Sci-Fi: Genre and Women's Writing in the Postmodern World*, ed. Helen Carr (London: Pandora Press, 1989), 63, argues that romance novels address women's "desire, fantasies and longings for a better world and for states of individual and collective transcendence."

46. For instance, interpreters suppress Mary's total silence and passivity and Martha's muteness at the end of Lk. 10:38–42, when they refer to Jesus' commendation of Mary's listening to support women's right to the formal study of the Scriptures. See Schüssler Fiorenza, *But She Said*, 62.

47. Schweickart, "Reading Ourselves," 26.

48. Ibid.

49. Eve K. Sedgwick, *Between Men: English Literature and Male Homosocial Desire* (New York: Columbia University Press, 1985).

50. Gayle Rubin, "The Traffic in Women: Notes on the 'Political Economy' of Sex," *Toward an Anthropology of Women*, ed. Rayna R. Reiter (New York: Monthly Review Press, 1975), 157–210. See esp. 174.

51. The reading process for women who are lesbians has its own particular dynamics and of course will vary among lesbians. Some lesbians may reject my term "woman reader" since they do not consider themselves "women." See Bonnie Zimmerman, "In Academia, and Out: The Experience of a Lesbian Feminist Literary Critic," in *Changing Subjects: The Making of Feminist Literary Criticism*, ed. Gayle Greene and Coppélia Khan (New York: Routledge, 1993), 112–20; Leslie Feinberg, *Stone Butch Blues* (Ithaca, N.Y.: Firebrand Books, 1993). Nevertheless, my feminist commitments demand that I define "woman reader" to include lesbians and offer these strategies to any women that may find them useful.

52. Maggie Humm (*Feminist Criticism*, 13–16) stresses that race, class, and sexual preferences must be addressed along with gender. Elisabeth Schüssler Fiorenza holds a similar position, articulated in "The Politics of Otherness: Biblical Interpretation as a Critical Praxis for Liberation," in *The Future of Liberation Theology*, ed. Marc H. Ellis and Otto Maduro (Maryknoll, N.Y.: Orbis Books, 1989), 311–25.

3. Gender Reversal

1. Moore (*Feminism and Anthropology*, 25–30) reviews some of the anthropological studies that address the social construction of the role of mother. Cf. Rosemarie Tong, *Feminist Thought: A Comprehensive Introduction* (Boulder: Westview Press, 1989), 84–87.

2. Sherry Ortner, "Is Female to Male as Nature Is to Culture?" 67–88.

3. For example, Moore, *Feminism and Anthropology*, 18–19; Marilyn Strathern, "No Nature, No Culture: The Hagen Case," in *Nature, Culture and Gender*, ed. C. MacCormack and M. Strathern (Cambridge: Cambridge University Press, 1980), 175–76; Jane Goodale, "Gender, Sexuality and Marriage: A Kaulong Model of Nature and Culture," in ibid., 130–31; Greene and Khan, "Feminist Scholarship," 9–11.

4. Some anthropologists have focused on how access to economic resources affects women's status. For example, Eleanor Leacock, "Women's Status in Egalitarian Society: Implications for Social Evolution," *Current Anthropology* 19, no. 2 (1978): 247–75; Mona Etienne and Eleanor Leacock, *Women and Colonization* (New York: Praeger, 1980); Diane Bell, *Daughters of the Dreaming* (Melbourne: McPhee Gribble, 1983); Karen Sacks, *Sisters and Wives: The Past and Future of Sexual Equality* (Westport, Conn.: Greenwood Press, 1979).

5. Collier and Rosaldo, "Politics and Gender," 275–329.

6. Moore, *Feminism and Anthropology*, 37–38.

7. Ibid., 38.

8. Greene and Khan, "Feminist Scholarship," 2–5, 18; Weedon, *Feminist Practice*, 25–32; Moi, *Sexual/Textual Politics*, 92–94.

9. Greene and Khan, "Feminist Scholarship," 3, 18–19, 22. Janice Radway, "Women Read the Romance: The Interaction of Text and Context," *Feminist Studies* 9 (1983): 68–71; Elizabeth Long, "Women, Reading, and Cultural Authority: Some Implications of the Audience Perspective in Cultural Studies," *American Quarterly* 38 (1986): 608–10.

10. Greene and Khan, "Feminist Scholarship," 21–22.

11. Meese (*Crossing the Double-Cross*, 85) refers to reversal as a way to uncover "assumptions of correctness or naturalness that discourse masks."

12. Jean Kennard, "Convention Coverage," 83–84.

13. For example, plots that focus on the battle of two strong women for supremacy in the early West or a young girl's attainment of womanhood by killing a bear in Minnesota sound strange because readers know them as actions that fit male gender roles as modern society has constructed them and not female gender roles. See Joanna Russ, "What Can a Heroine Do? or Why Women Can't Write," in *To Write Like a Woman: Essays in Feminism and Science Fiction* (Indianapolis: Indiana University Press, 1995), 79–93.

14. Quotations from the Old Testament and allusions to Old Testament figures have been continually recognized as distinctive features in Matthew.

15. Mary Ann Tolbert (*Sowing the Gospel*, 59–78) claims that the gospels "belong to the realm of popular literature" and share the conventions of other popular literature, namely, the ancient romance novels.

16. Richard A. Burridge argues that the gospels are ancient biographies because they display many of the generic features of ancient biographies (*What are the Gospels?* [New York: Cambridge University Press, 1992], 240–59). Although the literary style of most of the biographies in Burridge's study suggests a more educated audience than Matthew's, these biographies can still be helpful.

The author of Matthew could have used some of the same plots and motifs but conveyed them in a more informal literary style. Thomas Hägg claims that interchange occurred between the two genres, the ancient novel and biographies (*The Novel in Antiquity*, 115–17).

17. John J. Winkler, *The Constraints of Desire* (New York: Routledge, 1990), 4–10.

18. Some scholars insist that ἔθνη (*ethnē*) refers only to "Gentiles" because the Jews have rejected Jesus: Douglas Hare and Daniel Harrington, "'Make Disciples of all the Gentiles' (Mt. 28:19)," *CBQ* 37 (1975): 359–69 and Frank Matera, "The Plot of Matthew's Gospel," *CBQ* 49 (1987): 233–53. Amy-Jill Levine argues convincingly that Jews lose their privileged position but are still included with those whom the disciples will make disciples. The commission in chapter 28 focuses on the extension of the mission to Gentiles and assumes a continued mission to the Jews (*The Social and Ethnic Dimensions of Matthean Salvation History*, 165–92). See also, B. Rod Doyle, "Matthew's Intention as Discerned by His Structure," *RB* 95 (1988): 48; Pheme Perkins, "Matthew 28:16–20, Resurrection, Ecclesiology and Mission," *SBL Seminar Papers 1993*, ed. Eugene H. Lovering, Jr. (SBLSP 32; Atlanta: Scholars Press, 1993), 575, n. 8. Since women are marginalized in Matthew, what would be interesting to explore is whether *ethnē* includes women.

19. Although it is true that the main verb in Mt. 28:19 is "make disciples" (μαθητεύσατε *mathēteusate*), the participle "going" (πορευθέντες *poreuthentes*) defines the manner in which they will make disciples of all the nations: they will go to them. See Benjamin J. Hubbard, *The Matthean Redaction of a Primitive Apostolic Commissioning: An Exegesis of Matthew 28:16–20* (SBLDS 19; Missoula, Mont.: Scholars Press, 1974), 83, who notes that the verb "go" (πορεύομαι *poreuomai*) is associated with the commissioning activity in Mt. 2:20, 10:7, 28:7. All three texts necessitate travel in order to fulfill the command. Robert Harry Smith claims that the participle intensifies the imperative to convey "Throw yourself into forming disciples" ("Anticlimax or Key," 595). Making disciples of all the nations, however, could hardly be accomplished without traveling.

20. Five ancient novels in complete form exist. Emphasis will be placed on Chariton's *Chaereas and Callirhoe* and Xenophon of Ephesus' *An Ephesian Tale*, since these two novels share more of the same conventions with the gospels than the other three. Cf. Tolbert, *Sowing the Gospel*, 62.

21. Since it is beyond the confines of this study to examine all of the ancient biographies, emphasis will be placed on examining eight of the ten in Burridge's study. Copies of Nepos' *Atticus* and Satyr's *Euripides* were unavailable.

22. Scholars have debated whether the author of Matthew used the Septuagint or the Masoretic text, but most agree that the book shows a dependence upon the Old Testament. See Graham Stanton, *A Gospel for a New People* (Edinburgh: T. & T. Clark, 1992), 358. Stanton thinks that Matthew copied the textual form of the quotations found in his sources, which depended on the

Septuagint. Matthew himself, he claims, was responsible for mixing Greek and Hebrew textual traditions in some of the formula quotations.

23. Wolfgang Trilling, *Das wahre Israel: Studien zur Theologie des Matthäus-Evangeliums* (Munich: Kösel, 1968), 48–49; Benjamin J. Hubbard, *The Matthean Redaction*, 99.

24. Hubbard, *Matthean Redaction*, 33, 69–72.

25. Robert Alter, *The Art of Biblical Narrative* (New York: Basic Books, 1981), 47–52. Alter discusses the differences between the goals of form criticism and the study of type-scenes, but does not address the possibility of using the data of form criticism. Hubbard's study has been criticized because some of the components are missing or occur in a different order in the texts he cites (David R. Baur, *The Structure of Matthew's Gospel: A Study in Literary Design* JSNTSup, no. 31 [Sheffield: Almond Press, 1988], 113; G. Friedrich, "Die formale Struktur von Mt. 28.18–20," *ZThK* 80 [1983]: 161–62). If the texts are understood as type-scenes, then a missing component or a different order would have a rhetorical purpose.

26. Hubbard, *Matthean Redaction*, 35–36.

27. Hubbard does not mention the commissions of Hagar and the widow of Zarephath, although the pattern of the texts is similar to the ones he cites. Ruth 1:6–19a, where Naomi tells Orpah and Ruth to go and return home, also has some of the seven components of commissioning scenes.

28. Gen. 11:28–30, 12:1–4a; Gen. 15:1–6; Gen. 17:1–14; Gen. 26:1–6; Gen. 28:10–22; Gen. 35:9–15; Gen. 46:1–5a. Hubbard, *Matthean Redaction*, 33–62.

29. Gen. 24:1–9; Ex. 3:1–4:16 (J Version); Ex. 3:1–4:16 (E Version); Ex. 6:2–13, 7:1–6; Num. 22:22–35; Deut. 31:14–15, 23; Josh. 1:1–11; Judg. 4:6–10; Judg. 6:11–24; 1 Kings 19:1–19a; Isa. 6; Jer. 1:1–10; Ezek. 1:1–3:15. Hubbard, *Matthean Redaction*, 33–62.

30. Gen. 3:1–4:16 (J Version); Gen. 3:1–4:16 (E Version); Ex. 6:2–13, 7:1–6; Num. 22:22–35; Isa. 6; Jer. 1:1–10; Ezek. 1:1–3:15. Hubbard, *Matthean Redaction*, 33–62.

31. In both cases the women help with goals that focus on the needs of men. Judith's slave assists Judith in the murder of Holofernes and thus enables Uzziah to remain Israel's ruler. The friends of Jephthah's daughter give her companionship and do not challenge her commitment to fulfill her father's oath.

32. Numerous other texts can be cited where a leader sends messengers, but their gender cannot be determined. Leaders sometimes sent out two men: Josh. 2:1, 6:25; 2 Sam. 17:15–21, 18:19–32; 2 Kings 9:17, 19.

33. I used the translations of *An Ephesian Tale* and *Chaereas and Callirhoe* in the volume edited by B. P. Reardon, *Collected Ancient Greek Novels* (Los Angeles: University of California Press, 1989).

34. The Greek and Latin texts of these and other biographies that I consulted are those found in *The Loeb Classical Library Series*. Although the

quality of the texts in the series is uneven, the texts were adequate for the present study.

35. Burridge, *What Are the Gospels?*, 154–79.

36. Scholars have noted that women receive a commission in Mt. 28:8–10. For example, Levine, "Matthew," 262; Elaine Mary Wainwright, *Toward a Feminist Critical Reading of the Gospel According to Matthew* (New York: Walter de Gruyter, 1991), 151; Heil, *The Death and Resurrection of Jesus*, 101–2.

37. The novelty of a group of traveling women in Mt. 27:55–56 is mitigated by the designation of one of the women as the mother of the sons of Zebedee, two of the disciples. The reference to their following Jesus, whose loyalty at this point would not be diminished by the presence of women, diverts the audience's attention away from questioning the loyalty of James and John because their mother is with them.

38. Winkler, *Constraints of Desire*, 4–10.

39. The disciples here are the twelve male disciples. Michael J. Wilkins argues that the term "disciples" is used ambiguously and refers to a group larger than the twelve male disciples ("Named and Unnamed Disciples," 436). Although the identity of the disciples may be unclear in 5:1, after chapter 10 where the twelve disciples are listed, this ambiguity has been resolved. The terms "the disciples" and "the twelve disciples" are used synonymously, except in 17:6 where "disciples" refers to the three in 17:1 (Ulrich Luz, "The Disciples in the Gospel According to Matthew," *The Interpretation of Matthew*, ed. Graham Stanton [Philadelphia: Fortress Press, 1983], 119, note 13). Only late in the gospel, in 27:57, where Joseph of Arimathea is named as a disciple, is there any indication that the disciples are more than the twelve. The reference to Joseph prepares the audience for the addition of disciples in 28:19–20. The audience can choose to revise their assumptions about the number of the disciples, but they are still all male. The women in 27:55 are not designated as disciples. See Anderson, "Gender and Reading," 18–20; Jack Dean Kingsbury, "The Verb *Akolouthein* ('To Follow') as an Index to Matthew's View of His Community," *JBL* 97 (1978): 61.

40. Tikva Frymer-Kensky, "Deuteronomy" in *The Women's Bible Commentary*, ed. Carol A. Newsom and Sharon H. Ringe (Louisville, Ky.: Westminster/ John Knox Press, 1992), 53–54. She concludes that except for Deut. 5:21, the Decalogue and the laws in Deuteronomy address women, although women's rights are not identical to men's.

41. Danna Nolan Fewell, "Joshua," 65.

42. 1 Chr. 28:2–10, for instance, where David addresses "my brothers and my people," is only directed to men because in 28:1 he only summons his sons, officials, stewards, commanders, and warriors before he starts speaking.

43. Rebekah insures that Isaac blesses Jacob instead of Esau (Gen. 27:5–17). Bathsheba asks David to keep his promise to make their son Solomon succeed him as king (1 Kings 1:15–21). Esther does not seek to become queen; but, once she is queen, she uses her position to save her people at her uncle's prodding (Esther 8). In Mt. 20:20–28, the mother of James and John is seeking

positions of power for them. In *Chaereas and Callirhoe*, Chaereas wants to give the Persian queen to his wife Callirhoe as a slave whereas Callirhoe refuses the gift and sends her back to her husband. Miriam is jealous of Moses' greater status among the people; but it is important to acknowledge that she already has status over the people and wants Aaron and herself, also prophets, to be treated as Moses' equals (Num. 12). Miriam is punished to demonstrate that Moses is "first" among God's prophets.

44. David E. Garland asks whether the disciples and the crowds are addressed on the same level and concludes that Matthew directs the chapter to leaders of his own church to caution them not to become like the crowds who initially follow Jesus and then change their minds (*The Intention of Matthew 23* [Leiden: E. J. Brill, 1979], 40–41). Even if the disciples are seen positively and the crowds negatively in this chapter, the instruction is directed to both to be appropriated by both as they see fit.

45. Winkler, *Constraints of Desire*, 1–10.

46. Four additional texts, which stipulate how the Passover meal is to be celebrated, emphasize that all the people must participate and eat: Ex. 12:1–20; Num. 9:1–14; Deut. 16:1–8; Ezek. 45:21–25. Women appear to be included among "the people," "the whole congregation," "household," and "the Israelites."

47. Hannah may be another example of a woman who eats with her husband. The Greek text of 1 Sam. 1:18 reads that she ate and drank with her husband; the Hebrew text omits "and drank with her husband."

48. Sometimes "the people" at the meals are actually men (Esth. 1:5, 9; Neh. 5:1, 17–18) or the emphasis is on the men at the meal (2 Sam. 15:16, 17:27–29).

49. Philo's other biographies do not depict groups of women at banquets, but sometimes imply their presence with men. In *Abraham* 22, when Philo tells about the feast that Abraham and Sarah provided for the "three men," Sarah's presence is suggested. At the Egyptian king's feast in *Joseph* 18, celebrated by "the magistrates" (τῶν ἐν τέλει *tōn en telei*) and "the palace attendants" (θεραπείας *therapeias*), the presence of women is implied in the category of the attendants. The feast that Joseph provides his brothers and "Egyptian dignitaries" (ἄλλοι τῶν παρ' Αἰγυπτίοις δοκίμων *alloi ton par' Aigyptiois dokimōn*) is not attended by women (*Joseph* 33–34).

50. In his biography about Claudius, Suetonius mentions that Claudius invited his children to sit with him at banquets and also the sons and daughters of the male guests (*Claud.* 32).

51. Dennis Smith, "Table Fellowship as a Literary Motif in the Gospel of Luke," *JBL* 106 (1987): 613–38; David Aune, "Septem Sapientum Convivium," in *Plutarch's Ethical Writings and Early Christian Literature*, ed. Hans Dieter Betz (Leiden: E. J. Brill, 1978), 51–105; Gordon J. Bahr, "The Seder of Passover and Eucharistic Words," *Nov Test* 12 (1970): 181–202; S. Stein, "The Influence of Symposia Literature on the Literary Form of the Pesah Haggadah," *JJS* 8 (1957): 13–44.

52. Because the women in the feeding stories (Mt. 14:21; 15:38) are not eating with the disciples and cannot be construed as members of their household, their presence does not challenge the disciples' loyalty to Jesus.

53. The widow of Tekoa speaks to David (2 Sam. 14); Judith, to three elders (Jdt. 8:11–27); and a mother, to her son (2 Macc. 7:22–23, 27–29). Hannah (1 Sam. 2:1–10), Susannah (Sus. 42–43), and Sarah (Tob. 3:11–15) offer prayers. In *Chaereas and Callirhoe,* Callirhoe gives seven laments, five of which a female slave overhears. In *An Ephesian Tale,* Anthia gives eleven laments. Although her husband Habrocomes gives many laments too, it is significant that at the end, he tells about their adventures to the crowds in their hometown, but she prays to Aphrodite.

54. Critical evaluation of these writings must be done since they can also convey patriarchal perspectives.

4. Analogy

1. Schweickart, "Reading Ourselves," 28. Tolbert ("Protestant Feminists," 13–14) concurs with Schweickart. Schüssler Fiorenza (*But She Said,* 200–201) argues differently: female readers are not necessarily forced to pretend they are male; they unconsciously suppress the literal meaning of biblical texts and read its generic language to mean they are included. She proposes that when women become aware that the language of biblical texts privileges men, they provide biblical texts antipatriarchal contexts, especially by focusing on the female characters. Her position, however, does not account for why female readers identify with Jesus and other male characters even after they recognize the androcentric dynamics of biblical texts.

2. Schweickart, "Reading Ourselves," 28.

3. Delores Williams, *Sisters in the Wilderness: The Challenges of Womanist God-Talk* (Maryknoll, N.Y.: Orbis Books, 1993), 122–30.

4. Louisa Enright, "Let's Stop Using the Bible to Buttress Misogynist Views," *Daughters of Sarah* 19, no. 1 (1993): 36–37.

5. Lillian Sigal, "Models of Love and Hate," *Daughters of Sarah* 16, no. 2 (1990): 10.

6. Emily Sampson, "Who's Afraid of the Big Bad Wolf," *Daughters of Sarah* 16, no. 4 (1990): 16.

7. Marsha Wilfong, "Genesis 22:1–18," *Int* 45, no. 4 (1991): 397.

8. Sarah Cunningham, "A Meeting of the Minds," in *Women of Faith in Dialogue,* ed. Virginia Ramey Mollenkott (New York: Crossroad, 1987), 14–15.

9. Letty M. Russell, "Women and Ministry: Problem or Possibility?" in *Christian Feminism: Visions of Humanity,* ed. Judith L. Weidman (New York: Harper & Row, 1984), 87–88.

10. Rosemary Radford Ruether, "Feminism and Religious Faith: Renewal or New Creation?" *RIL* 3 (1986): 14. Ruether provides a different analogy in "Feminist Interpretation," 122.

11. For instance, although Ruether intentionally forms an analogy that will not perpetuate antagonism between Jews and Christians, she does not address how some elements are ignored and others added when bag ladies and homeless people are used to understand Lk. 4:17–27.

12. Sharon Seiem, "Writing Poetry: Harrowing the Earth of Me," *Daughters of Sarah* 15, no. 4 (1989): 12–13.

13. Roberta Nobleman, "Once Upon a Time," *Daughters of Sarah* 15, no. 4 (1989): 4.

14. Naomi P. F. Southard, "An Asian-American Woman Reflects on Racism, Classism, and Sexism," in *Women of Faith in Dialogue,* ed. Virginia Ramey Mollenkott (New York: Crossroad, 1987), 58.

15. Virginia Ramey Mollenkott, *Women, Men, and the Bible,* rev. ed. (New York: Crossroad, 1988), 98–99.

16. Schweickart, "Reading Ourselves," 28.

17. Ibid., 27.

18. Ibid., 28.

19. Iser, *The Act of Reading,* 37.

20. Iser leaves the impression that the text contains all the conventions and interpretive strategies (See also Mailloux, *Interpretive Conventions,* 49). His recognition of the creative role of the reader and the influence of the reader's own experiences on the outcome allows for his theory to be expanded to include the strategy discussed in this chapter.

21. Culler discusses readers' literary competence (*Structuralist Poetics*); and Mailloux elaborates on interpretive conventions which include both literary and extraliterary conventions (*Interpretive Conventions*).

22. See Sharon Ringe, "Reading from Context to Context: Contributions of a Feminist Hermeneutic to Theologies of Liberation," in *Lift Every Voice: Constructing Christian Theologies from the Underside,* ed. Susan Brooks Thistlethwaite and Mary Potter Engel (New York: HarperCollins, 1990), 290. Ringe defines patriarchy broadly and includes the critique of dualistic categories as a part of her critique of patriarchy. Feminists, such as Sheila Collins (*A Different Heaven and Earth* [Valley Forge, Pa.: Judson Press, 1974], 166–69), have noted for a long time the way that dualistic categories have been used to subordinate women and blacks and perpetuate sexism, racism, and colonialism.

23. Jean Kennard ("Convention Coverage," 77–78) argues that readers are always dependent on interpretive strategies and reading conventions for their interpretations. She identifies new conventions that enabled feminists to read "The Yellow Wallpaper" differently, conventions that highlighted certain textual elements and ignored others. Earlier critics of the story, using other conventions, had focused on different aspects.

24. Ministry leads to persecution which leads to ministry in another place which leads to persecution which leads to ministry in still another place and so on. Dorothy Jean Weaver, *Matthew's Missionary Discourse,* JSNTSup, no. 38 (Sheffield: JSOT Press, 1990), 99.

25. As mentioned in chapter 2, the reading experience for the male reader

is "a meeting ground of the personal and the universal" (Schweickart, "Reading Ourselves," 26). The experience of the male protagonist is presented to the male reader as a normative experience. What implicitly happens when the male reader identifies with the male protagonist and agrees that the experience is universal is that he validates his own maleness and equates it with humanity. For a similar argument, see Florence Howe, "Feminism and Literature," in *Images of Women in Fiction: Feminist Perspectives*, ed. Susan Koppelman Cornillon, rev. ed (Bowling Green, Ohio: Bowling Green University Popular Press, 1973), 262–63. More recently Maria Clara Bingemer ("Women in the Future of the Theology of Liberation," in *Feminist Theology from the Third World: A Reader*, ed. Ursula King [Maryknoll, N.Y.: Orbis Books, 1994], 312) has argued that a poor man can feel himself affirmed and protected in the Bible, but a poor woman does not know how to handle texts that marginalize and denigrate her.

26. Some feminists have insisted that the maleness of Jesus does not preclude women from accepting Jesus as savior because the New Testament stresses his humanness (Mollenkott, *Women, Men, and the Bible*, 54) or because he called for egalitarian relationships and elevated people to greater equality (Jacquelyn Grant, "Subjectification as a Requirement for Christological Construction," in *Lift Every Voice: Constructing Christian Theologies from the Underside*, ed. Susan Brooks Thistlethwaite and Mary Potter Engel [New York: HarperCollins, 1990], 201–14; Ellen M. Ross, "Human Persons as Images of the Divine: A Reconsideration," in *The Pleasure of Her Text: Feminist Reading of Biblical and Historical Texts*, ed. Alice Bach [Philadelphia: Trinity Press International, 1990], 110–11; Ruether, *Sexism and God-Talk*, 116–38). In the reading process, however, where the male gender functions to draw the male reader into the story to validate the universality of the experiences of the male protagonist, the reversal of Jesus' gender is necessary in order for women to have a similar reading experience. Cf. Isasi-Díaz, "The Bible and *Mujerista* Theology," 264; Luce Irigaray, *Sexes and Genealogies*, trans. Gillian C. Gill (New York: Columbia University Press, 1993), 67–68.

27. Role reversal does not completely convert the reading experience of men into the same one for women. Female readers validate their female identities but still do not presume that the experience of the characters is universal or normative.

28. Levine (*Social and Ethnic Dimensions of Matthean Salvation History*, 13–57) claims that the mission to the Jews in chapter 10 need not be interpreted as racist if read within the context of the whole gospel. Mission to the Jews was Jesus' focus before his death and the promise of inclusion in this mission was always offered to the Gentiles; after his death, the mission was extended to the Gentiles. Bauer (*The Structure of Matthew's Gospel*, 121–24) cites texts throughout the gospel that anticipate the extension of mission to the Gentiles.

29. Kingsbury (*Matthew as Story*, 71) claims that the absence of references to the disciples' departure and return allows the reader to assume that the disciples ministered to Israel but avoids the contradiction that their mission

was completed before Jesus' return (10:23). Portrayal of their return, however, would not necessarily have to convey completion of their mission.

30. Weaver, *Matthew's Missionary Discourse*, 127–28.

31. Jesus' dialogues with the centurion and the paralytic and other sick people include admiration for the faith expressed and response to their needs. Jesus leaves the country of the Gadarenes at the people's request.

32. The reference to God's judgment on those who do not welcome them would also have to be ignored, since it presumes that the perspective of those who reject them is inferior rather than different.

33. Catherine Keller (*From a Broken Web* [Boston: Beacon Press, 1986], 12) discusses how traditional understandings of sin as pride and self-assertion have perpetuated the subordination of women. Keller refers to Valerie Saiving's, Judith Plaskow's, and Susan Nelson Dunfee's critiques of traditional views of sin. For more recent critiques, see Sally Ann McReynolds and Ann O'Hara Graff, "When Women Are the Context," in *In the Embrace of God*, ed. Ann O'Hara Graff (Maryknoll, N.Y.: Orbis Books, 1995), 161–72; Delores Williams, "A Womanist Perspective on Sin," in *A Troubling in My Soul: Womanist Perspectives on Evil and Suffering*, ed. Emilie M. Townes (Maryknoll, N.Y.: Orbis Books, 1993), 130–49.

34. Mara E. Donaldson, "Woman as Hero in Margaret Atwood's *Surfacing* and Maxine Hong Kingston's *The Woman Warrior*," in *Heroines of Popular Culture*, ed. Pat Browne (Bowling Green, Ohio: Bowling Green University Popular Press, 1987), 101–13. See also Mara E. Donaldson, "The Hero in Contemporary Women's Fantasy," *Listening* 25 (1990): 141–52; Carol Pearson and Katherine Pope, *The Female Hero in American and British Literature* (New York: R. R. Bowker, 1981), 10, 223.

35. Joseph Campbell, *The Power of Myth*, ed. Betty Sue Flowers (New York: Doubleday, 1988), 123–63.

36. Donaldson, "The Hero," 143; Pearson and Pope, *The Female Hero*, 10.

37. Donaldson, "The Hero," 146–47. See Keller, *From a Broken Web*, 9–11, who discusses the separative self of male heroes.

38. Donaldson, "The Hero," 145–49, and "The Woman as Hero," 104–9.

39. Bruce Malina uses cultural anthropology to read New Testament texts and claims that the modern understanding of a person as a distinct and unique being found in the culture of the United States is not the way people understood themselves in the first-century Mediterranean world. Ancient people can be called people with dyadic personalities: they always understood who they were and how they were valued in terms of what others expected of them, especially one specific group ("Dealing with Biblical [Mediterranean] Characters: A Guide for U.S. Consumers," *BTB* 19 [1989]: 128).

40. Commentators have commented that Jesus' words do not attack familial relationships: David Hill, *The Gospel of Matthew* (Grand Rapids: Eerdmans, 1981), 194–95; Eduard Schweizer, *The Good News According to Matthew*, trans. D. E. Green (Atlanta: John Knox Press, 1975), 250. See also Marla Selvidge, *Daughters of Jerusalem* (Scottdale, Pa.: Herald Press, 1987), 61–87. The por-

trayal of the disciples in the rest of the gospel, however, does imply an attack on familial relationships.

41. James' and John's mother appears in 20:20–21, but James and John do not help her. She is attempting to help them. Jesus refuses her request and proceeds to teach the twelve about serving each other.

42. Edwards, *Matthew's Story of Jesus*, 36; Michael H. Crosby, *House of Disciples: Church, Economics, and Justice in Matthew* (Maryknoll, N.Y.: Orbis Books, 1988), 109.

43. Weaver, *Matthew's Missionary Discourse*, 114; Patte, *The Gospel According to Matthew*, 154–55; Paul S. Minear, *Matthew: The Teacher's Gospel* (New York: Pilgrim Press, 1982), 70; Robert C. Tannehill, *The Sword of His Mouth: Forceful and Imaginative Language in Synoptic Sayings*, ed. William A. Beardslee (SBLSS 1, Missoula, Mont.: Scholars Press, 1975), 143.

44. Patte's exegesis highlights the dualism (*The Gospel According to Matthew*, 155). Love for family members means putting trust in things of the human realm whereas loving Jesus means belonging to the realm of the kingdom. Feminists could use structural exegesis or commentaries such as Patte's to pinpoint dualistic perspectives that need to be challenged. For some of the complexities in using structuralism, see Milne, "The Patriarchal Stamp of Scripture," 17–34.

45. In three of the narratives that Mara Donaldson studies, the affirmation and renewal of family relationships are significant elements in the quest of the female protagonist: "A Hero," 144–45; "Woman as Hero," 104–9. See also Charlotte Spivak, *Merlin's Daughters: Contemporary Women Writers of Fantasy* (New York: Greenwood Press, 1987), 11–12, 164.

46. Rosemary Radford Ruether, "The Call of Women in the Church Today," in *Women of Faith in Dialogue*, ed. Virginia Ramey Mollenkott (New York: Crossroad, 1987), 78; Schüssler Fiorenza, *In Memory of Her*, 149–51; Kathryn Allen Rabuzzi, *The Sacred and the Feminine: Toward a Theology of Housework* (New York: Seabury Press, 1982), 47.

47. Wilkins ("Named and Unnamed Disciples," 436), for instance, argues that "disciples" is used ambiguously. W. G. Thompson (*Matthew's Advice to a Divided Community. Mt. 17, 22–18, 35* [AnBib 44; Rome: Biblical Institute Press, 1970], 71–72) claims that the term "disciples" includes a larger group than the twelve. See also Benno Przybylski, *Righteousness in Matthew and His World of Thought* (Cambridge: Cambridge University Press, 1980), 108–10, and P. S. Minear, "The Disciples and the Crowds in the Gospel of Matthew," *ATRSup* 3 (1974): 31, 37.

48. Kingsbury, "The Verb *Akolouthein*," 61; Anderson, "Gender and Reading," 18–20. Both insist that the women do not belong to the character group of disciples.

49. Luz, "The Disciples in the Gospel According to Matthew," 99, 119, n. 13. Mark Sheridan argues that "disciples" refers to the twelve, but the twelve represent the Christian community ("Disciples and Discipleship in the Gospel of Matthew and Luke," *BTB* 3 [1973]: 254).

50. Levine (*The Social and Ethnic Dimensions of Matthean Salvation History*, 46–47) contends that the mission is extended to the Gentiles but the mission to Israel continues.

51. Contrasts between female characters and their harmful effects on female readers have been studied. See, for example, Schüssler Fiorenza's exegesis of the Lucan account of Mary and Martha in *But She Said*, 57–62. Role reversal reveals that texts with male characters can have a similar impact on female readers.

52. Donald Senior notes the one-dimensional role of the religious leaders (*The Passion of Jesus in the Gospel of Matthew* [Wilmington, Del.: Michael Glazier, 1985], 178–79). Kingsbury classifies them as flat characters (*Matthew as Story*, 17–24). In highlighting the stereotypical portrayal of the religious leaders, I am giving a modern reading of the text. As mentioned in the Introduction, ancient audiences would have viewed some characters in Matthew as flat and others as somewhat less flat. Modern readers, however, perceive some of the characters in Matthew as flat and others as round because they have been influenced by modern literature. Here modern readers perceive the religious leaders as flat and the disciples as round.

53. Collins, *A Different Heaven and Earth*, 169.

54. Howell, *Matthew's Inclusive Story*, 236–38; Bauer, *The Structure of Matthew's Gospel*, 65–71; Senior, *Passion of Jesus*, 36.

55. Some women have reacted positively to images of the Christa or a crucified woman: Edwina Hunter, "Reflections on the Christa from a Christian Theologian," *Journal of Women and Religion* 4, no. 2 (1985): 22–32; Gloria Smallwood, "Reflections on the Christa from a Pastor," *Journal of Women and Religion* 4, no. 2 (1985): 41–43; Elizabeth Morris, "Reflections on the Christa from a Storyteller," *Journal of Women and Religion* 4, no. 2 (1985): 44–45. See also Doris Jean Dyke, *Crucified Woman* (Toronto: United Church Publishing House, 1991). Others have mixed opinions: Ruether, "Feminism and Religious Faith," 15–16; Christine M. Smith, *Weaving the Sermon: Preaching in a Feminist Perspective* (Louisville: Westminster/John Knox Press, 1989), 84.

56. Schüssler Fiorenza (*But She Said*, 71–73) argues that the stance of ministry as service must be rejected because women and other subordinated groups have been socialized to be subservient and cannot choose servanthood. See also Collins, *A Different Heaven and Earth*, 87–89. Grant ("Subjectification," 208) and Ruether (*Sexism and God-Talk*, 207) redefine service.

57. Some commentators claim that suffering and death is a possible consequence of discipleship (Patte, *The Gospel According to Matthew*, 363) or that the disciples participate sacramentally in Jesus' suffering and death (Senior, *Passion of Jesus*, 66–67). Given that Jesus has told them that they can expect to be persecuted and that they will drink the "cup" he will drink, suffering is a much more integral aspect of discipleship. See Weaver, *Matthew's Missionary Discourse*, 115; Heil, *The Death and Resurrection of Jesus*, 36.

58. Emphasis can be shifted to Jesus' identification with and empowerment of "outcasts," "sinners," or "the least of these," who do not choose to suffer but

suffer because of their subordination and marginalization (See Grant, "Subjectification," 209–10). This shift tends to turn Jesus into a victim and does not challenge the implications of the portrayal of Jesus in the Gospel of Matthew as one who chooses to suffer and die to fulfill God's will and expects disciples to suffer. Sandra Browders, for instance, offers a stronger critique with her position that the purpose of love is to end crucifixions, not to perpetuate them (cited by Beverly W. Harrison in *Making the Connections: Essays in Feminist Social Ethics*, ed. Carol S. Robb [Boston: Beacon Press, 1985], 19).

59. Tolbert, *Sowing the Gospel*, 155, n. 44; Edwards, "Uncertain Faith," 59 and *Matthew's Story of Jesus*, 94.

60. Tolbert (*Sowing the Gospel*, 155, n. 44) comments that the disciples are learners and at the resurrection become qualified to teach. Jesus' promise of his presence can be read as an indication that they are still learners who need the guidance of the risen Jesus.

61. Levine (*The Social and Ethnic Dimensions of Matthean Salvation History*, 111–12) explains that when Jesus hesitates, the centurion demonstrates that he knows that Jesus' mission is to Israel because he asks Jesus to heal his slave at a distance.

62. Some feminists (e.g., Mary Daly) view the ascendancy of women as the goal of women's liberation whereas others (e.g., Rosemary Radford Ruether) understand its goal to be the equality of both the oppressed and the oppressor. For a fuller discussion of these two views, see C. Christ and J. Plaskow, eds., *Womanspirit Rising: A Feminist Reader in Religion* (New York: Harper & Row, 1979), 13–14. For a more recent presentation and evaluation of these views (and others), see Tong, *Feminist Thought: A Comprehensive Introduction*, 1–9, 11–38, 95–138.

63. Heil (*The Death and Resurrection of Jesus*, 101), Kingsbury (*Matthew as Story*, 27, 89–91), Anderson ("Gender and Reading," 17), and Norman Perrin (*The Resurrection according to Matthew, Mark and Luke* [Philadelphia: Fortress, 1977], 29–31) claim that the women are substitutes for the disciples. The women do for Jesus what the disciples should have done. This position overlooks the concern that the disciples not be implicated in any way for the theft of Jesus' body.

64. Perrin (*Resurrection*, 47) argues that 28:16–20 focuses so much on Jesus' words to the disciples that his appearance has little significance. Dorothy Jean Weaver argues in a similar way in "Matthew 28:1–10," *Int* 46, no. 4 (1992): 401.

5. Women as Exchange Objects

1. Schweickart, "Reading Ourselves," 26; Howe, "Feminism and Literature," 262–63. Others have referred to the use of female characters to bond the reader and the author. Mary Jacobus mentions Stanley Fish's anecdote about a female student's question to his colleague in his book *Is There a Text in This Class? The Authority of Interpretive Communities*. Fish uses the female student's

question to expose her oversimplification of his approach and to insure that his readers will not misunderstand his reading theory as she did. (Jacobus, "Is There a Woman in This Text?" *NewLitHis* 14 (1982): 117–19.)

2. Fetterley, *The Resisting Reader*, xii, xxi–xxii, 11, 21; Morris, *Literature and Feminism*, 28–29; Schweickart, "Reading Ourselves," 27–28.

3. Claude Levi-Strauss, *Structural Anthropology*, trans. Claire Jacobson and Brooke Grunfest Shoepf (New York: Basic Books, 1963), 1:55–66.

4. Schweickart, "Reading Ourselves," 26.

5. Sedgwick, *Between Men*, 3, 16, 25–26; Rubin, "The Traffic in Women," 169–210.

6. Iser, *Act of Reading*, 141–49 and *The Implied Reader* (Baltimore: Johns Hopkins University Press, 1974), 283–88; Mailloux, *Interpretive Conventions*, 67–90.

7. Sedgwick's analysis relies heavily on the use of the erotic triangle (two men competing to possess one woman). Her choice of literature and the complex development of characters in these works justify her dependence. The characters in the Gospel of Matthew develop little and eroticism is not a theme; however, her use of Rubin's assessment of women as "objects of exchange" or "conduits of a relationship" between men can still help me explore and understand the power relationships among characters in the Gospel of Matthew. Ken Stone examines the role of wives and concubines but claims marital and sexual relationships are not the only ones that can be examined to assess the relationships between men ("Sexual Practice and the Structure of Prestige: The Case of the Disputed Concubines," *SBL Seminar Papers 1993*, ed. Eugene H. Lovering, Jr. [SBLSP 32; Atlanta: Scholars Press, 1993], 565).

8. Ben Witherington, *Women and the Genesis of Christianity*, ed. Ann Witherington (New York: Cambridge University Press, 1990), 82; Kingsbury, *Matthew as Story*, 27; Anderson, "Gender and Reading," 12–14, 16.

9. Anderson, "Gender and Reading," 23–24; R. H. Smith, "Anticlimax or Key," 602; Wilkins, "Named and Unnamed Disciples," 438–39; Howell, *Matthew's Inclusive Story*, 248. They all argue that modern readers need not identify with one character group but can evaluate the perspectives of all characters from the viewpoint of the narrator and Jesus. As discussed in the Introduction and chapter 1, I am convinced that modern readers would examine the various perspectives and still identify more with the disciples.

10. Anderson ("Gender and Reading," 16–20) and Wainwright (*Toward a Feminist Critical Reading*, 151) observe the positive depiction of female characters and their exclusion from the character group of the disciples. Anderson attributes their exclusion to their gender; Wainwright, to female power.

11. Herodias and her daughter (Mt. 14:1–12) are the only female characters that the audience is asked to despise as they identify against them.

12. Durber, "The Female Reader," 76–77.

13. Weaver (*Matthew's Missionary Discourse*, 71) and Baur (*The Structure of Matthew's Gospel*, 58) note the prominent place of the disciples in Jesus' ministry.

14. I am focusing on those specified with female gender. The two demoniacs and the two blind men whose gender is obscured by the Greek plural form could include women.

15. Dewey, "Jesus' Healings of Women: Conformity and Nonconformity to Dominant Cultural Values as Clues for Historical Reconstruction," in *SBL Seminar Papers 1993*, ed. Eugene H. Lovering, Jr. (SBLSP 32; Atlanta: Scholars Press, 1993), 186–87; Levine, "Matthew," 256; Witherington, *Women and Genesis*, 77, 83; Bingemer, "Women in the Future," 484; Mollenkott, *Women, Men, and the Bible*, 3–5; Selvidge, *Daughters of Jerusalem*, 77–78.

16. Levine, "Matthew," 256.

17. Dewey, "Jesus' Healings," 186; Witherington, *Women and Genesis*, 77–78. Anderson ("Gender and Reading," 19) concurs but suggests that her serving might also reflect what the disciples should do. Selvidge (*Daughters of Jerusalem*, 84) argues that her service indicates she is a disciple. Wainwright (*Toward a Feminist Critical Reading*, 78–87) claims that the pericope was formerly a call story similar to those in Mt. 4:18–22 and 9:9.

18. In Mt. 8:1–4 and 9:18–26, Jesus risks becoming unclean. In Mt. 9:1–8, the notion that sickness involves sinfulness is introduced, and in Mt. 9:10–13, Jesus eats with sinners.

19. Anderson ("Gender and Reading," 16) observes that both male and female supplicants in chapters 8–9 do not become disciples.

20. Minear, "Disciples and Crowds," 30.

21. That Jesus does not tell the eleven disciples to heal the sick in Mt. 28:16–20 may mean that the command to heal in the commission in chapter 10 has been rescinded or is secondary. Weaver (*Matthew's Missionary Discourse*, 151) argues that the mission of chapter 10 becomes an inclusive mission in Mt. 28:16–20, but does not discuss whether healing is still a part of the mission. Perkins ("Matthew 28:16–20," 584) argues that the mission shifts away from healing and preaching.

22. Although the seven commissioned disciples unnamed until Mt. 10:2–4 could have come from among the crowds whom Jesus healed, the narrator does not give any allusions to persuade the reader in this direction.

23. The intercalation of the two healings has been often observed. For example, Edwards, *Matthew's Story of Jesus*, 31; Anderson, "Gender and Reading," 12.

24. Biblical scholars who have used anthropological studies of Mediterranean society in their research have proposed that New Testament texts reflect a society where the men protected the women of their households. See Bruce Malina, *The New Testament World* (Atlanta: John Knox Press, 1981), 42–44.

25. In her study of the Marcan account, Tolbert ("Mark," 268) discusses how Jesus becomes the kinsman that the woman needs.

26. Witherington (*Women and Genesis*, 82) argues that she is "an example of faith for all to emulate." Although the audience is encouraged to emulate her, this imitation is due to Jesus' affirmation of her action. Jesus remains the center

of the audience's attention. Jesus, who can heal the sick and affirms those who believe in his power, is someone the audience wants to follow.

27. Peter's wife, for instance, could have been listed among them, since Jesus upholds marriage.

28. According to Kennard ("Convention Coverage," 83), the reversal of negative evaluations of women is a technique that female writers have used to affirm women. Adrienne Munich discusses this technique for reading ("Notorious Signs, Feminist Criticism and Literary Tradition," in *Making a Difference: Feminist Literary Criticism*, ed. Gayle Greene and Coppélia Khan [New York: Routledge, 1985], 252–55).

29. Mary John Mananzan and Sun Ai Park recount a Korean woman's struggle to survive and her efforts to improve the working conditions in a textile company. She organized a union and a strike ("Emerging Spirituality of Asian Women," in *With Passion and Compassion: Third World Women Doing Theology*, ed. Virginia Fabella and Mercy Amba Oduyoye [Maryknoll, N.Y.: Orbis Books, 1989], 82–83). In their account, what the Korean woman who had been trained in a mission program does to preserve her own life is not separate from what she does to help the other women who work in the factory.

30. In Mt. 23:1, the narrator introduces Jesus' speech to the crowds and his disciples without any reference to his summoning them or their approach to him. These omissions suggest that they were already with Jesus. See Patte (*The Gospel According to Matthew*, 319), who argues that Jesus is reinforcing his position in Mt. 23 to insure that the disciples and the crowds get the import of his disputes in Mt. 21:14–22:46.

31. Levine, "Matthew," 260; Daniel Harrington, *The Gospel of Matthew* (Sacra Pagina Series 1; Collegeville, Minn.: Liturgical Press, 1991), 312.

32. For a discussion of levirate marriage, see Frymer-Kensky, "Deuteronomy," 60–61.

33. The Sadducees, who accepted only the Pentateuch as authoritative, objected to the notion of the resurrection because it was based on texts in other writings (Isa. 25:8, 26:19; Ps. 73:24–25; Dan. 12:1–3).

34. Commentators have interpreted Jesus' answer: Since God speaks to Moses, saying "I am the God of Abraham, Isaac, and Jacob," these men must be alive in Moses' time; yet, since there is evidence that they died, this life must be the resurrected life. See Harrington, *The Gospel of Matthew*, 314; Patte, *The Gospel According to Matthew*, 312.

35. If the woman had not died, maybe she could have married the next closest kinsman to her husband as Ruth had and then provided her husband an heir.

36. In the way that the story is told, the woman is not given any choice but to comply with the subsequent marriages. She is treated like property passed from one brother to the next. They all "had" (ἔσχον *eschon*) her. See Crosby, *House of Disciples*, 113.

37. Jesus is doing more than criticizing the practice of the law of levirate marriage. His formation of a new family based on nonbiological ties undermines its observance. See Crosby, *House of Disciples*, 112–13.

38. That men are disciples is clear from Mt. 4:18–22, 9:9, 10:1, 27:57; but women are never specifically designated as disciples.

39. According to Frymer-Kensky, a widow might actively demand her husband's brother to fulfill his obligation so that she would not become economically bereft ("Deuteronomy," 61). See also Niditch, "Genesis," 22.

40. Schüssler-Fiorenza (*But She Said*, 205–7) argues that identification with female characters will enable women to extricate themselves from the patriarchal designs of the text. In her treatment of Lk. 13:10–17, she accomplishes this extrication by reading the female character as though she were in the subject-position of the text. She does not provide female readers the means to examine the negative attributes of female characters and the positive attributes of the male protagonists, which could give them the choice to reject female characters and affirm male characters.

41. Levine, "Matthew," 261; Heil, *The Death and Resurrection of Jesus*, 27; Joachim Gnilka, *Das Matthäusevangelium*, vol. 1, pt. 2 (Freiburg: Herder, 1988), 386; Patte, *The Gospel According to Matthew*, 356–57; Frank J. Matera, *Passion Narratives and Gospel Theologies* (New York: Paulist Press, 1986), 88; Senior, *The Passion of Jesus*, 53–54; Anderson, "Gender and Reading," 18; Schweizer, *The Good News According to Matthew*, 487.

42. R. T. France, *The Gospel According to Matthew*, Tyndale New Testament Commentaries (Grand Rapids: Eerdmans, 1985), 364; Minear, *Teacher's Gospel*, 129; Paul Meier, *The Vision of Matthew* (New York: Paulist Press, 1979), 182.

43. F. W. Beare, *The Gospel According to Matthew* (San Francisco: Harper & Row, 1981), 505; Meier, *Vision of Matthew*, 182.

44. Heil, *The Death and Resurrection of Jesus*, 101; Anderson, "Gender and Reading," 17; Perrin, *Resurrection*, 29–31. They all claim that the woman plays the role that the disciples should have. This is Jesus' judgment of Simon in the Lucan account. Here her action becomes an opportunity for the disciples to learn. Cf. Weaver, *Matthew's Missionary Discourse*, 218, n. 67.

45. Malina (*New Testament World*, 25–50) offers a way to understand New Testament texts by utilizing the concepts of honor and shame found in cultural anthropological studies on Mediterranean society. For the limitations of this type of study of Mediterranean peoples, see Unni Wikan, "Shame and Honor: A Contestable Pair," *Man* 19 (1984): 635–52.

46. Malina, *New Testament World*, 38.

47. Initiating and responding to a challenge occurred only between equals. A challenge could be ignored if the initiator was considered one's inferior (Malina, *New Testament World*, 36.) Jesus' acceptance of the disciples as equals is reinforced grammatically, for his response begins with a question and the pronoun "why" (τί ti) just as the disciples' challenge had.

48. That decorum prevented her from debating with Jesus only accentuates that her view is unknown.

49. Kjeld Nielsen, "Ancient Aromas: Good and Bad," *Bible Review* 7, no. 3 (1991): 28.

50. If it is true, as discussed in chapter 3, that literary conventions would have permitted the author of Matthew to portray wives at the meal, then female readers could have had at least one group of women with whom to identify, although obviously a too narrowly defined group of women. It might be argued that the absence of women is good because it keeps female readers from limiting their identification to a small group such as wives. For modern women who want to affirm their female identities, the absence of women is not good, because they have no women with whom they can identify.

51. Elizabeth Amoah and Mercy Amba Oduyoye, for instance, claim that in African charismatic churches the suffering Christ is an appealing figure but Jesus is seen more as a companion who displayed in his encounters with people that "suffering is not in the plan of God" ("The Christ for African Women," in *With Passion and Compassion: Third World Women Doing Theology,* ed. Virginia B. Fabella and Mercy Amba Oduyoye [Maryknoll, N.Y.: Orbis Books, 1989], 39). See also Delores S. Williams, "Black Women's Surrogate Experience and the Christian Notion of Redemption," in *After Patriarchy: Feminist Transformations of the World Religions,* ed. Paula M. Cooey, William R. Eakin, and Jay B. McDaniel (Maryknoll, N.Y.: Orbis Books, 1990), 9.

52. Heil (*The Death and Resurrection of Jesus,* 102) argues that the address "my brothers" emphasizes the importance of the women's role to get Jesus and his disciples reunited. It stresses more the women's exclusion. Cf. Anderson, "Gender and Reading," 20.

53. Heil, *The Death and Resurrection of Jesus,* 171; Weaver, *Matthew's Missionary Discourse,* 150; Ben Witherington, *Women in the Earliest Churches* (Cambridge: Cambridge University Press, 1988), 173–74.

54. The positive response of the women is sometimes contrasted to the disciples' response to argue that the women are better models of discipleship (Witherington, *Women and the Genesis,* 232; Patte, *The Gospel According to Matthew,* 392). Their positive behavior, however, is necessary in order to convince the audience that they will deliver the message.

55. Witherington (*Women in the Earliest Churches,* 173–74) stresses how devoted the women are, how dependent the eleven disciples are upon the women, and how the women have been given a new role (messengers to the eleven disciples). The shift in identification, however, lessens the importance of the women's activities.

56. Doyle, "Matthew's Intention," 51; Perrin, *Resurrection,* 49, 52.

57. The women are often interpreted as loyal because they watch him die and visit the tomb, and the disciples are often described as disloyal because they are absent at the cross and the tomb. That Jesus foretells the disciples' desertion and promises to meet them in Galilee makes their behavior less negative.

58. The two women, therefore, are not substitutes for the disciples. Contra: Heil, *The Death and Resurrection of Jesus,* 106; Anderson, "Gender and Reading," 17–20; Perrin, *Resurrection,* 29–31.

6. Application of the Strategies to Mt. 1:18–25

1. For example, *Common Lectionary: The Lectionary Proposed by the Consultation on Common Texts* (New York: Church Hymnal Corporation, 1983); *An Inclusive Language Lectionary: Readings for Year A* (New York: Division of Education and Ministry, National Council of the Churches of Christ in the U.S.A., 1983); Gordon Lathrop and Gail Ramshaw-Schmidt, eds., *Lectionary for the Christian People: Cycle A of the Roman, Episcopal, Lutheran Lectionaries* (New York: Pueblo Publishing Co., 1986).

2. Ibid.

3. According to Raymond E. Brown, when Joseph accepts Jesus as his son and thus becomes his legal father, he is doing what every father was required to do after his wife gave birth. Joseph is not an adoptive or foster father ("The Annunciation to Joseph," *Worship* 61 [1987]: 488). Edwin Freed concurs ("The Women in Matthew's Genealogy," *JSNT* 2 [1987]: 17).

4. Brown ("Annunciation," 485) argues that vs. 18 is directed to the audience and that the major purpose of the angel's message in vs. 20 is to tell Joseph about Jesus' divine origin. Jane Schaberg, who agrees that vs. 18 is directed to the audience, claims that the spirit is generative in any birth and can also mark the special relationship between God and certain persons, such as kings, prophets, and the messiah. Joseph accepts Jesus because he learns about the special role of the spirit in Jesus' conception (*The Illegitimacy of Jesus: A Feminist Theological Interpretation of the Infancy Narratives* [San Francisco: Harper & Row, 1987], 60, 62, 66–67, 74). Fred L. Horton, Jr., arguing somewhat differently, states that if the spirit is understood as operative in every human birth, then knowledge about the role of the spirit in Jesus' birth would not have persuaded him to continue his marriage. The purpose of the angel's message is to tell Joseph about Jesus' role among his people ("Parenthetical Pregnancy: The Conception and Birth of Jesus in Matthew 1:18–25," in *SBL Seminar Papers 1987* [SBLSP 26; Atlanta: Scholars Press, 1987], 185–86).

5. Horton ("Parenthetical Pregnancy," 188) stresses that "by the spirit" (ἐκ πνεύματός ἁγίου *ek pneumatos hagiou*) affirms that the child represents God's will, not Mary's chastity. The narrator does not establish Mary's virginity through Mary's words or the angel's words. The narrator affirms her virginity by interpreting the event of Mary's conception as the fulfillment of the Scriptures.

6. Gail Patterson Corrington, *Her Image of Salvation: Female Saviors and Formative Christianity* (Louisville: Westminster/John Knox Press, 1992), 152; Crouch, "How Early Christians Viewed the Birth of Jesus," *Bible Review* 7, no. 5 (1991): 35; Schaberg, *Illegitimacy*, 74; Freed, "The Women in the Genealogy," 15; Herman C. Waetjen, "The Genealogy as the Key to the Gospel of Matthew," *JBL* 95, no. 2 (1976): 224.

7. Brooten argues that according to one strand of legal practice in ancient Judaism, both men and women had the legal right to initiate a divorce ("Early Christian Women and Their Cultural Context," 73–74). Eva Cantarella (*Pandora's Daughters: The Role and Status of Women in Greek and Roman Antiquity*, trans. Maureen B. Fant [Baltimore: Johns Hopkins University Press, 1987],

136–37) claims that during the time of the Roman Republic, a husband or wife could obtain a divorce by one of them ceasing to live with the other spouse and that later the practice of confirming the dissolution with a written statement was established. What needs to be explored, therefore, is whether women would be portrayed in narrative texts as the initiators of a divorce.

8. According to Naomi Steinberg, Hagar remains secondary to Sarah in status, but Ishmael is a legitimate heir to Abraham. Sarah is worried about her status even though she is the primary wife. After Sarah gives birth to Isaac, she wants to guarantee that Isaac will be Abraham's heir. By securing Isaac's future, she guarantees her own future under Isaac's care if Abraham should die before her. See *Kinship and Marriage in Genesis: A Household Economics Perspective* (Minneapolis: Fortress Press, 1993), 17, 26–27, 61–65, 77–81.

9. See Gen. 27, where Rachel takes the initiative to make Jacob Isaac's heir but needs Isaac's blessing to validate her choice.

10. Bathsheba is passive throughout most of the account (Jo Ann Hackett, "1 and 2 Samuel," *WBC*, ed. Carol A. Newsom and Sharon H. Ringe [Louisville: Westminster/John Knox Press, 1992], 92; Schaberg, *Illegitimacy*, 30–31; Adele Berlin, *Poetics and Interpretation of Biblical Narrative*, ed. David Gunn [Sheffield: Almond Press, 1983], 26).

11. Schaberg (*Illegitimacy*, 23) points out that the charge against Tamar is based on her adultery as a betrothed woman.

12. Hackett, "1 and 2 Samuel," 92–93.

13. According to Reardon, this action was legal (Reardon, ed., *Collected Ancient Greek Novels*, 27).

14. In another Greek romance novel, *Leucippe and Clitophon*, written in the late second century, Thersandros takes Clitophon and his wife Melite to court on the grounds of adultery.

15. Isocrates does not mention Evagoras' wife. Xenophon does not tell about Agesilaus' wife. The children of both men are included. Tacitus records that Agricola's marriage was harmonious and that his wife and daughter survived him (6, 44). Philo includes the account of Moses taking his wife and sons with him when he returned to Egypt (1.15). Philostratus claims that Apollonius rejected marriage. Lucian mentions nothing about Demonax's marital status or views about marriage.

16. As discussed in chapter 3, this issue of normativeness is a modern one, since the ancient protocols of male public language would have led the audience to assume a male audience.

17. Ulrich Luz (*Matthew 1–7: A Commentary*, trans. Wilhelm C. Linss [Minneapolis: Augsburg, 1989], 117) thinks that the author of Matthew had oral traditions about the naming of Jesus, which he gave a fresh interpretation. Jack Dean Kingsbury (*Matthew: Structure, Christology, Kingdom* [Philadelphia: Fortress Press, 1975], 80,) and Waetjen ("The Genealogy as the Key," 220) claim that the author of Matthew was responsible for the writing of Mt. 1:18–25.

18. Fuchs notes that the woman is always a mother and the child is always a son ("The Literary Characterization of Mothers and Sexual Politics," 131, 134–

35). Janice Capel Anderson claims that the second-century Protoevangelium of James is the first to use the biblical annunciation type-scene to portray the birth of a female ("Mary's Difference," 201).

19. R. Alter, "How Conventions Help Us Read: The Case of the Bible's Annunciation Type-Scene," *Prooftexts* 3, no. 2 (May 1983): 115–30.

20. Alter, *Art of Biblical Narrative*, 101.

21. Fuchs, "Literary Characterization of Mothers," 119–28.

22. Ibid., 128–29.

23. Fuchs ("The Literary Characterization of Mothers," 120–21) correctly interprets Sarah's position in the tent as subordinate, but it is better than Mary's position. Mary does not hear the promise at all.

24. Schaberg, *Illegitimacy*, 106.

25. Crouch refers to Gen. 16:7–16 as an annunciation ("How Early Christians Viewed," 37). Brown (*The Birth of the Messiah* [Garden City, N.Y.: Image Books, 1979], 157) also cites Gen. 16:7–16 as an annunciation scene.

26. Isa. 7:10–17 could imply a newly married woman. Actually the text offers nothing about her marital status. 1 Kings 13:1–6 and 1 Chr. 22:7–10 do not mention the mothers.

27. Anderson ("Mary's Difference," 186, 190, 199) refers to Mary's conception outside marriage. Mary *is* married, although she has not yet had sexual relations with Joseph and has not completed the second stage of marriage. See Brown ("Annunciation," 484), who stresses that Mary and Joseph are married.

28. Alter, *Art of Biblical Narrative*, 54.

29. In the annunciation scenes about Isaac, Samson, and the Shunammite woman's son, the mother is given a promise of a *future* conception. In the type-scenes about Ishmael, Jacob and Esau, and Samson, the mother is told about their futures. In the scenes about Jacob and Esau, Joseph, Samuel, Samson, and Immanuel, the mothers name their sons.

30. In *Chaereas and Callirhoe*, Callirhoe's deception is effective because her son remains in the background of the narrative.

31. I am not suggesting that Mary actually tried and failed to deceive Joseph. I am exploring why deception would not work here (although it is found in a similar scene in *Chaereas and Callirhoe*) as a way to understand why Matthew's scene is written the way it is.

32. In a third-century novel based on earlier sources, *The Alexander Romance*, Olympias has a dream in which the god Ammon promises she will conceive a son who will be her avenger. Her husband also has a dream in which he hears a god telling his wife that she will conceive a son who will avenge the death of his father.

33. Anderson ("Mary's Difference," 190) notes that Mary is marginalized as Sarah is in Gen. 17 and 18. Mary is actually more marginalized than Sarah. She does not hear the promise at all.

34. Fuchs, "Literary Characterization of Mothers," 128–29.

35. Hubbard (*Matthean Redaction*, 35–36) identifies two of the annunciation scenes, Gen. 17:1–21 and 1 Chron. 22:7–10, as commissioning scenes.

Both scenes demand the fulfillment of a task and promise a son to continue it. Other commissioning scenes cited by Hubbard also include the promise of many descendants: Gen. 11:28–30, 12:1–4a; 15:1–6, 26:1–6; 28:10–22; 35:9–15; 46:1–5a. There is a relationship between the annunciation scene and commissioning scenes in Matthew. The annunciation scene in Mt. 1 prepares the audience for commissions that do not depend on procreation in Mt. 10 and Mt. 28.

36. As previously discussed, male readers receive affirmation of their gender identities as they identify with the male protagonists of the text.

37. Jesus' male gender still has an effect on the audience, as I will show in the rereading of the genealogy in this section.

38. The audience is in a position superior to that of the character Joseph who remains in the narrative world and cannot hear the narrator. See Horton, "Parenthetical Pregnancy," 188. Schaberg (*Illegitimacy*, 71–72) argues that the author is thinking of a woman who had been a virgin and then conceived naturally; but the text allows the audience to fill in the gap of the biological father and imagine a miraculous conception comparable to the births of other figures of that period.

39. Compare, however, Gen. 2, where a female adult is created out of a man's rib, and the account of the birth of Athena from the head of Zeus.

40. As I talked with colleagues about reversing Mary's and Joseph's roles, one reaction was "How can they be reversed? Joseph can't bear a child." Role reversal helps to emphasize the physical aspects of Jesus' conception and birth that are so overshadowed that Mary often appears to have no role.

41. We cannot assume that Mt. 1:18–25 reflects divorce practices that allowed the husband to divorce without consulting his wife. The flippant way that many of the upper-class men in the ancient biographies divorced their wives may not have been the predominant way divorces were handled. However, within Matthew's narrative world, Mary's silence stresses the importance of the law and the angel's message and conceals her needs.

42. Howell (*Matthew's Inclusive Story*, 248–59) argues that Jesus is the model of discipleship for the implied reader. Although Jesus shares his powers of healing and control over nature with his disciples, his powers are not always meant to be imitated. His superhuman abilities and omniscience also function to evoke belief in him.

43. Of course, available genealogies show that ancient audiences would not usually trace a daughter's ancestral history. Women's names were rarely included in genealogies (Corrington, *Her Image of Salvation*, 150; Schaberg, *Illegitimacy*, 20; Raymond E. Brown et al., eds., *Mary in the New Testament* [Philadelphia: Fortress Press, 1978], 78; Waetjen, "The Genealogy as the Key," 215). Role reversal, applied to those characters with whom the narrator encourages identification, highlights the patriarchal context of Mt. 1:18–25 for modern readers.

44. Brian M. Nolan, *The Royal Son of David: The Christology of Matthew 1–2 in the Setting of the Gospel* (Orbis Biblicus et Orientalis 23; Göttingen: Van-

denhoeck & Ruprecht, 1979), 26–28; Rodney T. Hood, "The Genealogies of Jesus," in *Early Christian Origins: Studies in Honor of Harold R. Willoughby*, ed. Allen Wikgren (Chicago: Quadrangle, 1961), 5–6; Gerard Mussies, "Parallels to Matthew's Version of the Pedigree of Jesus," *NovTest* 28 (1986): 33; Lucretia Yaghijan, "How Shall We Read? A Preface to Matthew's Protocols of Reading," 3 (unpublished paper cited by Andries G. van Aarde, "The *Evangelium Infantium*, the Abandonment of Children, and the Infancy Narrative in Matthew 1 and 2 from a Social Scientific Perspective," in *SBL Seminar Papers 1992*, ed. Eugene H. Lovering, Jr. [SBLSP 31; Atlanta: Scholars Press, 1992], 445).

45. Levine ("Matthew," 253–54) compares Joseph to Tamar, Ruth, Rahab, and Uriah and claims that they all express a higher righteousness, a quality that Jesus will also display in his ministry. Levine focuses on Uriah instead of Bathsheba because he is named and she is not. Since Bathsheba is often identified as Uriah's wife, there is no need to focus on Uriah as Levine does. It is unclear to me how the actions of Uriah, Ruth, and Rahab are more righteous than the actions of the other characters in the scenes; therefore, the actions of the four women (Tamar, Ruth, Rahab, Bathsheba) and Mary (from role reversal) will be examined to assess how they address the needs of the people of Israel. The primary source for this study will be the Hebrew Scriptures.

46. Retaining Jesus' male gender reveals this pattern. Jesus, too, puts male interests over those of women. Schaberg (*Illegitimacy*, 73–77) argues differently and claims that, although Mt. 1 is written primarily for and about men, the five women in the genealogy emphasize that "salvation history cannot be viewed essentially as a male enterprise."

47. Anderson, "Mary's Difference," 188. Anderson, of course, is not the only one who holds this position; she has combined the position with an audience-oriented literary analysis of Mt. 1.

48. Ibid., 189.

49. Schaberg, *Illegitimacy*, 46; A. M. Dubarle, "La conception virginale et la citation d'Is., VII, 14 dans l'Evangile de Matthieu," *RB* 85 (1978): 362–67.

50. Freed ("The Women in Matthew's Genealogy," 15) argues that the law permitted Joseph to condemn Mary to death publicly or divorce her. Brown ("Annunciation," 486) claims that Joseph could have demanded a public trial but decided against it. Schaberg (*Illegitimacy*, 47–62) discusses the range of options depending on whether the stricter or the more lenient halakah was observed.

51. Brown and Schaberg maintain that Joseph's decision does not contradict the law. See Brown, "Annunciation," 487; Schaberg, *Illegitimacy*, 61.

52. Brown ("Annunciation," 487) correctly points out that Joseph reverses his decision not for the sake of protecting Mary's reputation but for establishing Jesus' identity.

53. Waetjen ("The Genealogy as the Key," 217) is correct that the flow of the narrative is from 1:1 to 1:16 and then on to 1:18–25; however, the audience can also look back on what they have read and change their evaluations of it.

54. In Mt. 3:9 John the Baptist warns the Pharisees and the scribes not to presume that their descent from Abraham will save them from judgment.

55. Here is another instance where the audience is asked to identify against a woman without feeling revulsion for her.

56. Levine ("Matthew," 254) claims that Mary's passivity is used to undermine her privileged position. The narrator also undercuts her position by requiring the audience to identify against her.

57. Schaberg (Illegitimacy, 76) stresses that Mary, who was raped or seduced, survives and thus is depicted more positively than other biblical women who are raped or seduced. Mary must survive so that the narrator can depict Jesus' rejection of her.

Conclusion

1. Christine Smith, Weaving the Sermon, 92.

2. In some ways my position is similar to Elizabeth Cady Stanton's in The Woman's Bible (Boston: Northeastern University Press, 1993), 12–13.

BIBLIOGRAPHY OF
WORKS CITED

Abrams, M. H. *A Glossary of Literary Terms.* 6th ed. New York: Holt, Rinehart and Winston, 1993.

Achtemeier, Paul J. *Mark.* Proclamation Commentaries. Philadelphia: Fortress Press, 1975.

Ackerman, Susan. "'And the Women Knead Dough': The Worship of the Queen of Heaven in Sixth-Century Judah." In *Gender and Difference in Ancient Israel,* pp. 109–24. Ed. Peggy L. Day. Minneapolis: Fortress Press, 1989.

Alcoff, Linda. "Cultural Feminism Versus Post-Structuralism: The Identity Crisis in Feminist Theory." *Signs* 13, no. 3 (1988): 405–36.

Alter, Robert. *The Art of Biblical Narrative.* New York: Basic Books, 1981.

———. "How Conventions Help Us Read: The Case of the Bible's Annunciation Type-Scene." *Prooftexts* 3, no. 2 (1983): 115–30.

Amoah, Elizabeth, and Mercy Amba Oduyoye. "The Christ for African Women." In *With Passion and Compassion: Third World Women Doing Theology,* pp. 35–46. Ed. Virginia Fabella and Mercy Amba Oduyoye. Maryknoll, N.Y.: Orbis Books, 1989.

Anderson, Janice Capel. "Feminist Criticism: The Dancing Daughter." In *Mark and Method: New Approaches in Biblical Studies,* pp. 103–34. Ed. Janice Capel Anderson and Stephen D. Moore. Philadelphia: Fortress Press, 1992.

———. "Mary's Difference: Gender and Patriarchy in the Birth Narratives." *Journal of Religion* 67 (1987): 183–202.

———. "Matthew: Gender and Reading." *Semeia* 28 (1983): 3–27.

Aune, David. "Septem Sapientum Convivium." In *Plutarch's Ethical Writings and Early Christian Literature,* pp. 51–105. Ed. Hans Dieter Betz. Leiden: E. J. Brill, 1978.

Bahr, Gordon J. "The Seder of Passover and Eucharistic Words." *Novum Testamentum* 12 (1970): 181–202.

Bal, Mieke. *Death and Dissymmetry: The Politics of Coherence in the Book of Judges.* Chicago: University of Chicago Press, 1988.

———. *Lethal Love: Feminist Literary Readings of Biblical Love Stories.* Bloomington: Indiana University Press, 1987.

———. *Murder and Difference: Gender, Genre, and Scholarship on Sisera's Death.* Bloomington: Indiana University Press, 1988.

————. "Murder and Difference: Uncanny Sites in an Uncanny World." *Journal of Literature and Theology* 5, no. 1 (1991): 11–19.

Baur, David R. *The Structure of Matthew's Gospel: A Study in Literary Design.* Journal for the Study of the New Testament Supplement, no. 31. Sheffield: Almond Press, 1988.

Beare, F. W. *The Gospel According to Matthew.* San Francisco: Harper & Row, 1981.

Bell, Diane. *Daughters of the Dreaming.* Melbourne: McPhee Gribble, 1983.

Berlin, Adele. *Poetics and Interpretation of Biblical Narrative.* Ed. David Gunn. Sheffield: Almond Press, 1983.

Bingemer, Maria Clara. "Women in the Future of the Theology of Liberation." In *Feminist Theology from the Third World: A Reader,* pp. 308–17. Ed. Ursula King. Maryknoll, N.Y.: Orbis Books, 1994.

Booth, Wayne. *The Rhetoric of Fiction.* 2nd ed. Chicago: University of Chicago Press, 1983.

Brooten, Bernadette. "Early Christian Women and Their Cultural Context: Issues of Method in Historical Reconstruction." In *Feminist Perspectives on Biblical Scholarship,* pp. 65–91. Ed. Adela Yarbro Collins. Chico, Calif.: Scholars Press, 1985.

Brown, Raymond E. "The Annunciation to Joseph." *Worship* 61 (1987): 482–92.

————. *The Birth of the Messiah.* Garden City, N.Y.: Image Books, 1979.

Brown, Raymond E. et al., eds. *Mary in the New Testament.* Philadelphia: Fortress Press, 1978.

Bulkin, Elly. *Lesbian Fiction.* Watertown, Mass.: Persephone Press, 1981.

Burnett, Fred W. "Characterization and Reader Construction of Characters in the Gospels." *Semeia* 63 (1993): 3–28.

Burridge, Richard A. *What Are the Gospels?* New York: Cambridge University Press, 1992.

Cameron, Deborah. *Feminism and Linguistic Theory.* London: Macmillan, 1985.

Campbell, Joseph. *The Power of Myth.* Ed. Betty Sue Flowers. New York: Doubleday, 1988.

Cantarella, Eva. *Pandora's Daughters: The Role and Status of Women in Greek and Roman Antiquity.* Trans. Maureen B. Fant. Baltimore: Johns Hopkins University Press, 1987.

Castelli, Elizabeth A. *Visions and Voyeurism: Holy Women and the Politics of Sight in Early Christianity.* Ed. Christopher Ocker. Berkeley: Center for Hermeneutical Studies, 1995.

Christ, C., and J. Plaskow. *Womanspirit Rising: A Feminist Reader in Religion.* New York: Harper & Row, 1979.

Collier, Jane, and Michelle Rosaldo. "Politics and Gender in Simple Societies." In *Sexual Meanings: The Cultural Construction of Gender and Sexuality,* pp. 275–329. Ed. Sherry Ortner and Harriet Whitehead. Cambridge: Cambridge University Press, 1981.

Collins, Sheila. *A Different Heaven and Earth.* Valley Forge, Pa.: Judson Press, 1974.

Common Lectionary: The Lectionary Proposed by the Consultation on Common Texts. New York: Church Hymnal Corporation, 1983.

Cooper, Kate. "Apostles, Ascetic Women, and Questions of Audience: New Reflections on the Rhetoric of Gender in the Apocryphal Acts." In *SBL Seminar Papers 1992,* pp. 147–53. Ed. Eugene H. Lovering. SBLSP 31. Atlanta: Scholars Press, 1992.

Corrington, Gail Patterson. *Her Image of Salvation: Female Saviors and Formative Christianity.* Louisville: Westminster/John Knox Press, 1992.

Craig, Kerry M., and Margret A. Kristjansson. "Women Reading as Men/ Women Reading as Women: A Structural Analysis for the Historical Project." *Semeia* 51 (1990): 119–36.

Crosby, Michael H. *House of Disciples: Church, Economics, and Justice in Matthew.* Maryknoll, N.Y.: Orbis Books, 1988.

Crouch, James E. "How Early Christians Viewed the Birth of Jesus." *Bible Review* 7, no. 5 (1991): 34–38.

Culler, Jonathan. *Structuralist Poetics: Structuralism, Linguistics, and the Study of Literature.* Ithaca, N.Y.: Cornell University Press, 1975.

Cunningham, Sarah. "A Meeting of the Minds." In *Women of Faith in Dialogue,* pp. 9–16. Ed. Virginia Ramey Mollenkott. New York: Crossroad, 1987.

Darr, John. *On Character Building: The Reader and the Rhetoric of Characterization in Luke-Acts.* Louisville: Westminster/John Knox Press, 1992.

Darr, Katheryn Pfisterer. *Far More Precious than Jewels: Perspectives on Biblical Women.* Louisville: Westminster/John Knox Press, 1991.

Davies, Stevan L. *The Revolt of the Widows: The Social World of the Apocryphal Acts.* Carbondale: Southern Illinois University Press, 1980.

Dewey, Joanna. "The Gospel of Mark." In *Searching the Scriptures,* pp. 470–509. Vol. 2. Ed. Elisabeth Schüssler Fiorenza. New York: Crossroad, 1994.

———. "Feminist Readings, Gospel Narrative, and Critical Theory." *Biblical Theology Bulletin* 22 (1992): 167–73.

———. "Jesus' Healings of Women: Conformity and Nonconformity to Dominant Cultural Values as Clues for Historical Reconstruction." *SBL Seminar Papers 1993,* pp. 178–93. Ed. Eugene H. Lovering, Jr. SBLSP 32. Atlanta: Scholars Press, 1993.

Dewey, Joanna, Peggy Hutaff, and Jane Schaberg. "Respondents to Elizabeth A. Castelli's and Clarice J. Martin's Articles." *Journal of Feminist Studies in Religion* 6, no. 2 (1990): 63–85.

Donaldson, Mara. "The Hero in Contemporary Women's Fantasy." *Listening* 25 (1990): 141–52.

———. "Woman as Hero in Margaret Atwood's *Surfacing* and Maxine Hong Kingston's *The Woman Warrior.*" In *Heroines of Popular Culture,* pp. 101–13. Ed. Pat Browne. Bowling Green, Ohio: Bowling Green University Popular Press, 1987.

Doyle, B. Rod. "Matthew's Intention as Discerned by His Structure." *Revue Biblique* 95 (1988): 34–54.

Dubarle, A. M. "La conception virginale et la citation d'Is., VII, 14 dans l'Evangile de Matthieu." *Revue Biblique* 85 (1978): 362–67.

Durber, Susan. "The Female Reader of the Parables of the Lost." *Journal for the Study of the New Testament* 45 (1992): 59–78.

Dyke, Doris Jean. *Crucified Woman.* Toronto: United Church Publishing House, 1991.

Edwards, Lee. "Women, Energy, and *Middlemarch*." *Massachusetts Review* 13 (1972): 223–38.

Edwards, Richard A. *Matthew's Story of Jesus.* Philadelphia: Fortress Press, 1985.

———. "Uncertain Faith: Matthew's Portrait of the Disciples." In *Discipleship in the New Testament*, pp. 47–61. Ed. F. F. Segovia. Philadelphia: Fortress Press, 1985.

Enright, Louisa. "Let's Stop Using the Bible to Buttress Misogynist Views." *Daughters of Sarah* 19, no. 1 (1993): 36–38.

Etienne, Mona, and Eleanor Leacock. *Women and Colonization.* New York: Praeger, 1980.

Exum, J. Cheryl. "Feminist Criticism: Whose Interests Are Being Served?" In *Judges and Method: New Approaches in Biblical Studies*, pp. 65–90. Ed. Gale A. Yee. Minneapolis: Fortress Press, 1995.

———. *Fragmented Women: Feminist (Sub)versions of Biblical Narratives.* Valley Forge, Pa.: Trinity Press International, 1993.

Feinberg, Leslie. *Stone Butch Blues.* Ithaca, N.Y.: Firebrand Books, 1993.

Felski, Rita. *Beyond Feminist Aesthetics: Feminist Literature and Social Change.* Cambridge: Harvard University Press, 1989.

Fetterley, Judith, ed. *Provisions: A Reader from 19th-Century American Women.* Bloomington: Indiana University Press, 1985.

———. *The Resisting Reader: A Feminist Approach to American Fiction.* Bloomington: Indiana University Press, 1978.

Fewell, Danna Nolan. "Joshua." In *The Women's Bible Commentary*, pp. 63–66. Ed. Carol A. Newsom and Sharon H. Ringe. Louisville: Westminster/John Knox Press, 1992.

Forster, E. M. *Aspects of the Novel.* New York: Harcourt, Brace & World, 1927.

France, R. T. *The Gospel According to Matthew.* Tyndale New Testament Commentaries. Grand Rapids: Eerdmans, 1985.

Freed, Edwin D. "The Women in Matthew's Genealogy." *Journal for the Study of the New Testament* 2 (1987): 3–19.

Friedrich, G. "Die formale Struktur von Mt. 28.18–20." *Zeitschrift für Theologie und Kirche* 80 (1983): 137–83.

Frymer-Kensky, Tikva. "Deuteronomy." In *The Women's Bible Commentary*, pp. 52–62. Ed. Carol A. Newsom and Sharon H. Ringe. Louisville: Westminster/John Knox Press, 1992.

Fuchs, Esther. " 'For I Have the Way of Women': Deception, Gender, and Ideology in Biblical Narrative." *Semeia* 42 (1988): 68–83.

————. "The Literary Characterization of Mothers and Sexual Politics in the Hebrew Bible." In *Feminist Perspectives on Biblical Scholarship*, pp. 117–36. Ed. Adela Yarbro Collins. Chico, Calif.: Scholars Press, 1985.

————. "Marginalization, Ambiguity, Silencing: The Story of Jephthah's Daughter." *Journal of Feminist Studies in Religion* 5 (1989): 35–45.

————. "Structure and Patriarchal Functions in the Biblical Betrothal Type-Scene." *Journal of Feminist Studies in Religion* 3 (1987): 7–13.

Furman, Nelly. "The Politics of Language: Beyond the Gender Principle?" In *Making a Difference: Feminist Literary Criticism*, pp. 59–79. Ed. Gayle Greene and Coppélia Khan. New York: Routledge, 1985.

————. "Textual Feminism." In *Women and Language in Literature*, pp. 45–54. Ed. Sally McConnell-Ginet, Ruth Borker, and Nelly Furman. New York: Praeger, 1980.

Fuss, Diana. "Reading Like a Feminist." *Differences* 1, no. 2 (1989): 77–92.

Garland, David E. *The Intention of Matthew 23*. Leiden: E. J. Brill, 1979.

Gnilka, Joachim. *Das Matthäusevangelium*. vol. 1, pt. 2. Freiburg: Herder, 1988.

Goodale, Jane. "Gender, Sexuality and Marriage: A Kaulong Model of Nature And Culture." In *Nature, Culture and Gender*, pp. 119–42. Ed. C. MacCormack and M. Strathern. Cambridge: Cambridge University Press, 1980.

Grant, Jacquelyn. "Subjectification as a Requirement for Christological Construction." In *Lift Every Voice: Constructing Christian Theologies from the Underside*, pp. 201–14. Ed. Susan Brooks Thistlethwaite and Mary Potter Engel. New York: HarperCollins, 1990.

Greene, Gayle. "Looking at History." In *Changing Subjects: The Making of Feminist Literary Criticism*, pp. 4–27. Ed. Gayle Greene and Coppélia Khan. New York: Routledge, 1993.

Greene, Gayle and Coppélia Khan. "Feminist Scholarship and the Social Construction of Woman." In *Making a Difference: Feminist Literary Criticism*, pp. 1–36. Ed. Gayle Greene and Coppélia Khan. New York: Routledge, 1985.

Hackett, Jo Ann. "1 and 2 Samuel." In *The Women's Bible Commentary*, pp. 85–95. Ed. Carol A. Newsom and Sharon H. Ringe. Louisville: Westminster/John Knox Press, 1992.

Hägg, Thomas. *The Novel in Antiquity*. Los Angeles: University of California Press, 1983.

Hare, Douglas, and Daniel Harrington. "'Make Disciples of all the Gentiles.' (Mt. 28:19)." *Catholic Biblical Quarterly* 37 (1975): 359–69.

Harrington, Daniel. *The Gospel of Matthew*. Sacra Pagina Series 1. Collegeville, Minn.: Liturgical Press, 1991.

Harrison, Beverly W. *Making the Connections: Essays in Feminist Social Ethics*. Ed. Carol S. Robb. Boston: Beacon Press, 1985.

Heil, John Paul. *The Death and Resurrection of Jesus: A Narrative-Critical Reading of Matthew 26–28*. Minneapolis: Fortress Press, 1991.

Hill, David. *The Gospel of Matthew*. Grand Rapids: Eerdmans, 1981.

Hollis, Susan Tower. "The Woman in Ancient Examples of the Potiphar's Wife Motif, K2111." In *Gender and Difference in Ancient Israel*, pp. 28–42. Ed. Peggy L. Day. Minneapolis: Fortress Press, 1989.

Hood, Rodney T. "The Genealogies of Jesus." In *Early Christian Origins: Studies in Honor of Harold R. Willoughby*, pp. 1–15. Ed. Allen Wikgren. Chicago: Quadrangle, 1961.

Hoppin, Ruth. *Priscilla: The Author of the Epistle to the Hebrews*. New York: Exposition Press, 1969.

Horton, Jr., Fred L. "Parenthetical Pregnancy: The Conception and Birth of Jesus in Matthew 1:18–25." In *SBL Seminar Papers 1987*, pp. 175–89. SBLSP 26. Atlanta: Scholars Press, 1987.

Howe, Florence. "Feminism and Literature." In *Images of Women in Fiction: Feminist Perspectives*, pp. 253–77. Ed. Susan Koppelman Cornillon. Rev. ed. Bowling Green, Ohio: Bowling Green University Popular Press, 1973.

Howell, David B. *Matthew's Inclusive Story*. Sheffield: JSOT Press, 1990.

Hubbard, Benjamin J. *The Matthean Redaction of a Primitive Apostolic Commissioning: An Exegesis of Matthew 28:16–20*. SBL Dissertation Series, no. 19. Missoula, Mont.: Scholars Press, 1974.

Humm, Maggie. *Feminist Criticism: Women as Contemporary Critics*. New York: St. Martin's Press, 1986.

Hunter, Edwina. "Reflections on the Christa from a Christian Theologian." *Journal of Women and Religion* 4, no. 2 (1985): 22–32.

Ifri, Pascal A. "Proust's Male Narratee." *Style* 22 (1988): 524–32.

An Inclusive Language Lectionary: Readings for Year A. New York: Division of Education and Ministry, National Council of the Churches of Christ in the U.S.A., 1983.

Irigaray, Luce. *Je, Tu, Nous: Toward a Culture of Difference*. Trans. Alison Martin. New York: Routledge, 1993.

———. *Sexes and Genealogies*. Trans. Gillian C. Gill. New York: Columbia University Press, 1993.

———. *This Sex Which Is Not One*. Trans. Catherine Porter. Ithaca, N.Y.: Cornell University Press, 1985.

Isasi-Díaz, Ada María. "The Bible and Mujerista Theology." In *Lift Every Voice: Constructing Christian Theologies from the Underside*, pp. 261–69. Ed. Susan Brooks Thistlethwaite and Mary Potter Engel. New York: HarperCollins Publishers, 1990.

Iser, Wolfgang. *The Act of Reading: A Theory of Aesthetic Response*. Baltimore: Johns Hopkins University Press, 1978.

———. *The Implied Reader*. Baltimore: Johns Hopkins University Press, 1974.

Jackson, J. de J. R. *Historical Criticism and the Meaning of Texts*. New York: Routledge, 1989.

Jacobus, Mary. "Is There a Woman in This Text?" *New Literary History* 14 (1982): 117–41.

Jameson, Fredric. *The Political Unconscious: Narrative as a Socially Symbolic Act*. Ithaca, N.Y.: Cornell University Press, 1981.

Jones, Ann Rosalind. "Inscribing Femininity: French Theories of the Feminine." In *Making a Difference: Feminist Literary Criticism*, pp. 80–112. Ed. Gayle Greene and Coppélia Khan. New York: Routledge, 1985.

Keller, Catherine. *From a Broken Web*. Boston: Beacon Press, 1986.

Kennard, Jean. "Convention Coverage or How to Read Your Own Life." *New Literary History* 13 (1981): 69–88.

Kermode, Frank. *The Genesis of Secrecy: On the Interpretation of Narrative*. Cambridge: Harvard University Press, 1977.

Kingsbury, Jack Dean. *Matthew as Story*. 2nd ed. Philadelphia: Fortress Press, 1988.

———. *Matthew: Structure, Christology, Kingdom*. Philadelphia: Fortress Press, 1975.

———. "The Verb *Akolouthein* ('To Follow') as an Index to Matthew's View of His Community." *Journal of Biblical Literature* 97 (1978): 56–73.

Kwok Pui-Lan. "Discovering the Bible in the Non-Biblical World." In *Lift Every Voice: Constructing Christian Theologies from the Underside*, pp. 270–82. Ed. Susan Brooks Thistlethwaite and Mary Potter Engel. New York: HarperCollins, 1990.

Lacan, Jacques. *Ecrits: A Selection*. London: Tavistock, 1977.

Laffey, Alice L. *An Introduction to the Old Testament: A Feminist Perspective*. Philadelphia: Fortress Press, 1988.

Lanser, Susan Sniader. *The Narrative Act: Point of View in Prose Fiction*. Princeton: Princeton University Press, 1981.

Lathrop, Gordon, and Gail Ramshaw-Schmidt, eds. *Lectionary for the Christian People: Cycle A of the Roman, Episcopal, Lutheran Lectionaries*. New York: Pueblo, 1986.

Leacock, Eleanor. "Women's Status in Egalitarian Society: Implications for Social Evolution." *Current Anthropology* 19, no. 2 (1978): 247–75.

Levine, Amy-Jill. "Matthew." In *The Women's Bible Commentary*, pp. 252–62. Ed. Carol A. Newsom and Sharon H. Ringe. Louisville: Westminster/John Knox Press, 1992.

———. *The Social and Ethnic Dimensions of Matthean Salvation History*. Lewiston, N.Y.: Edwin Mellen Press, 1988.

Levi-Strauss, Claude. *Structural Anthropology*. Trans. Claire Jacobson and Brooke Grunfest Shoepf. New York: Basic Books, 1963.

Lincoln, Andrew T. "Matthew — A Story for Teachers?" In *The Bible in Three Dimensions: Essays in Celebration of Biblical Studies in the University of Sheffield*, pp. 103–25. Ed. David J. A. Clines et al. Journal for the Study of the Old Testament Supplement Series 87. Sheffield: JSOT Press, 1990.

Long, Elizabeth. "Women, Reading, and Cultural Anthropology: Some Implications of the Audience Perspective in Cultural Studies." *American Quarterly* 38 (1986): 591–612.

Lucas, Caroline. *Writing for Women: The Example of Women as Reader in Elizabethan Romance*. Philadelphia: Open University Press, 1989.

Luz, Ulrich. "The Disciples in the Gospel According to Matthew." In *The Interpretation of Matthew*, pp. 98–128. Ed. Graham Stanton. Philadelphia: Fortress Press, 1983.

———. *Matthew 1–7: A Commentary*. Trans. Wilhelm C. Linss. Minneapolis: Augsburg, 1989.

Mailloux, Steven. *Interpretive Conventions: The Reader in the Study of American Fiction*. Ithaca, N.Y.: Cornell University Press, 1982.

Malina, Bruce. "Dealing with Biblical (Mediterranean) Characters: A Guide for U.S. Consumers." *Biblical Theology Bulletin* 19 (1989): 127–41.

———. *The New Testament World*. Atlanta: John Knox Press, 1981.

Mananzan, Mary John, and Sun Ai Park. "Emerging Spirituality of Asian Women." In *With Passion and Compassion: Third World Women Doing Theology*, pp. 77–88. Ed. Virginia Fabella and Mercy Amba Oduyoye. Maryknoll, N.Y.: Orbis Books, 1989.

Matera, Frank. *Passion Narratives and Gospel Theologies*. New York: Paulist Press, 1986.

———. "The Plot of Matthew's Gospel." *Catholic Biblical Quarterly* 49 (1987): 233–53.

McReynolds, Sally Ann, and Ann O'Hara Graff. "When Women Are the Context." In *In the Embrace of God*, pp. 161–72. Ed. Ann O'Hara Graff. Maryknoll, N.Y.: Orbis Books, 1995.

Meese, Elizabeth A. *Crossing the Double-Cross: The Practice of Feminist Criticism*. Chapel Hill: University of North Carolina Press, 1986.

Meier, Paul. *The Vision of Matthew*. New York: Paulist Press, 1979.

Meyers, Carol. *Discovering Eve: Ancient Israelite Women in Context*. New York: Oxford University Press, 1988.

Milne, Pamela J. "The Patriarchal Stamp of Scripture: The Implications of Structural Analyses for Feminist Hermeneutics." *Journal of Feminist Studies in Religion* 5, no. 1 (1989): 17–34.

Minear, Paul S. "The Disciples and the Crowds in the Gospel of Matthew." *Anglican Theological Review Supplement* 3 (1974): 235–55.

———. *Matthew: The Teacher's Gospel*. New York: Pilgrim Press, 1982.

Moi, Toril. *Sexual/Textual Politics: Feminist Literary Theory*. New York: Routledge, 1985.

Mollenkott, Virginia Ramey. *Women, Men, and the Bible*. Rev. ed. New York: Crossroad, 1988.

Moore, Henrietta. *Feminism and Anthropology*. Minneapolis: University of Minnesota Press, 1988.

———. *Space, Text and Gender: An Anthropological Study of the Marakwet of Kenya*. Cambridge: Cambridge University Press, 1986.

Morris, Elizabeth. "Reflection on the Christa from a Storyteller." *Journal of Women and Religion* 4, no. 2 (1985): 44–45.

Morris, Pam. *Literature and Feminism: An Introduction*. Cambridge: Blackwell Publishers, 1993.

Munich, Adrienne. "Notorious Signs, Feminist Criticism and Literary Tradition." In *Making a Difference: Feminist Literary Criticism*, pp. 238–59. Ed. Gayle Greene and Coppélia Khan. New York: Routledge, 1985.

Mussies, Gerard. "Parallels to Matthew's Version of the Pedigree of Jesus." *Novum Testamentum* 28 (1986): 32–47.

Niditch, Susan. "Genesis." In *The Women's Bible Commentary*, pp. 10–25. Ed. Carol A. Newsom and Sharon H. Ringe. Louisville: Westminster/John Knox Press, 1992.

Nielsen, Kjeld. "Ancient Aromas: Good and Bad." *Bible Review* 7, no. 3 (1991): 26–33.

Nobleman, Roberta. "Once Upon a Time." *Daughters of Sarah* 15, no. 4 (1989): 3–5.

Nolan, Brian M. *The Royal Son of David: The Christology of Matthew 1–2 in the Setting of the Gospel*. Orbis Biblicus et Orientalis 23. Göttingen: Vandenhoeck & Ruprecht, 1979.

O'Day, Gail R. "John." In *The Women's Bible Commentary*, pp. 293–304. Ed. Carol A. Newsom and Sharon H. Ringe. Louisville: Westminster/John Knox Press, 1992.

Ortner, Sherry. "Is Female to Male as Nature Is to Culture?" In *Woman, Culture and Society*, pp. 67–88. Ed. M. Rosaldo and L. Lamphere. Stanford: Stanford University Press, 1974.

Overman, J. Andrew. *Matthew's Gospel and Formative Judaism: The Social World of the Matthean Community*. Minneapolis: Fortress Press, 1990.

Patte, Daniel. *The Gospel According to Matthew: A Structural Commentary on Matthew's Faith*. Philadelphia: Fortress Press, 1987.

Pearson, Carol, and Katherine Pope. *The Female Hero in American and British Literature*. New York: R. R. Bowker, 1981.

Perkins, Pheme. "Matthew 28:16–20, Resurrection, Ecclesiology and Mission." In *SBL Seminar Papers 1993*, pp. 574–88. Ed. Eugene H. Lovering, Jr. SBLSP 32. Atlanta, Georgia, 1993.

Perrin, Norman. *The Resurrection according to Matthew, Mark, and Luke*. Philadelphia: Fortress Press, 1977.

Pippin, Tina. "Eros and the End: Reading for Gender in the Apocalypse of John." *Semeia* 59 (1992): 193–210.

Powell, Mark Alan. *What Is Narrative Criticism?* Minneapolis: Fortress Press, 1990.

Przybylski, Benno. *Righteousness in Matthew and His World of Thought*. Cambridge: Cambridge University Press, 1980.

Rabinowitz, P. J. *Before Reading: Narrative Conventions and the Politics of Conventions*. Ithaca, N.Y.: Cornell University Press, 1987.

Rabuzzi, Kathryn Allen. *The Sacred and the Feminine: Toward a Theology of Housework*. New York: Seabury Press, 1982.

Radway, Janice. "Women Read the Romance: The Interaction of Text and Context." *Feminist Studies* 9 (1983): 53–78.

Reardon, B. P., ed. *Collected Ancient Greek Novels*. Los Angeles: University of California Press, 1989.

Reeves, Keith Howard. *The Resurrection Narrative in Matthew: A Literary Critical Examination*. Lewiston, N.Y.: Mellen Biblical Press, 1993.

Reinhartz, Adele. "The Gospel of John." In *Searching the Scriptures*, pp. 561–600. Vol. 2. Ed. Elisabeth Schüssler Fiorenza. New York: Crossroad, 1994.

Ringe, Sharon H. "Luke 9:28–36: The Beginning of an Exodus." *Semeia* (1983): 83–99.

————. "Reading from Context to Context: Contributions of a Feminist Hermeneutic to Theologies of Liberation." In *Lift Every Voice: Constructing Christian Theologies from the Underside*, pp. 283–91. Ed. Susan Brooks Thistlethwaite and Mary Potter Engel. New York: HarperCollins Publishers, 1990.

————. "When Women Read the Bible." In *The Women's Bible Commentary*, pp. 1–9. Ed. Carol A. Newsom and Sharon H. Ringe. Louisville: Westminster/John Knox Press, 1992.

Ross, Ellen M. "Human Persons as Images of the Divine: A Reconsideration." In *The Pleasure of Her Text: Feminist Readings of Biblical and Historical Texts*, pp. 97–116. Ed. Alice Bach. Philadelphia: Trinity Press International, 1990.

Rubin, Gayle. "The Traffic in Women: Notes on the 'Political Economy' of Sex." In *Toward an Anthropology of Women*, pp. 157–210. Ed. Rayna R. Reiter. New York: Monthly Review Press, 1975.

Ruether, Rosemary Radford. "The Call of Women in the Church Today." In *Women of Faith in Dialogue*, pp. 77–88. Ed. Virginia Ramey Mollenkott. New York: Crossroad, 1987.

————. "Christian Quest for Redemptive Community." *Cross Currents* 38 (1988): 3–16.

————. "Feminism and Religious Faith: Renewal or New Creation?" *Religion and Intellectual Life* 3 (1986): 7–20.

————. "Feminist Interpretation: A Method of Correlation." In *Feminist Interpretation of the Bible*, pp. 111–24. Ed. Letty M. Russell. Philadelphia: Fortress Press, 1985.

————. "Recontextualizing Theology." *Theology Today* 43 (1986): 22–27.

————. *Sexism and God-Talk: Toward a Feminist Theology*. Boston: Beacon Press, 1983.

————. *Women-Church: Theology and Practice*. New York: Harper & Row, 1985.

Russ, Joanna. "What Can a Heroine Do? or Why Women Can't Write." In *To Write Like a Woman: Essays in Feminism and Science Fiction*, pp. 79–93. Indianapolis: Indiana University Press, 1995.

Russell, Letty M. "Women and Ministry: Problem or Possibility?" In *Christian Feminism: Visions of Humanity*, pp. 75–92. Ed. Judith L. Weidman. New York: Harper & Row, 1984.

Sacks, Karen. *Sisters and Wives: The Past and Future of Sexuality*. Westport, Conn.: Greenwood Press, 1979.

Sacks, Kenneth S. "Rhetorical Approaches to Greek History Writing in the Hellenistic Period." In *SBL Seminar Papers 1984*, pp. 123–33. Ed. K. Richards. SBLSP 23. Chico, Calif.: Scholars Press, 1984.

Sakenfeld, Katharine Doob. "Feminist Uses of Biblical Materials." In *Feminist Interpretation of the Bible*, pp. 55–64. Ed. Letty M. Russell. Philadelphia: Fortress Press, 1985.

Sampson, Emily. "Who's Afraid of the Big Bad Wolf?" *Daughters of Sarah* 16, no. 4 (1990): 15–16.

Schaberg, Jane. *The Illegitimacy of Jesus: A Feminist Theological Interpretation of the Infancy Narratives*. San Francisco: Harper & Row, 1987.

Schibanoff, Susan. "Taking the Gold Out of Egypt: The Art of Reading as a Woman." In *Gender and Reading: Essays on Readers, Texts, and Contexts*, pp. 83–106. Ed. E. A. Flynn and P. P. Schweickart. Baltimore: Johns Hopkins University Press, 1986.

Schneiders, Sandra M. "Feminist Ideology Criticism and Biblical Hermeneutics." *Biblical Theology Bulletin* 19 (1989): 3–10.

———. *The Revelatory Text: Interpreting the New Testament as Sacred Scripture*. New York: HarperCollins, 1991.

Scholes, Robert, and Robert Kellogg. *The Nature of Narrative*. New York: Oxford University Press, 1966.

Schüssler Fiorenza, Elisabeth. *Bread Not Stone: The Challenge of Feminist Biblical Interpretation*. Boston: Beacon Press, 1984.

———. *But She Said: Feminist Practices of Biblical Interpretation*. Boston: Beacon Press, 1992.

———. "A Feminist Critical Interpretation for Liberation: Martha and Mary: Lk. 10:38–42." *Religion and Intellectual Life* 3 (1986): 21–36.

———. *Jesus: Miriam's Child, Sophia's Prophet*. New York: Continuum, 1994.

———. *In Memory of Her: A Feminist Theological Reconstruction of Christian Origins*. New York: Crossroad, 1983.

———. "The Politics of Otherness: Biblical Interpretation as a Critical Praxis for Liberation." In *The Future of Liberation Theology*, pp. 311–25. Ed. Marc H. Ellis and Otto Maduro. Maryknoll, N.Y.: Orbis Books, 1989.

———. "The Quilting of Women's History: Phoebe of Cenchreae." In *Embodied Love: Sensuality and Relationship as Feminist Values*, pp. 35–49. Ed. Paula M. Cooey et al. San Francisco: Harper & Row, 1987.

———. "Text and Reality — Reality as Text: The Problem of a Feminist Historical and Social Reconstruction Based on Texts." *Studia Theologica* 43 (1989): 19–34.

Schweickart, Patrocinio. "Reading Ourselves: Toward a Feminist Theory of Reading." In *Speaking of Gender*, pp. 17–44. Ed. Elaine Showalter. New York: Routledge, 1989.

Schweizer, Eduard. *The Good News According to Matthew*. Trans. D. E. Green. Atlanta: John Knox Press, 1975.

Sedgwick, Eve. *Between Men: English Literature and Male Homosocial Desire*. New York: Columbia University Press, 1985.

Seiem, Sharon. "Writing Poetry: Harrowing the Earth of Me." *Daughters of Sarah* 15, no. 4 (1989): 12–13.

Selvidge, Marla. *Daughters of Jerusalem.* Scottdale, Pa.: Herald Press, 1987.

Senior, Donald. *The Passion of Jesus in the Gospel of Matthew.* Wilmington, Del.: Michael Glazier, 1985.

Setel, Drorah O'Donnell. "Exodus." In *The Women's Bible Commentary,* pp. 26–35. Ed. Carol A. Newsom and Sharon H. Ringe. Louisville: Westminster/John Knox Press, 1992.

Sheridan, Mark. "Disciples and Discipleship in the Gospel of Matthew and Luke." *Biblical Theology Bulletin* 3 (1973): 235–55.

Showalter, Elaine. "Feminist Criticism in the Wilderness." In *The New Literary Criticism: Essays on Women, Literature, and Theory,* pp. 243–70. Ed. Elaine Showalter. New York: Pantheon, 1985.

———. "Towards a Feminist Poetics." In *The New Literary Criticism: Essays on Women, Literature, and Theory,* pp. 125–43. Ed. Elaine Showalter. New York: Pantheon, 1985.

———. "Women and the Literary Curriculum." *College English* 32 (1971): 855–62.

Sigal, Lillian. "Models of Love and Hate." *Daughters of Sarah* 16, no. 2 (1990): 8–10.

Sigal, Phillip. "Manifestations of Hellenistic Historiography in Select Judaic Literature. In *SBL Seminar Papers 1984,* pp. 161–85. Ed. K. Richards. Chico, Calif.: Scholars Press, 1984.

Smallwood, Gloria. "Reflections on the Christa from a Pastor." *Journal of Women and Religion* 4, no. 2 (1985): 41–43.

Smith, Christine. *Weaving the Sermon: Preaching in a Feminist Perspective.* Louisville: Westminster/John Knox Press, 1989.

Smith, Dennis. "Table Fellowship as a Literary Motif in the Gospel of Luke." *Journal of Biblical Literature* 106 (1987): 613–38.

Smith, Robert Harry. "Matthew 28:16–20, Anticlimax or Key to the Gospel?" In *SBL Seminar Papers 1993,* pp. 589–603. Ed. Eugene H. Lovering. SBLSP 32. Atlanta: Scholars Press, 1993.

Southard, Naomi P. F. "An Asian-American Woman Reflects on Racism, Classism, and Sexism." In *Women of Faith in Dialogue,* pp. 51–60. Ed. Virginia Ramey Mollenkott. New York: Crossroad, 1987.

Spivak, Charlotte. *Merlin's Daughters: Contemporary Women Writers of Fantasy.* New York: Greenwood Press, 1987.

Stanton, Elizabeth Cady. *The Woman's Bible.* Boston: Northeastern University Press, 1993.

Stanton, Graham. *A Gospel for a New People.* Edinburgh: T. & T. Clark, 1992.

Stein, S. "The Influence of Symposia Literature on the Literary Form of the Pesah Haggadah." *Journal of Jewish Studies* 8 (1957): 13–44.

Steinberg, Naomi. *Kinship and Marriage in Genesis: A Household Economics Perspective.* Minneapolis: Fortress Press, 1993.

Stone, Ken. "Sexual Practice and the Structure of Prestige: The Case of Disputed Concubines." In *SBL Seminar Papers 1993*, pp. 554–73. Ed. Eugene H. Lovering, Jr. SBLSP 32. Atlanta: Scholars Press, 1993.

Strathern, Marilyn. "No Nature, No Culture: The Hagen Case." In *Nature, Culture and Gender*, pp. 174–222. Ed. C. MacCormack and M. Strathern. Cambridge: Cambridge University Press, 1980.

Swidler, Leonard. *Biblical Affirmations of Woman*. Philadelphia: Westminster Press, 1979.

Tamez, Elsa. "Women's Rereading of the Bible." *Feminist Theology from the Third World: A Reader*, pp. 190–200. Ed. Ursula King. Maryknoll, N.Y.: Orbis Books, 1994.

Tannehill, Robert C. *The Sword of His Mouth: Forceful and Imaginative Language in Synoptic Sayings*. Ed. William A. Beardslee. SBLSS 1. Missoula, Mont.: Scholars Press, 1975.

Taylor, Helen. "Romantic Readers." In *From My Guy to Sci-Fi: Genre and Women's Writing in the Postmodern World*, pp. 58–77. Ed. Helen Carr. London: Pandora Press, 1989.

Thistlethwaite, Susan Brooks. "Every Two Minutes: Battered Women and Feminist Interpretation." In *Feminist Interpretation of the Bible*, pp. 96–107. Ed. Letty M. Russell. Philadelphia: Westminster Press, 1985.

Thompson, W. G. *Matthew's Advice to a Divided Community. Mt. 17,22–18,35*. Analecta Biblica 44. Rome: Biblical Institute Press, 1970.

Thurston, Bonnie Bowman. *The Widows: A Women's Ministry in the Early Church*. Minneapolis: Fortress Press, 1989.

Tolbert, Mary Ann. "Defining the Problem: The Bible and Feminist Hermeneutics." *Semeia* 28 (1983): 113–26.

———. "Mark." In *The Women's Bible Commentary*, pp. 263–74. Ed. Carol A. Newsom and Sharon H. Ringe. Louisville: Westminster/John Knox Press, 1992.

———. "Protestant Feminists and the Bible: On the Horns of a Dilemma." *Union Seminary Quarterly Review* 43 (1989): 1–17.

———. *Sowing the Gospel: Mark's World in Literary-Historical Perspective*. Minneapolis: Fortress Press, 1989.

Tong, Rosemarie. *Feminist Thought: A Comprehensive Introduction*. Boulder: Westview Press, 1989.

Torjesen, Karen Jo. *When Women Were Priests*. San Francisco: HarperCollins Publishers, 1993.

Trible, Phyllis. "Depatriarchalizing in Biblical Interpretation. *Journal of the American Academy of Religion* 41 (1973): 30–48.

———. *God and the Rhetoric of Sexuality*. Philadelphia: Fortress Press, 1978.

———. "The Pilgrim Bible on a Feminist Journey." *Daughters of Sarah* 15, no. 3 (1989): 4–7.

———. *Texts of Terror: Literary-Feminist Reading of Biblical Narratives*. Philadelphia: Fortress Press, 1984.

Trilling, Wolfgang. *Das Wahre Israel: Studien zur Theologie des Matthäus-Evangeliums.* Studien zum Alten und Neuen Testament, no. 10. Munich: Kösel, 1968.

Van Aarde, Andries G. "The *Evangelium Infantium,* the Abandonment of Children, and the Infancy Narrative in Matthew 1 and 2 from a Social Scientific Perspective." In *SBL Seminar Papers 1992,* pp. 435–53. Ed. Eugene H. Lovering, Jr. SBLSP 31. Atlanta: Scholars Press, 1992.

Van Leeuwen, Mary Stewart, ed. *After Eden: Facing the Challenge of Gender Reconciliation.* Grand Rapids: Eerdmans, 1993.

Waetjen, Herman C. "The Genealogy as the Key to the Gospel According to Matthew." *Journal of Biblical Literature* 95, no. 2 (1976): 205–30.

Wainwright, Elaine Mary. "The Gospel of Matthew," In *Searching the Scriptures,* pp. 635–77. Vol. 2. Ed. Elisabeth Schüssler Fiorenza. New York: Crossroad, 1994.

———. *Toward a Feminist Critical Reading of the Gospel According to Matthew.* New York: Walter de Gruyter, 1991.

Washington, Mary Helen. "Foreword." In *Their Eyes Were Watching God,* by Zora Neale Hurston. New York: Harper & Row, 1990.

Weaver, Dorothy Jean. "Matthew 28:16–20." *Interpretation* 46, no. 4 (1992): 398–402.

———. *Matthew's Missionary Discourse.* Journal for the Study of the New Testament Supplement, no. 38. Sheffield: JSOT Press, 1990.

Weedon, Chris. *Feminist Practice and Poststructuralist Theory.* New York: Basil Blackwell, 1987.

Weems, Renita. "Gomer: Victim of Violence or Victim of Metaphor?" *Semeia* 47 (1989): 87–104.

White, Sidnie Ann. "Esther." In *The Women's Bible Commentary,* pp. 124–29. Ed. Carol A. Newsom and Sharon H. Ringe. Louisville: Westminster/John Knox Press, 1992.

———. "Esther: A Feminine Model for Jewish Diaspora." In *Gender Difference in Ancient Israel,* pp. 161–77. Ed. Peggy L. Day. Minneapolis: Fortress Press, 1989.

Wikan, Unni. "Shame and Honor: A Contestable Pair." *Man* 19 (1984): 635–52.

Wilfong, Marsha. "Genesis 22:1–19." *Interpretation* 45, no. 4 (1991): 393–97.

Wilkins, Michael J. *The Concept of Disciple in Matthew's Gospel.* Novum Testamentum Supplement 59. New York: E. J. Brill, 1988.

———. "Named and Unnamed Disciples in Matthew: A Literary-Theological Study." In *SBL Seminar Papers 1991,* pp. 418–39. Ed. Eugene H. Lovering, Jr. SBLSP 30. Atlanta: Scholars Press, 1991.

Williams, Delores. "Black Women's Surrogate Experience and the Christian Notion of Redemption." In *After Patriarchy: Feminist Transformations of the World Religions.* Ed. Paula M. Cooey, William R. Eakin, and Jay B. McDaniel. Maryknoll, N.Y.: Orbis Books, 1990.

————. *Sisters in the Wilderness: The Challenges of Womanist God-Talk*. Maryknoll, N.Y.: Orbis Books, 1993.

————. "A Womanist Perspective on Sin." In *A Troubling in My Soul: Womanist Perspectives on Evil and Suffering*, pp. 130–49. Ed. Emilie M. Townes. Maryknoll, N.Y.: Orbis Books, 1993.

Winkler, John J. *The Constraints of Desire*. New York: Routledge, 1990.

Wire, Antoinette Clark. *The Corinthian Women Prophets: A Reconstruction through Paul's Rhetoric*. Minneapolis: Fortress Press, 1990.

Witherington, Ben. *Women and the Genesis of Christianity*. Ed. Ann Witherington. New York: Cambridge University Press, 1990.

————. *Women in the Earliest Churches*. Cambridge: Cambridge University Press, 1988.

Zimmerman, Bonnie. "In Academia, and Out: The Experience of a Lesbian Feminist Literary Critic." In *Changing Subjects: The Making of Feminist Literary Criticism*, pp. 112–20. Ed. Gayle Greene and Coppélia Khan. New York: Routledge, 1993.

SCRIPTURE INDEX

GENERAL INDEX

DATE DUE

APR 0 4 1999			
MAR 1 8	2004		
APR 2 0	2004		
SEP 1 0	2007		
OCT 1 3	2013		
GAYLORD			PRINTED IN U.S.A.